9783987411663
I0727805

like we could almost live forever

CARLOTTA GUERRA

like we could almost live forever

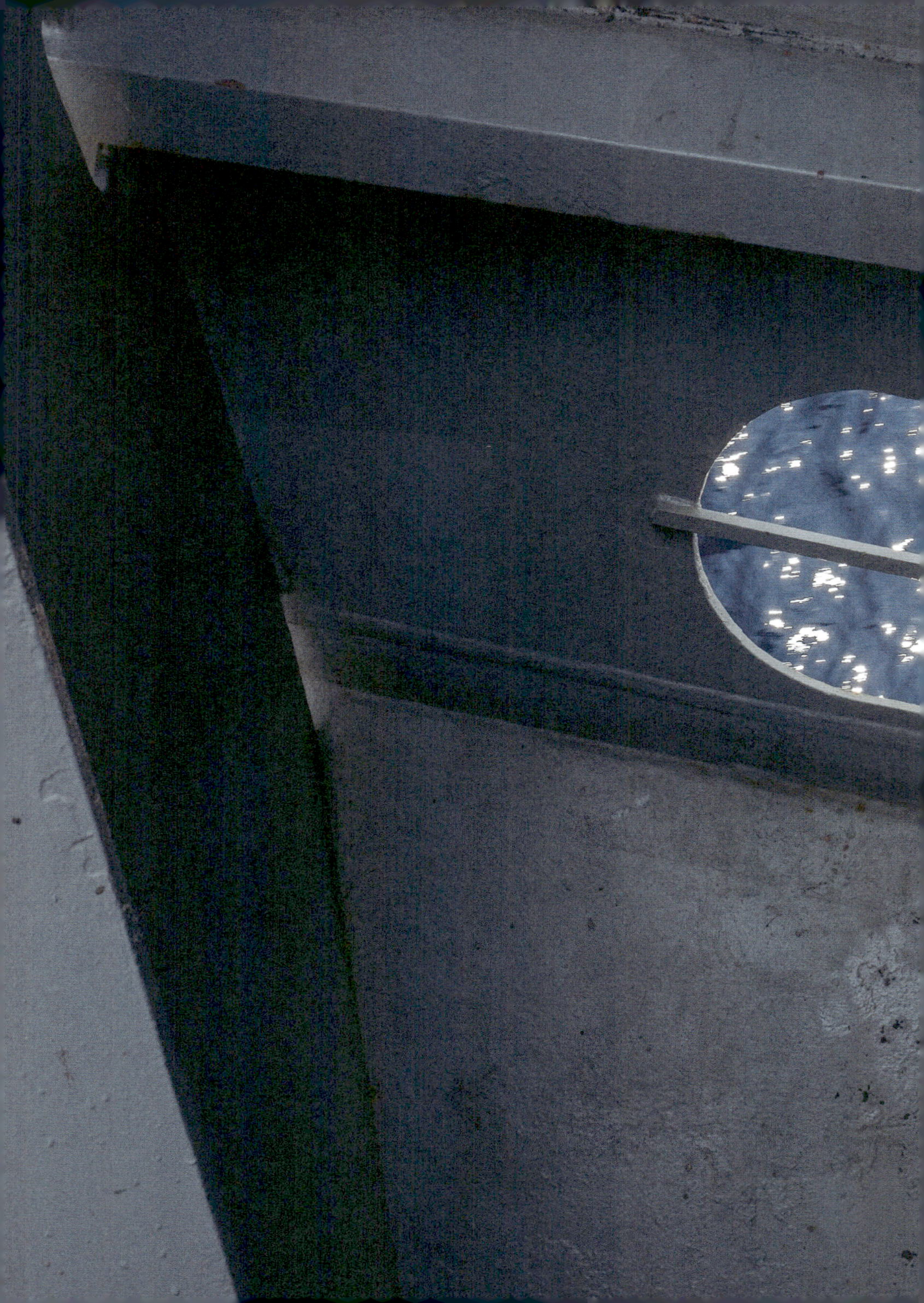

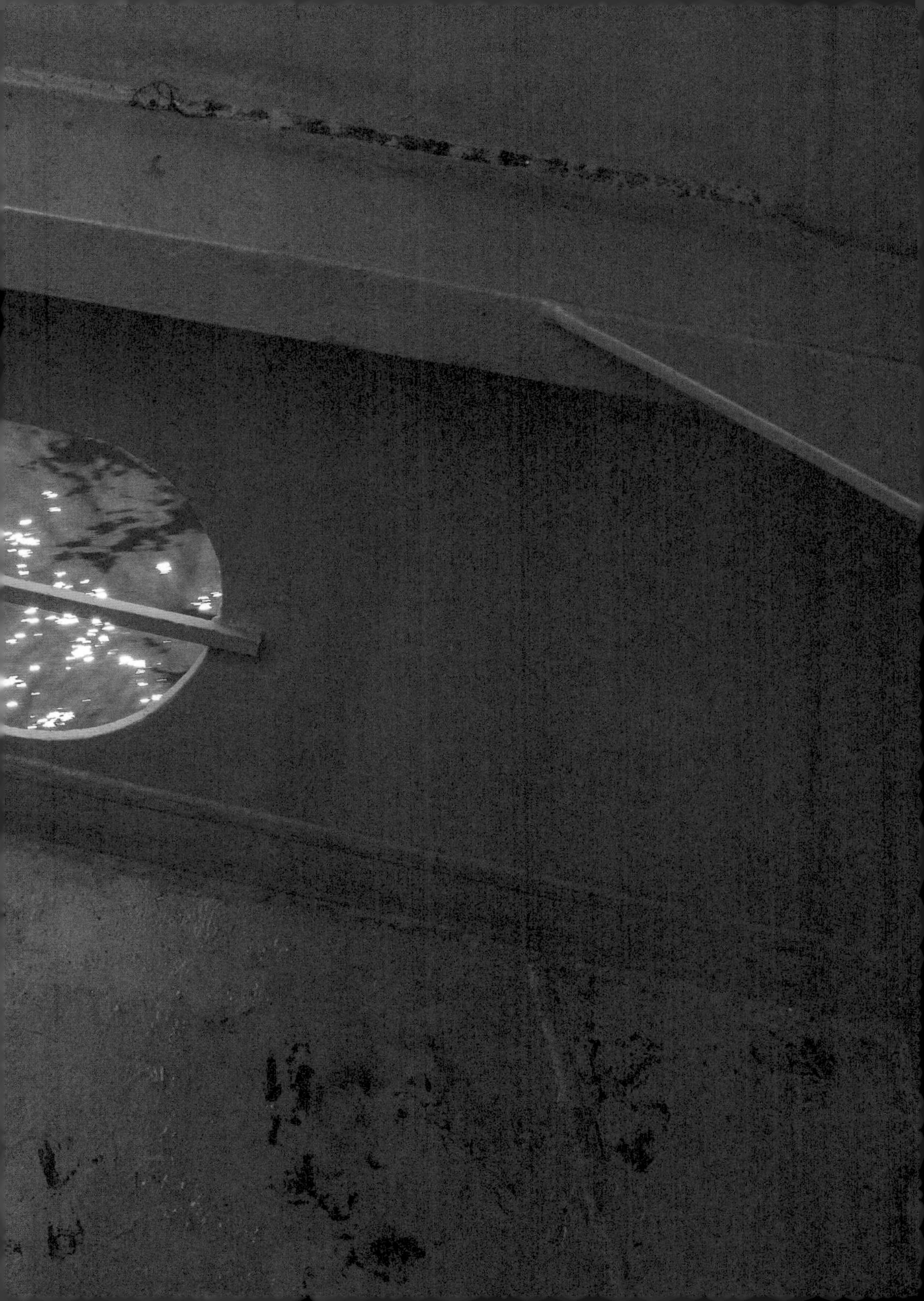

Sometimes I wish I could be invisible.
So I wouldn't have to explain or defend myself.

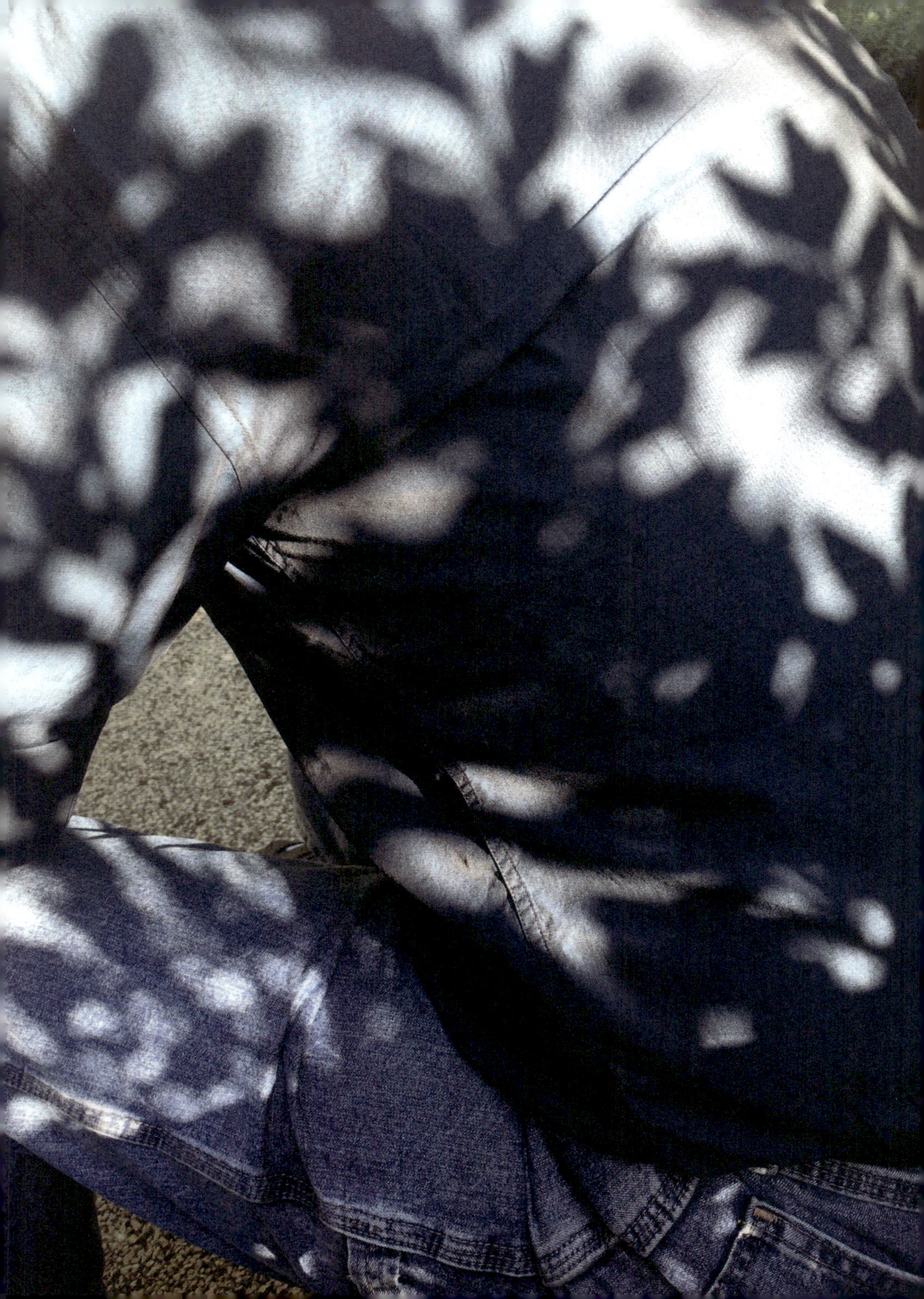

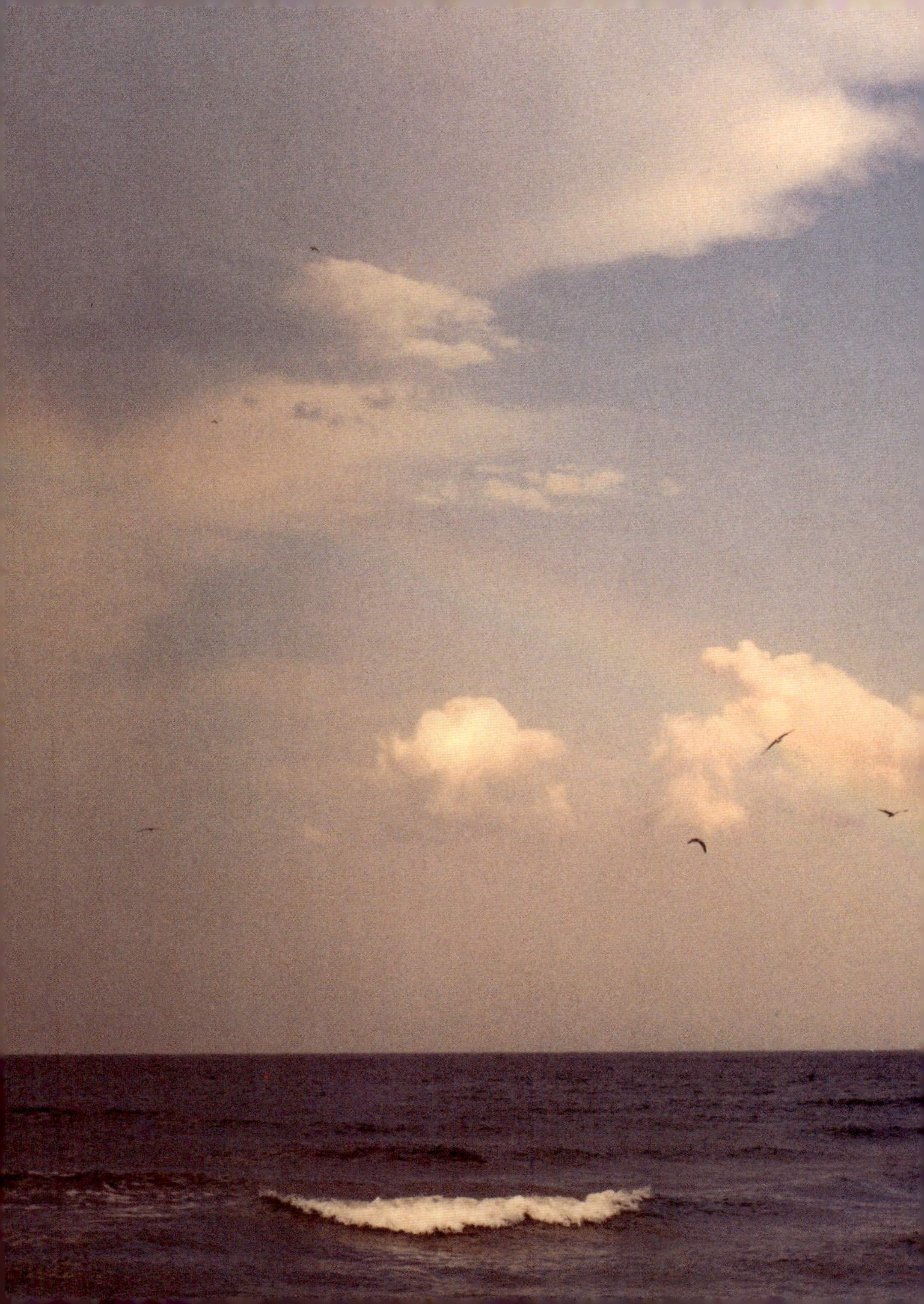

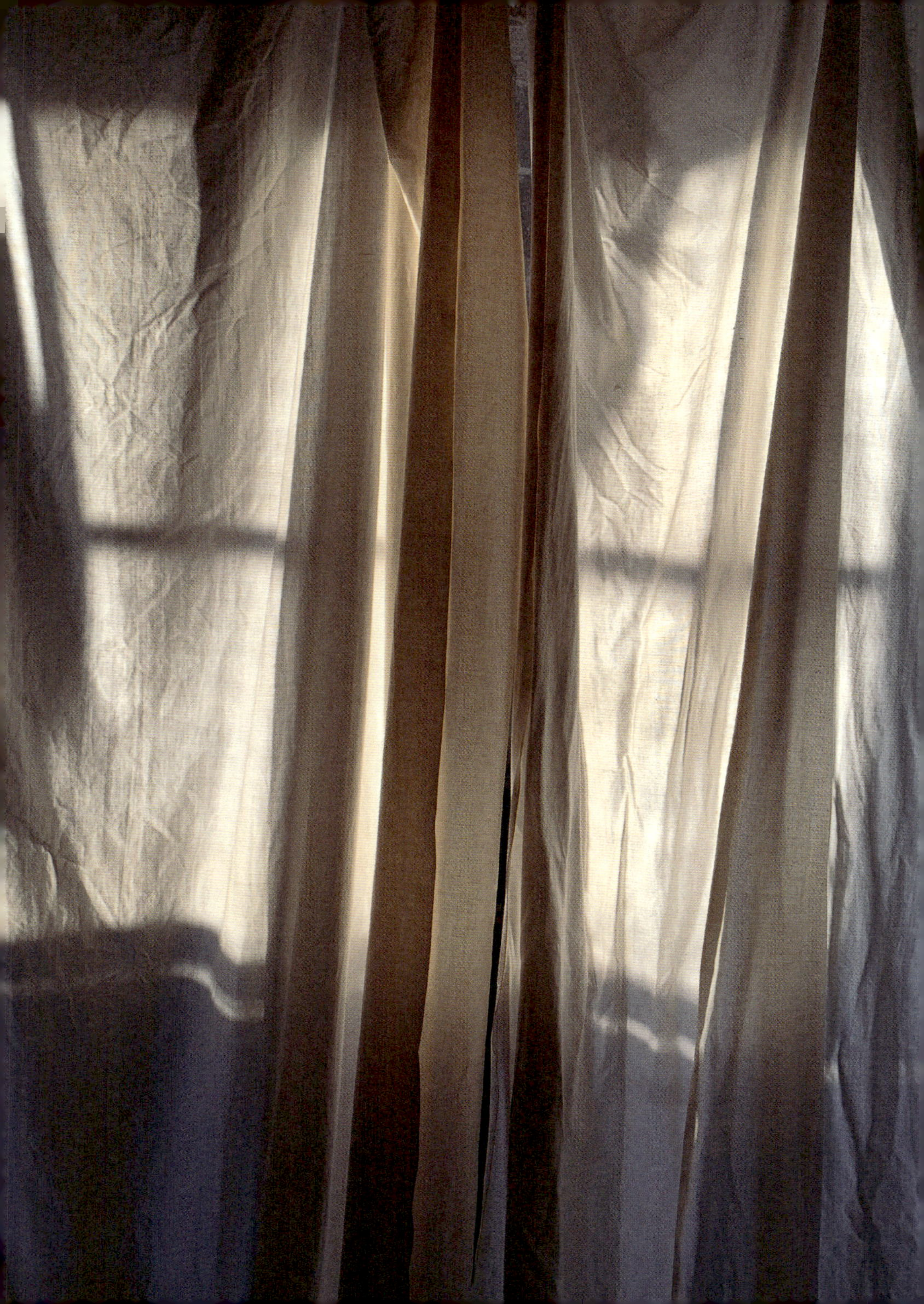

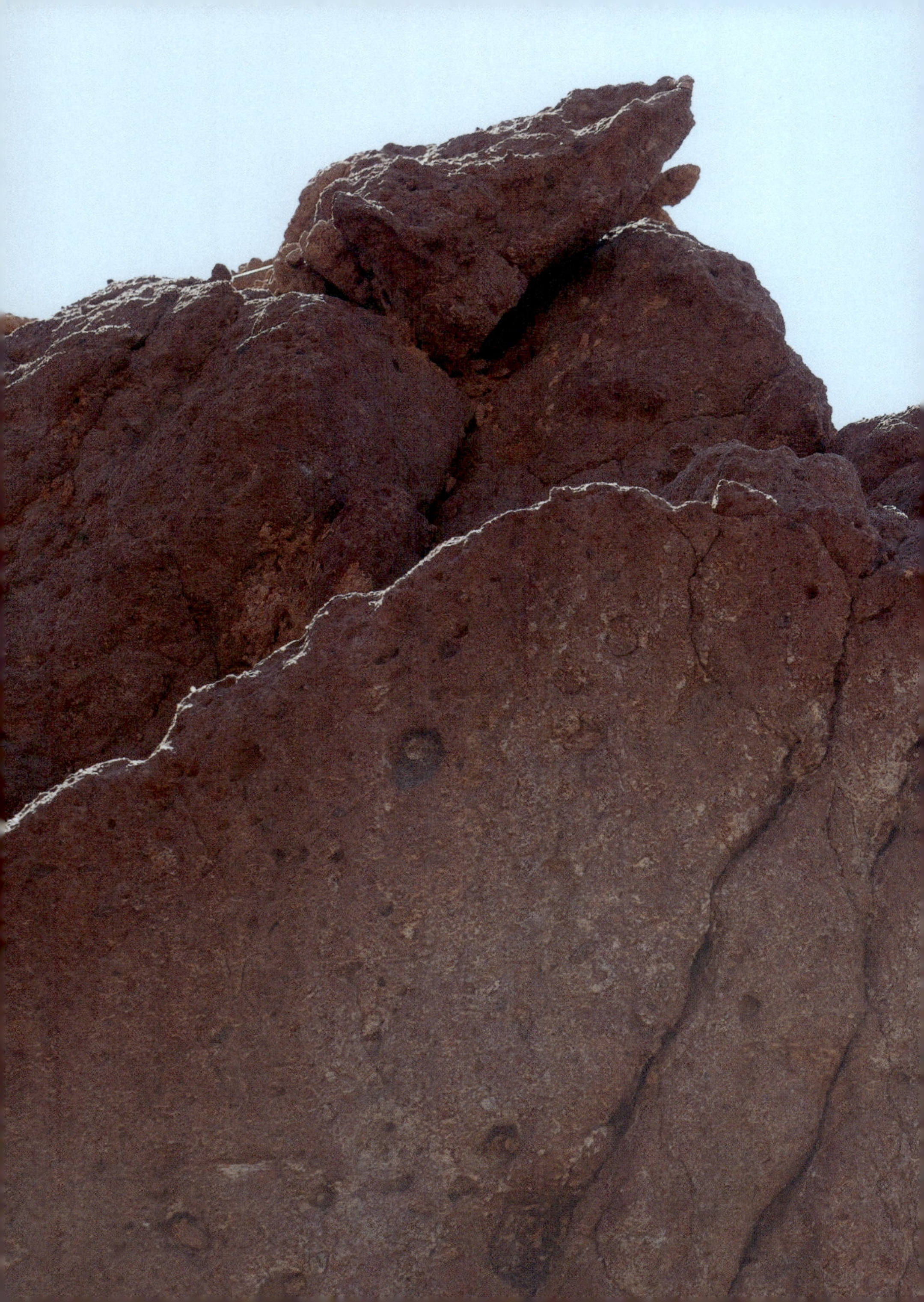

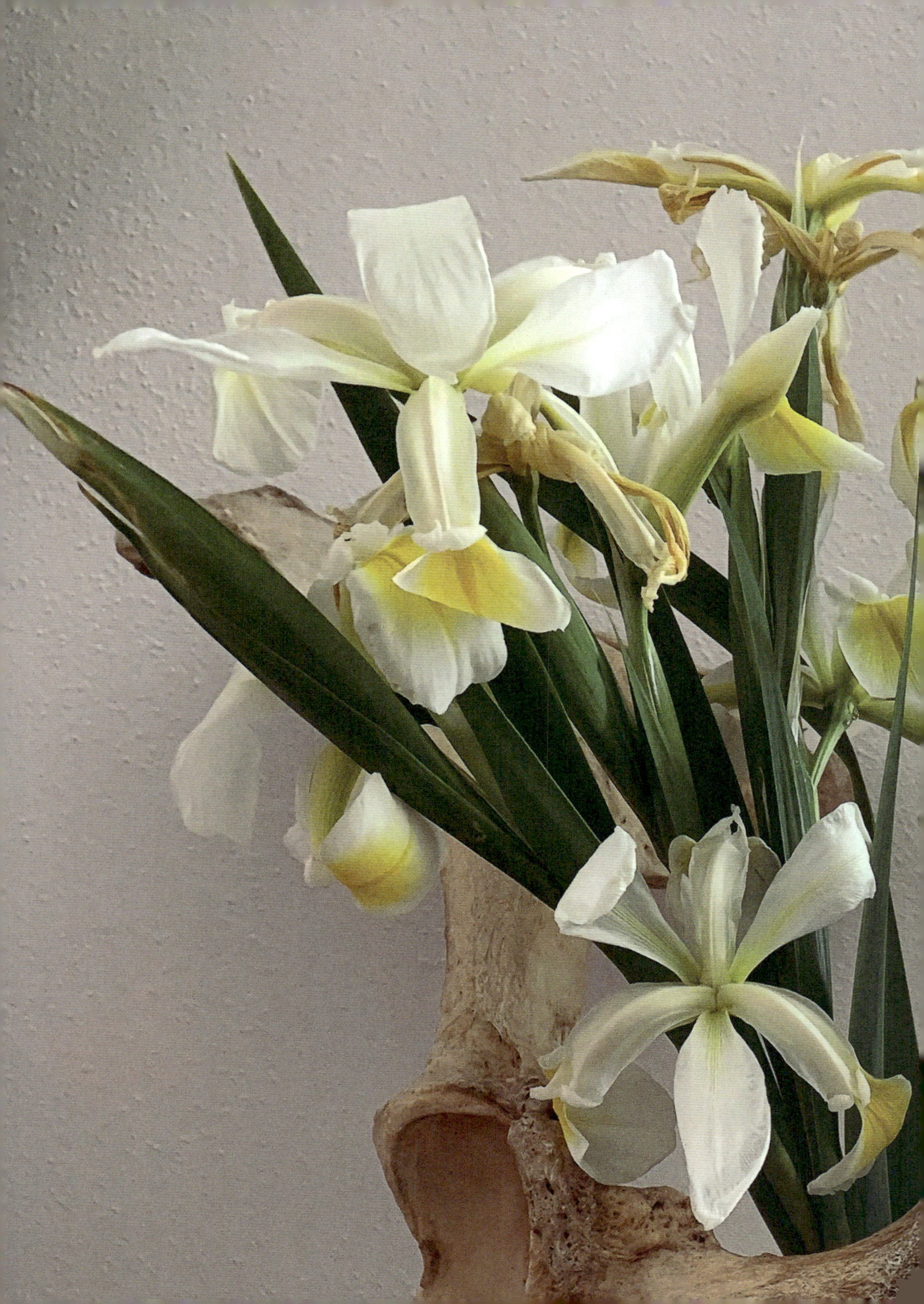

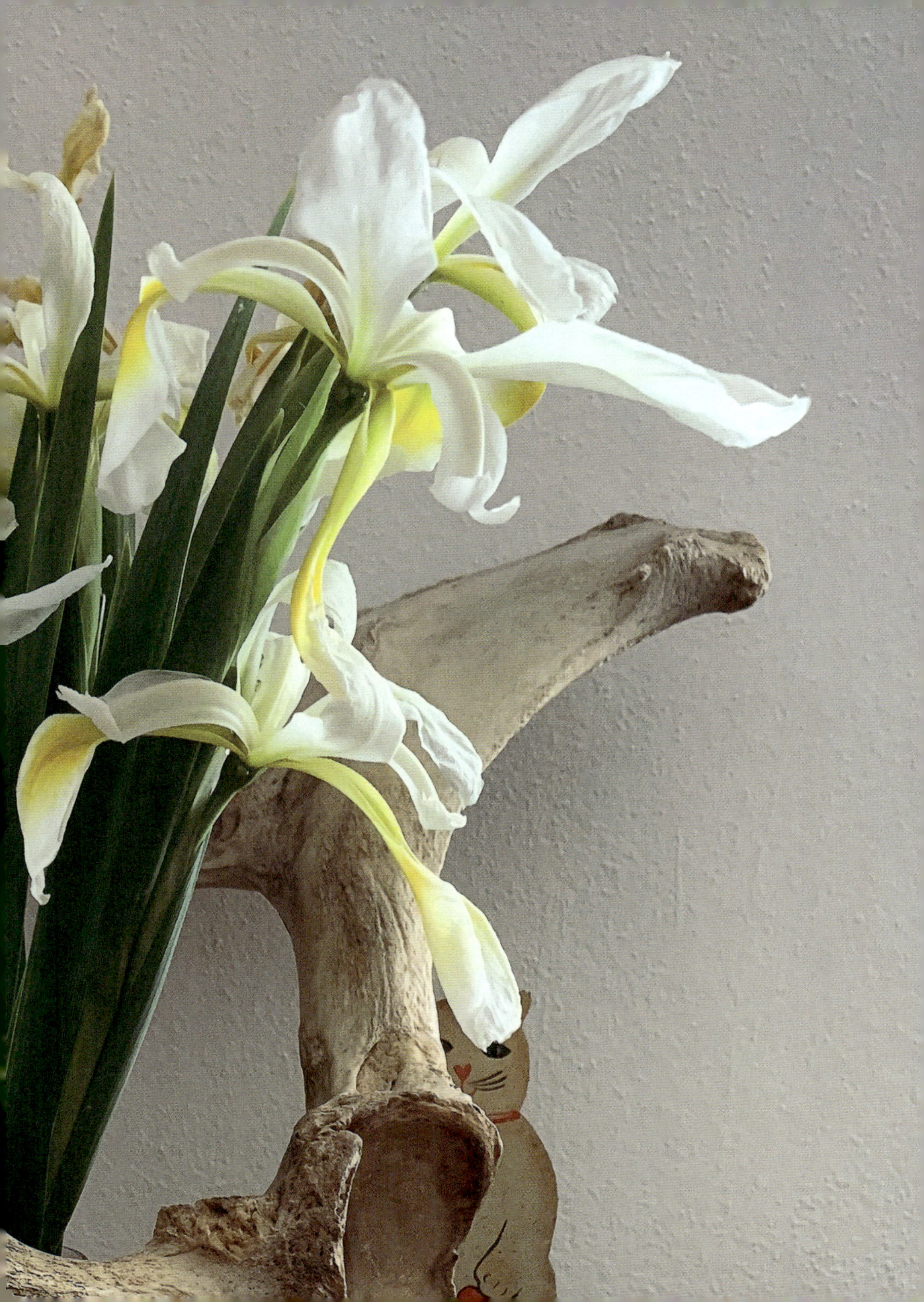

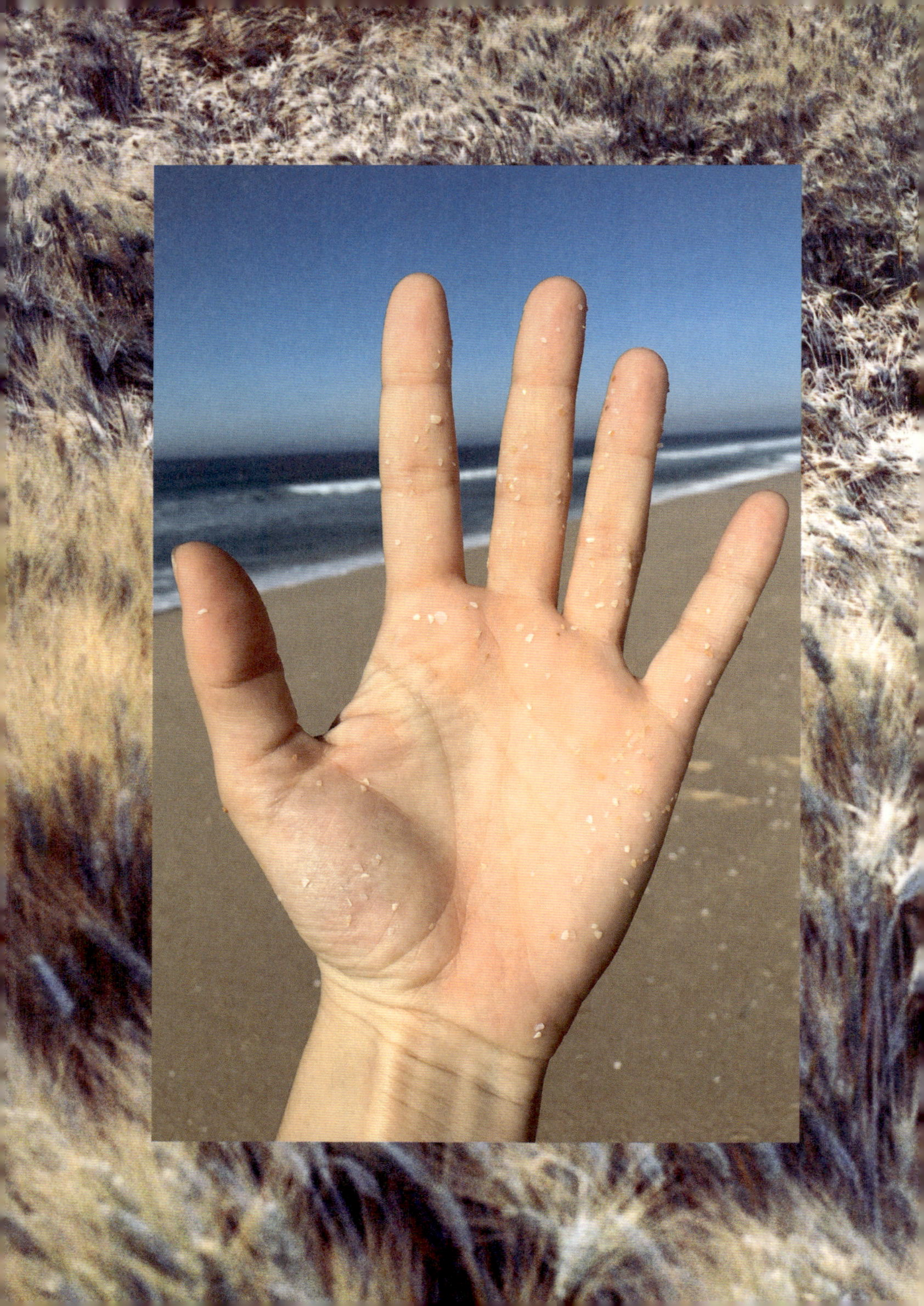

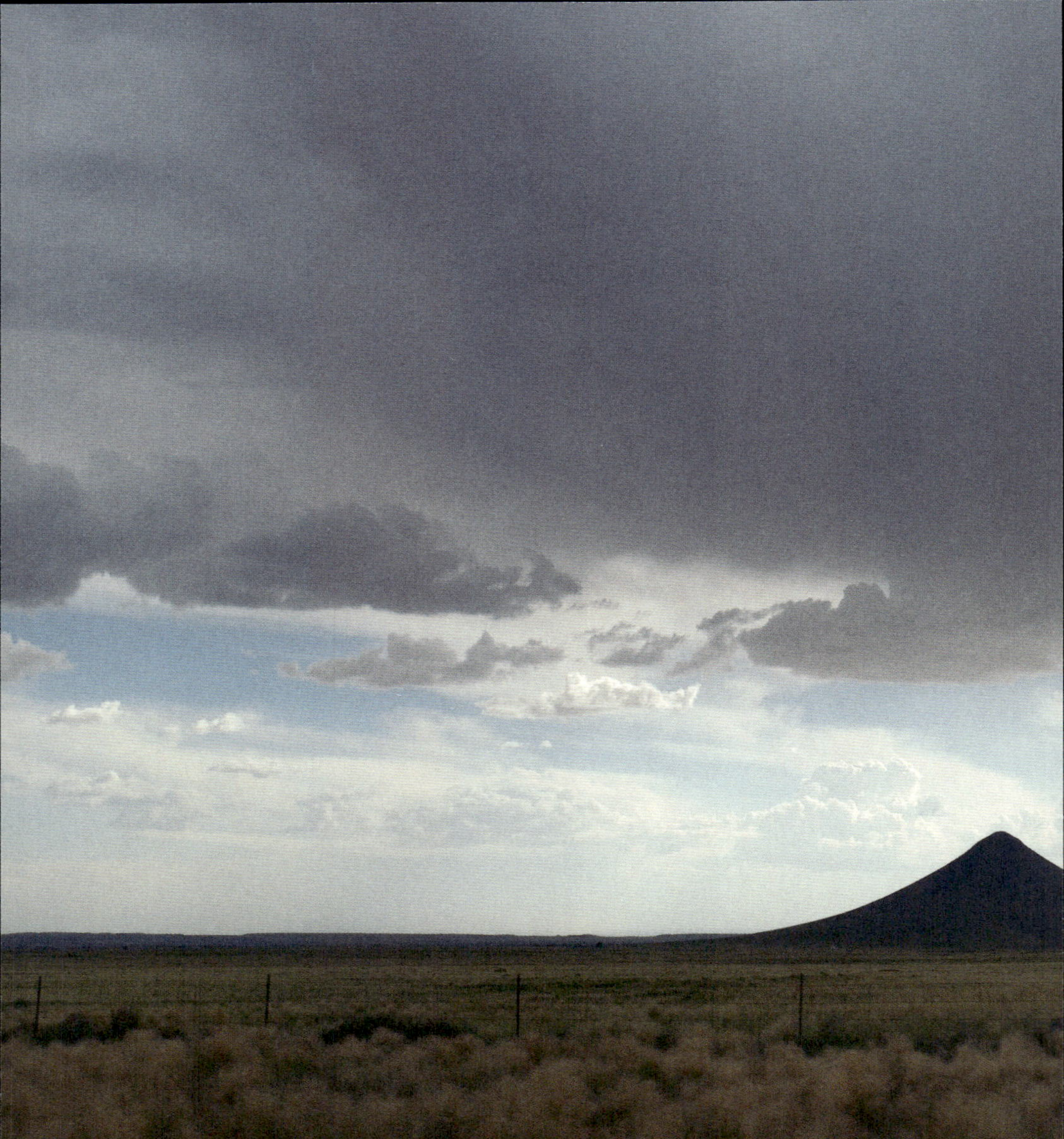

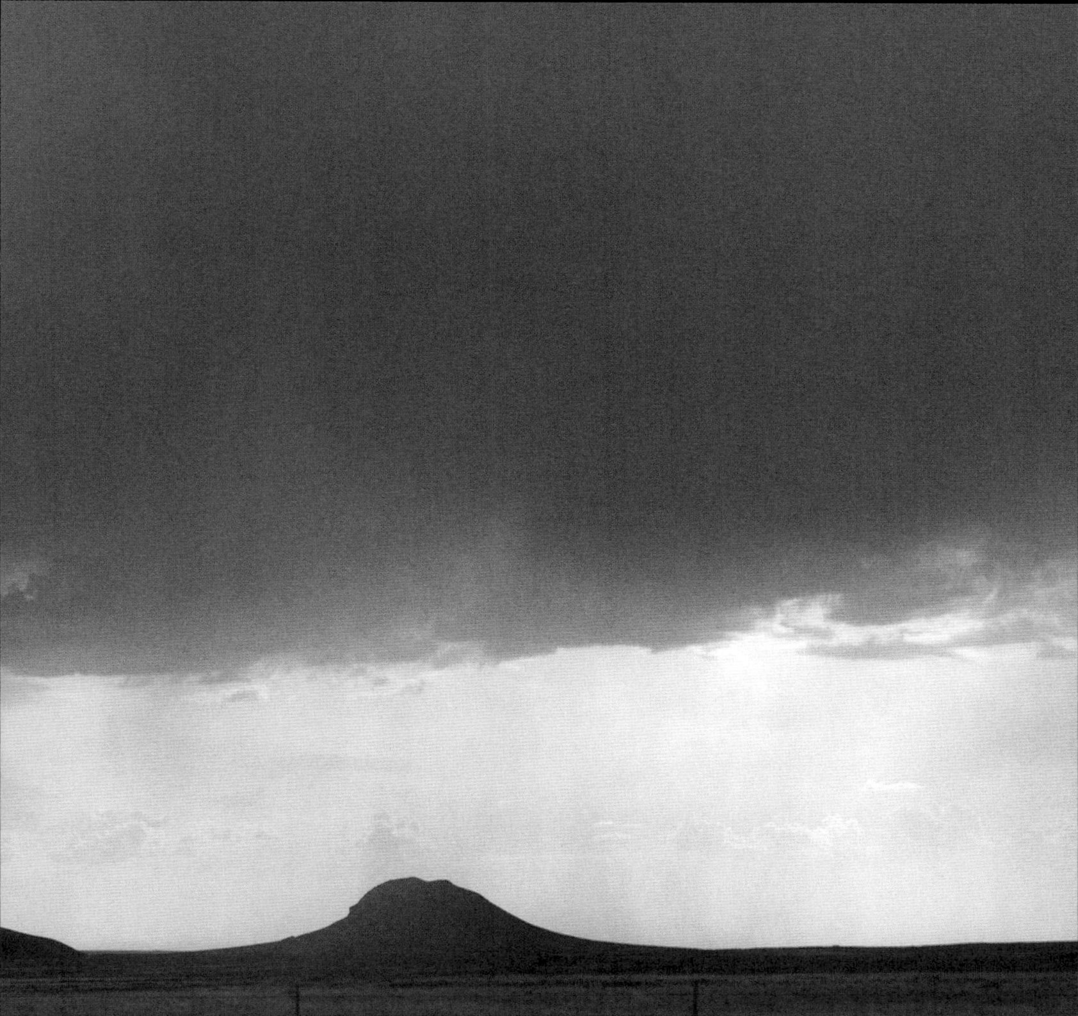

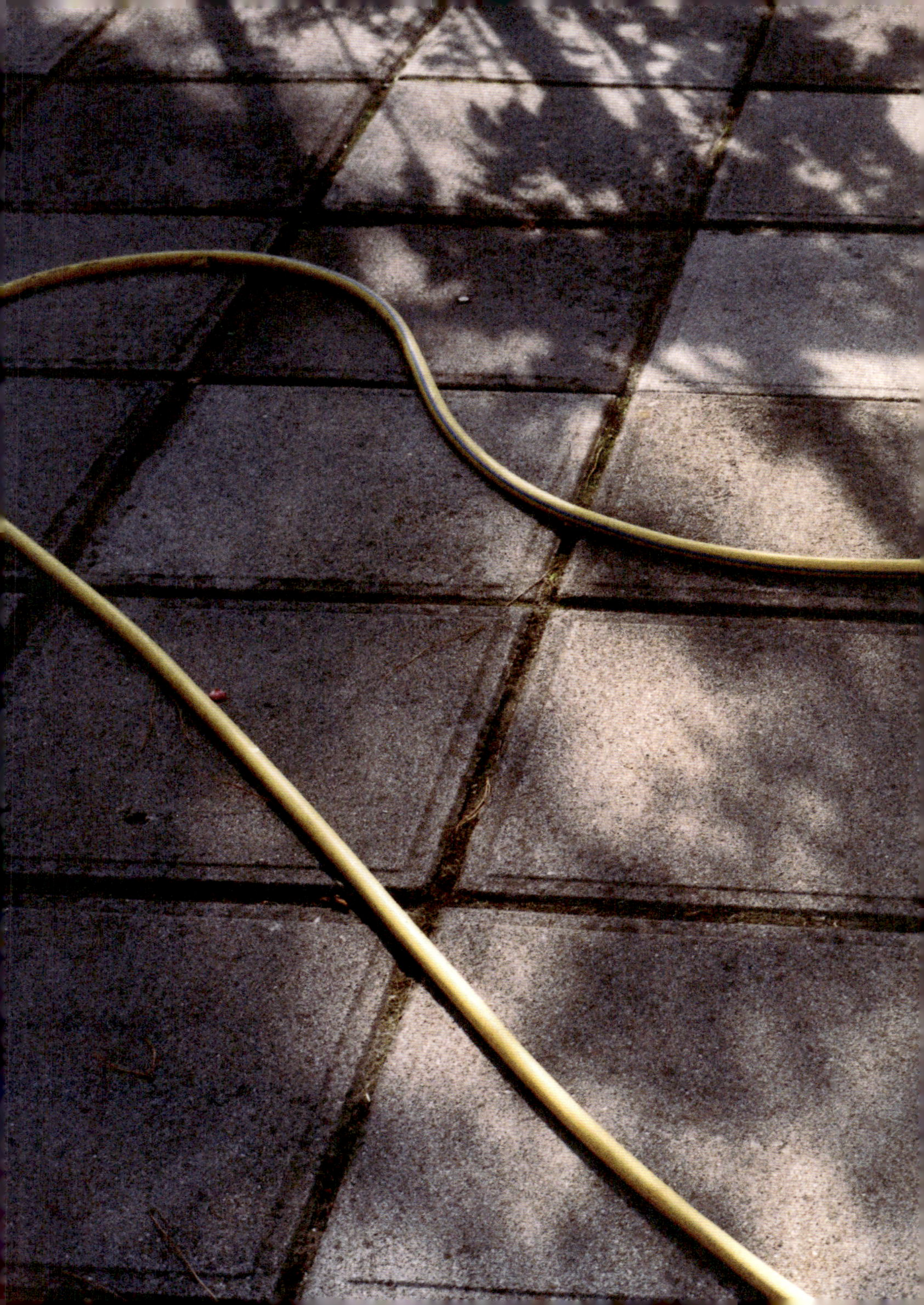

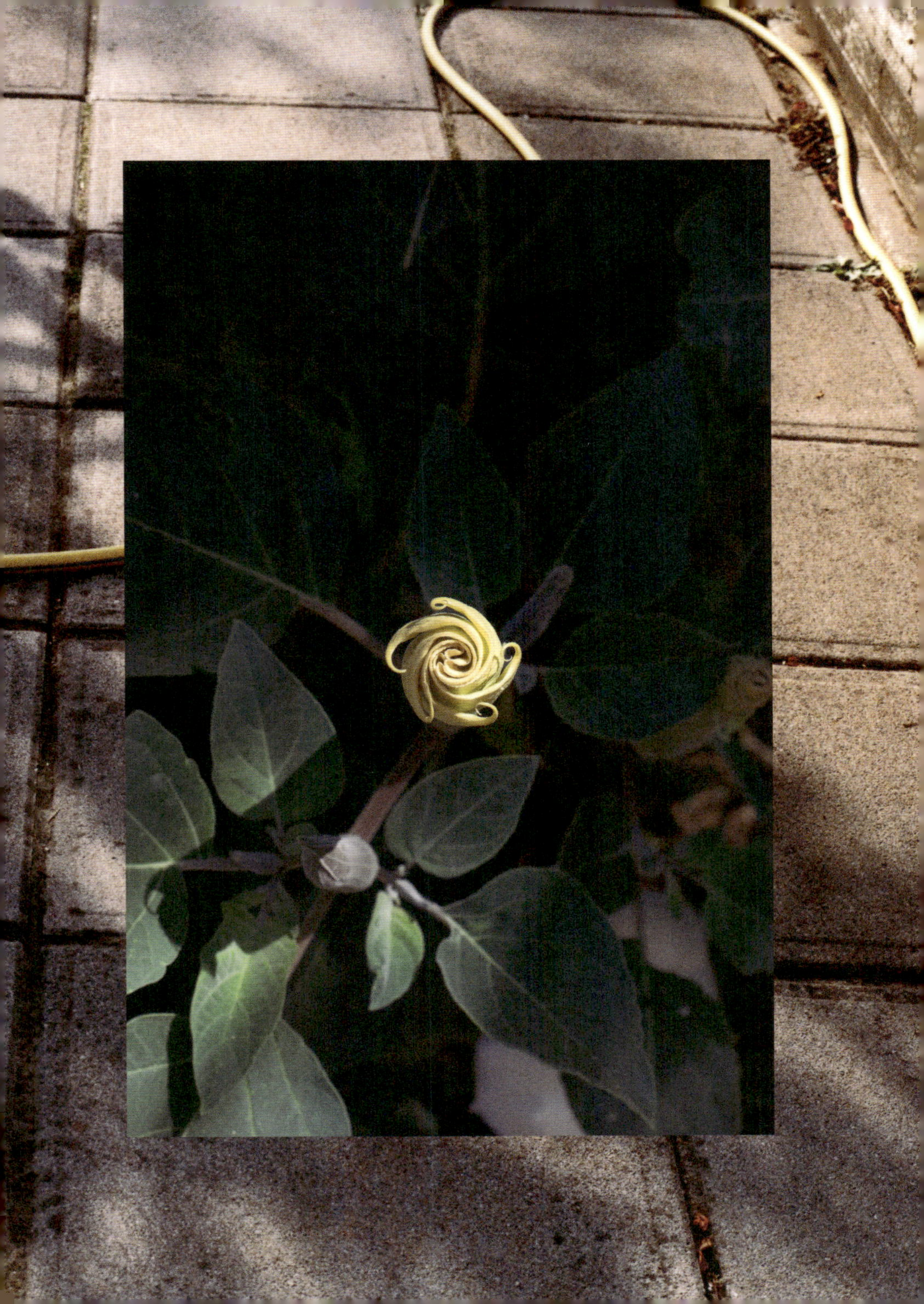

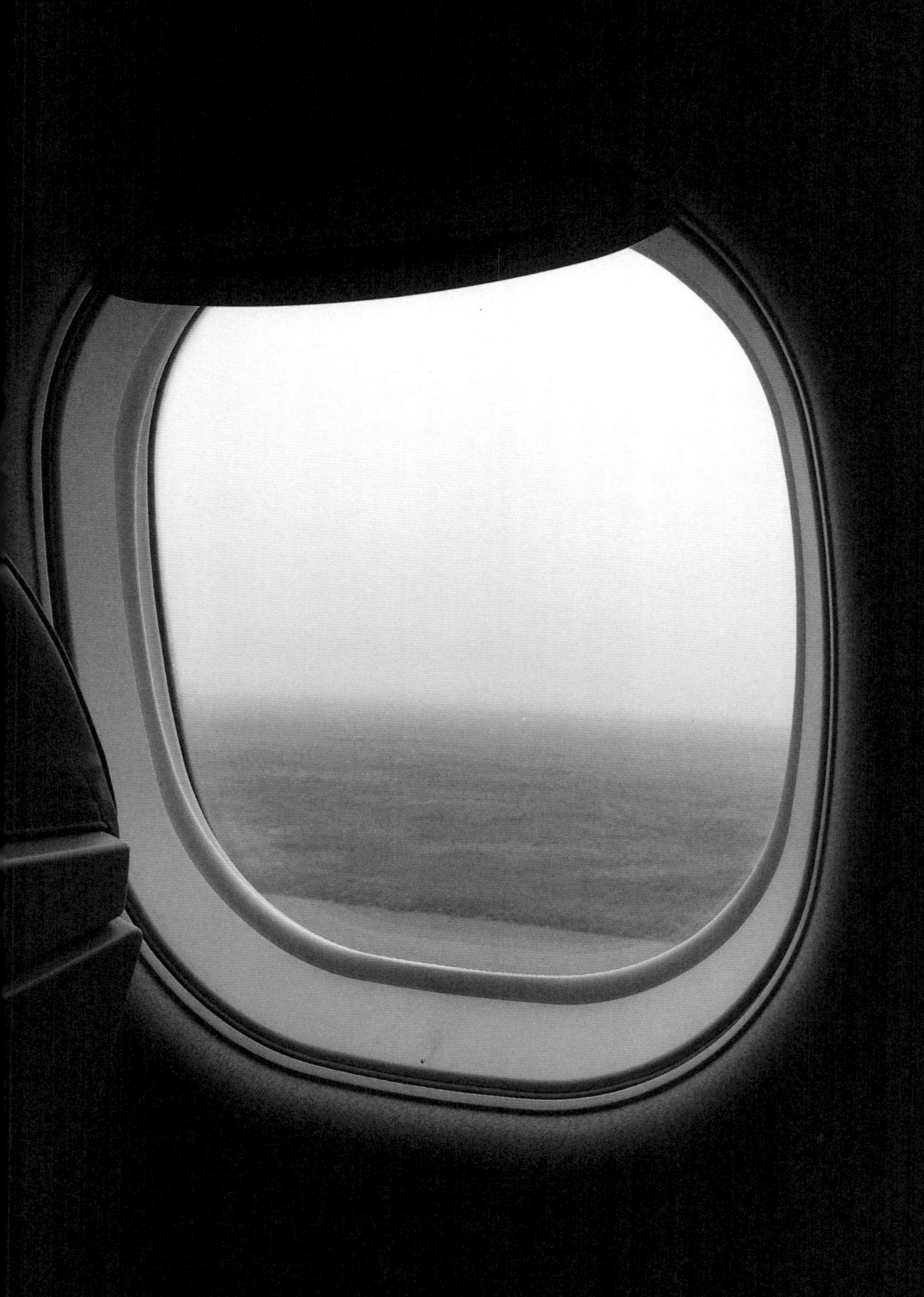

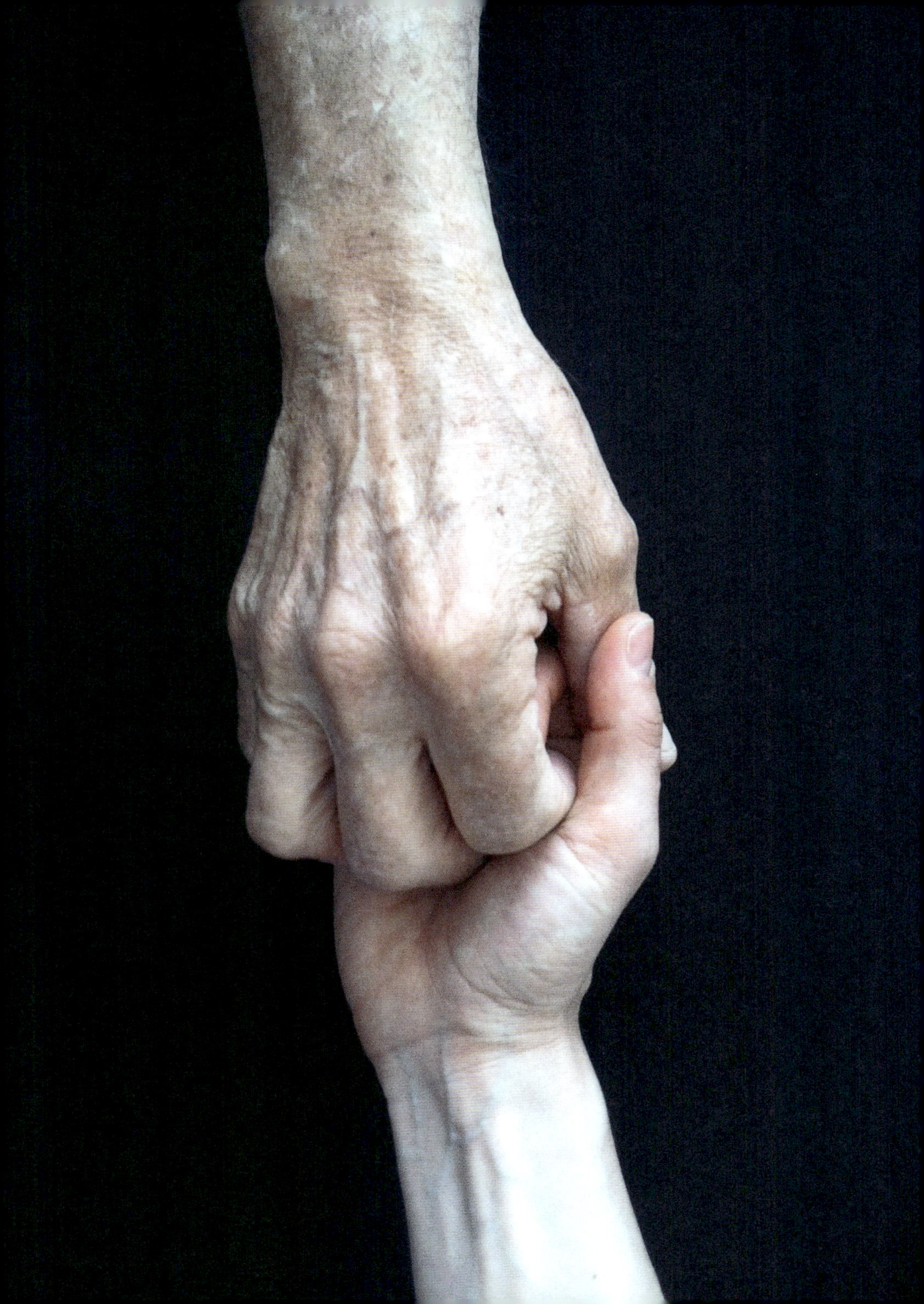

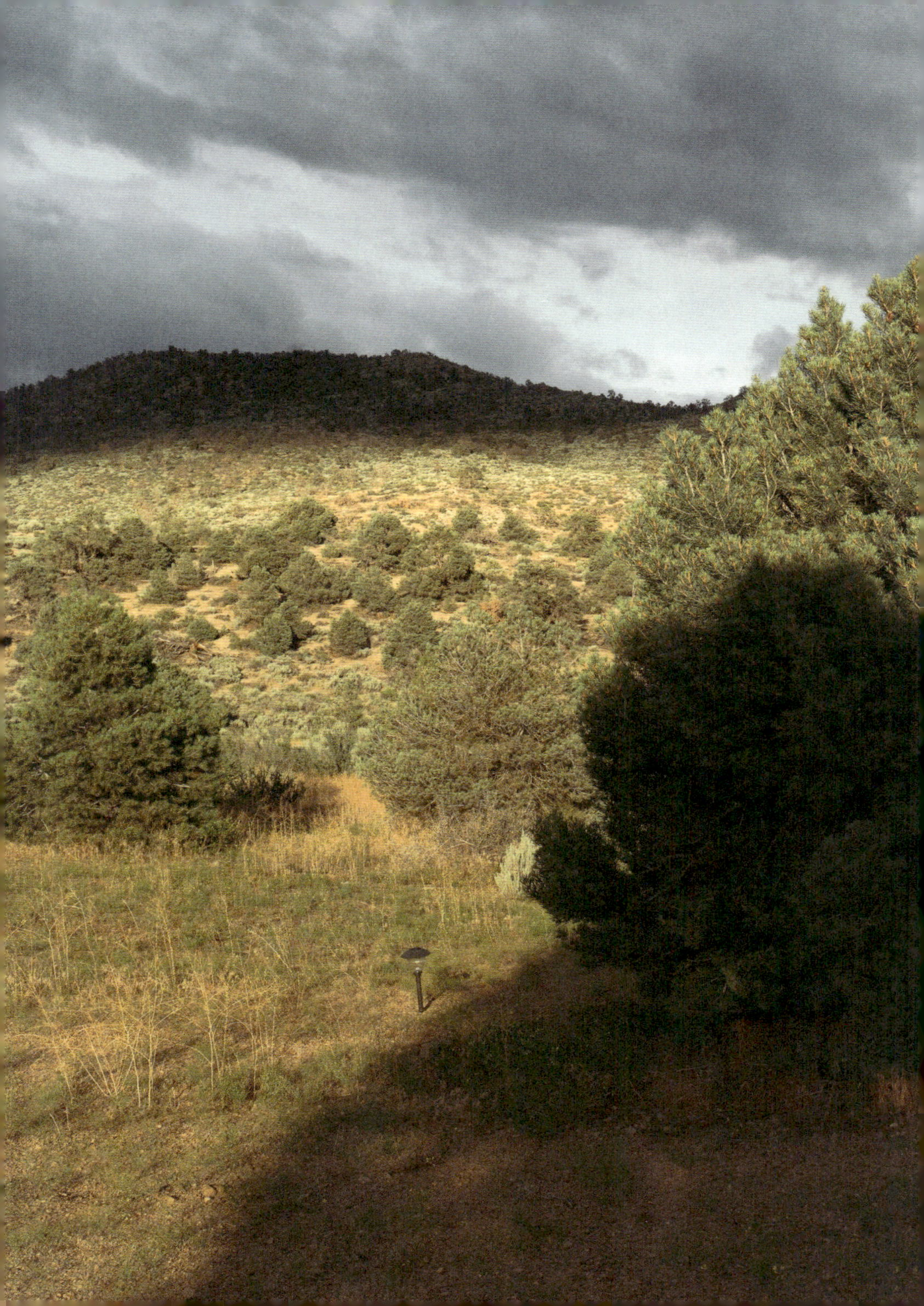

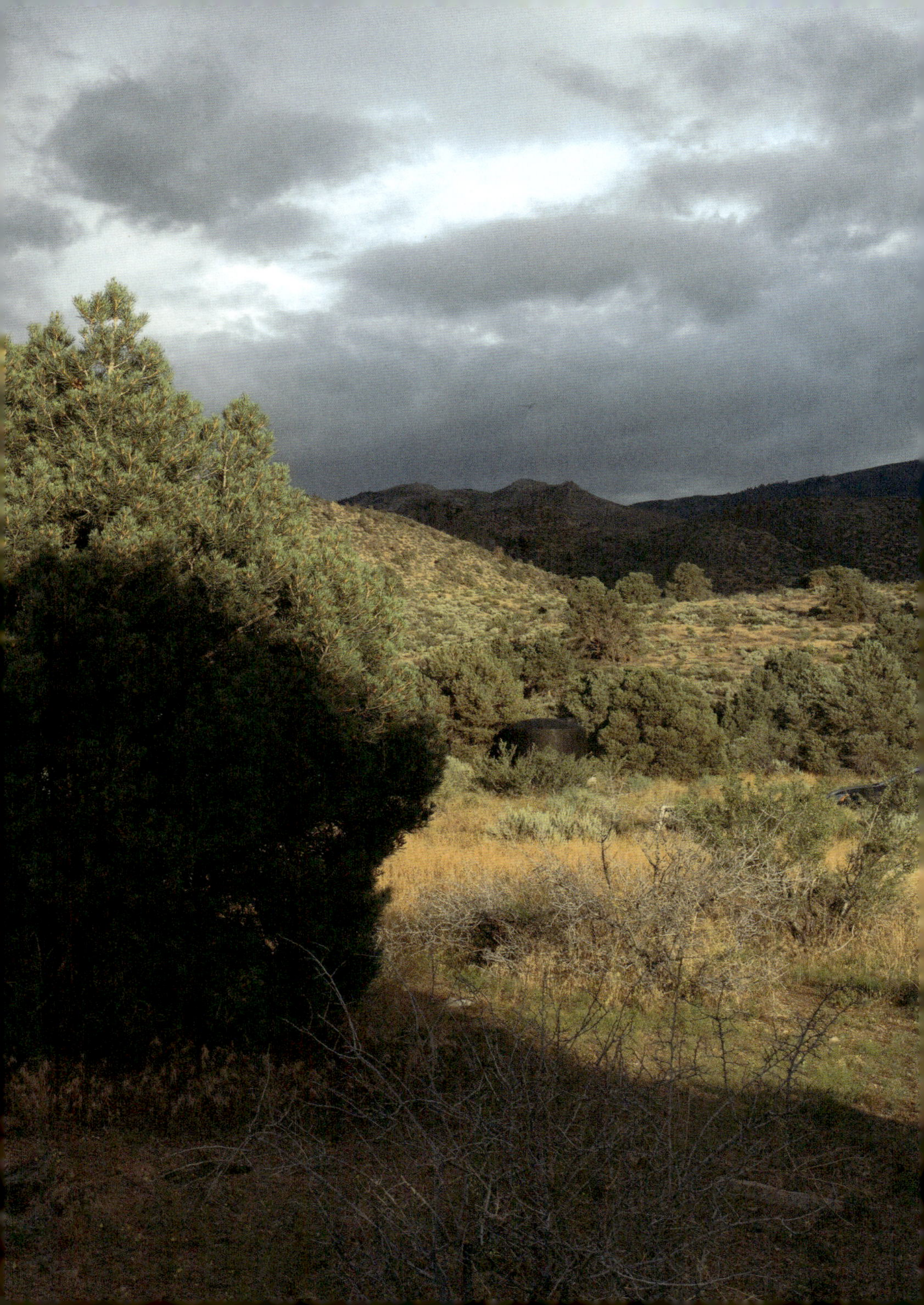

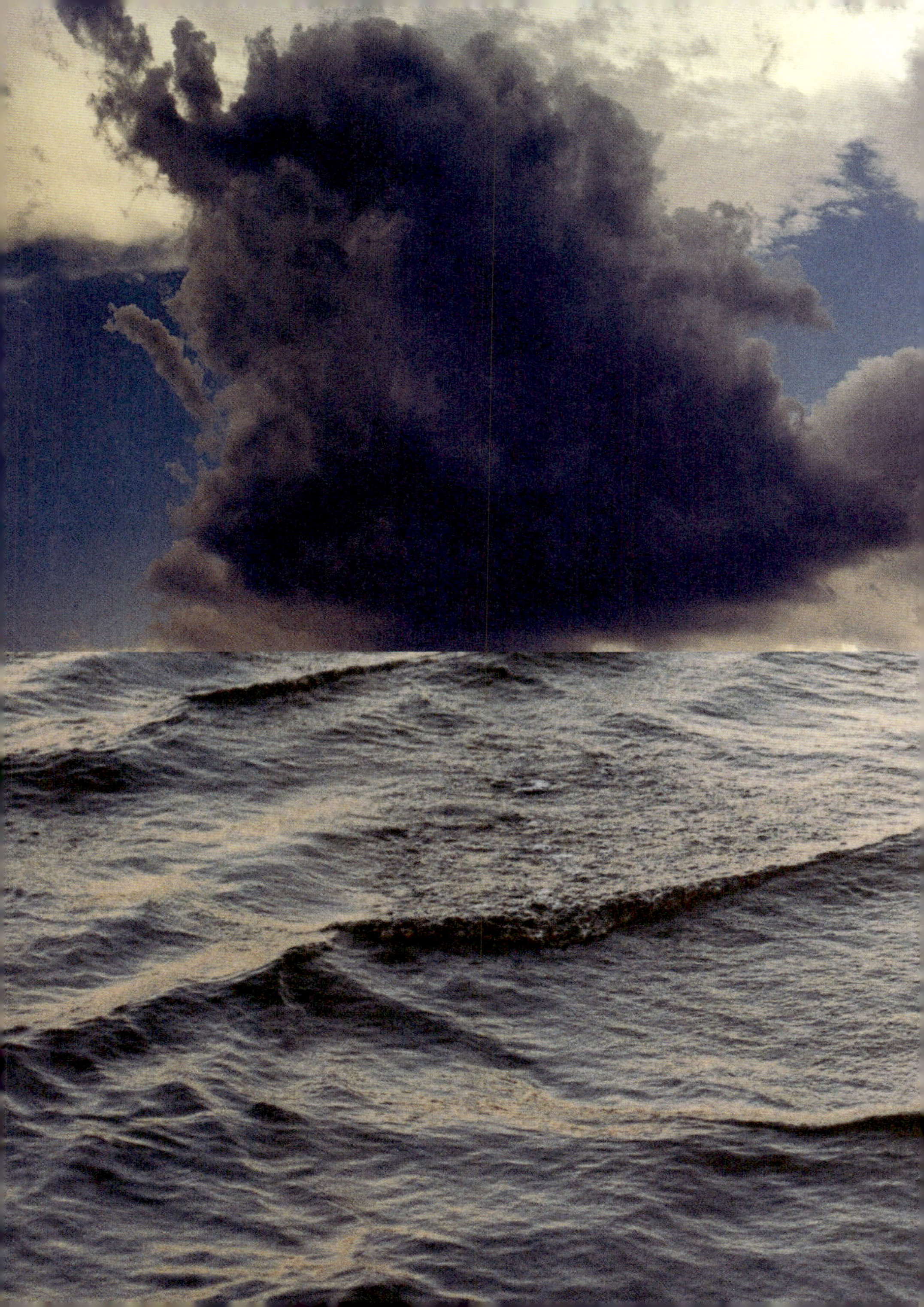

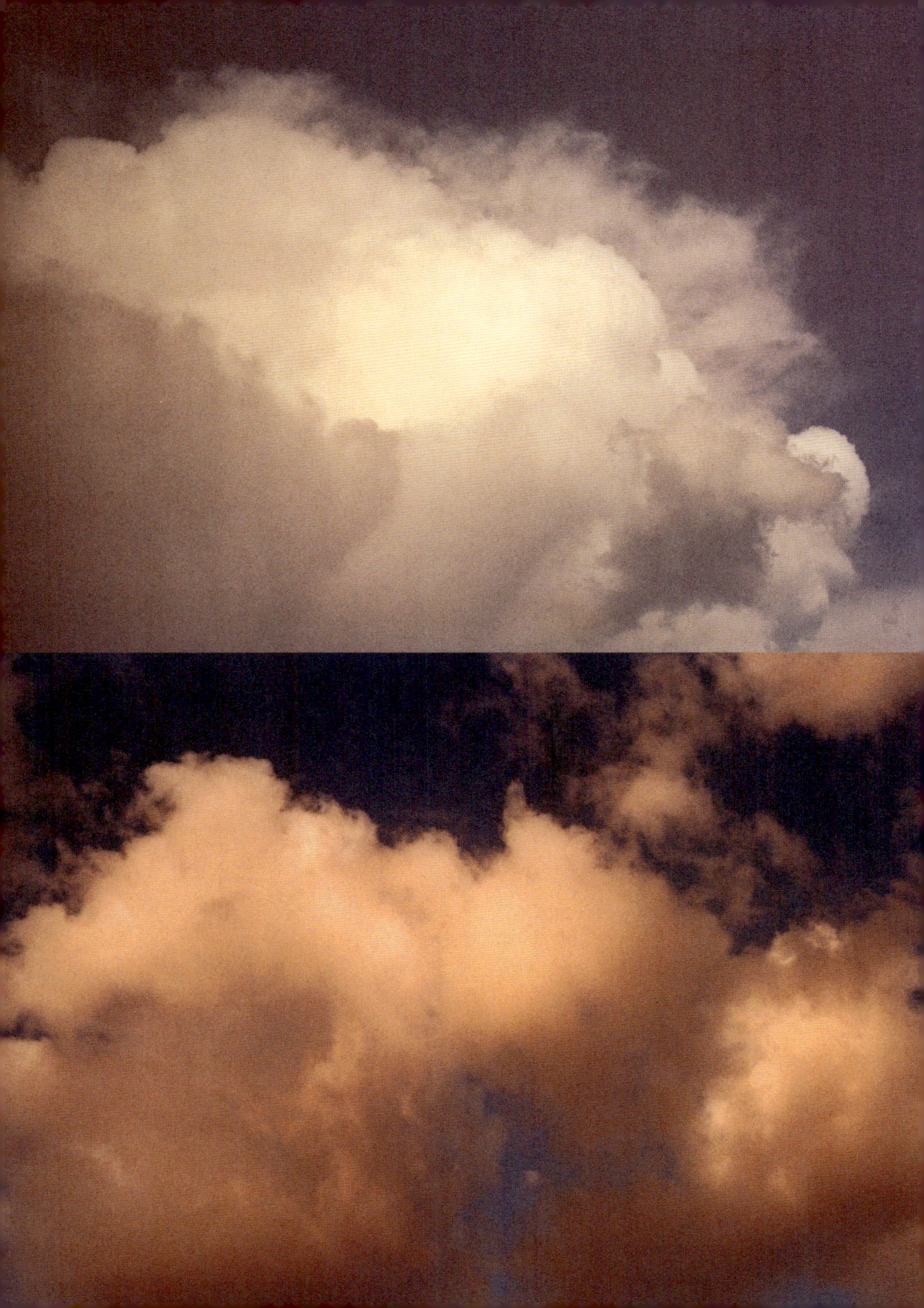

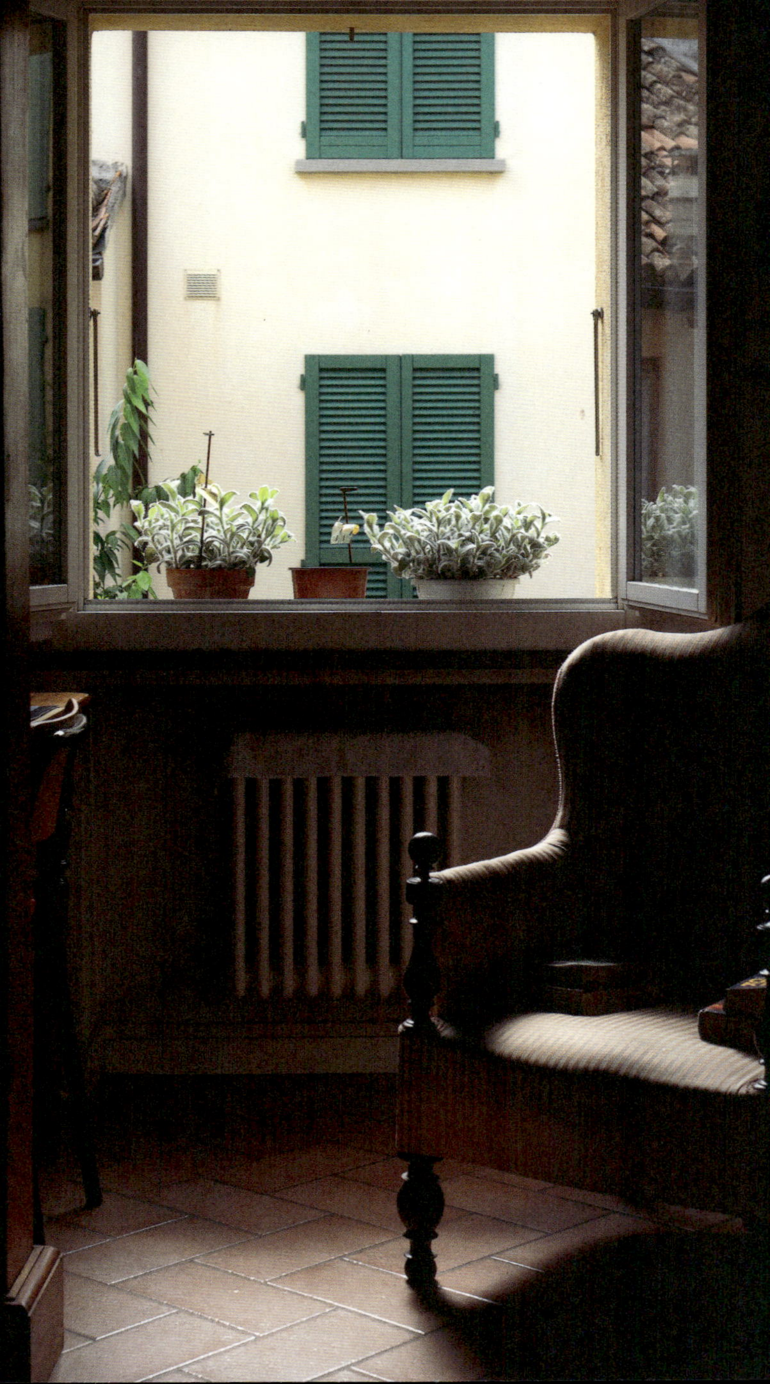

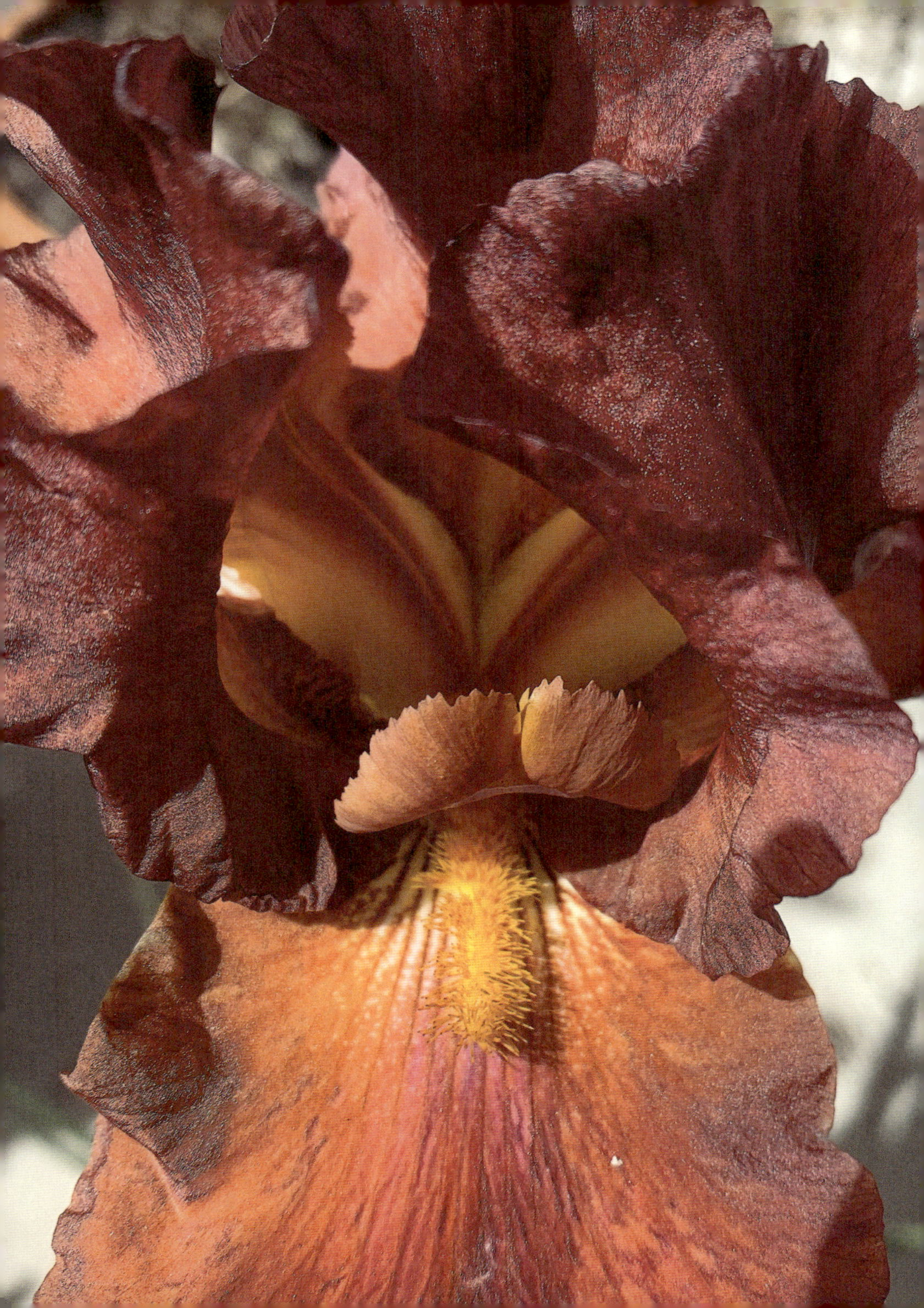

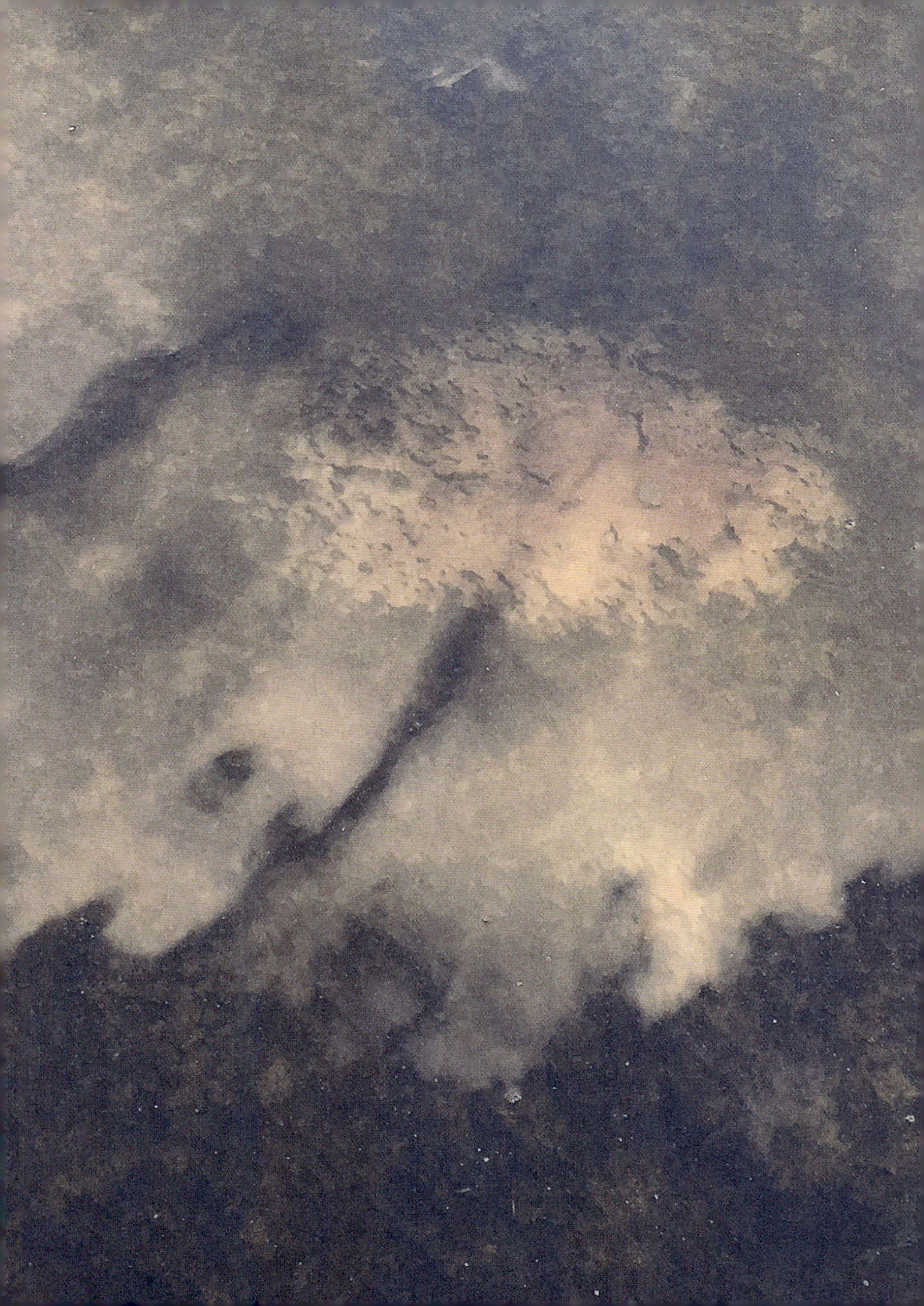

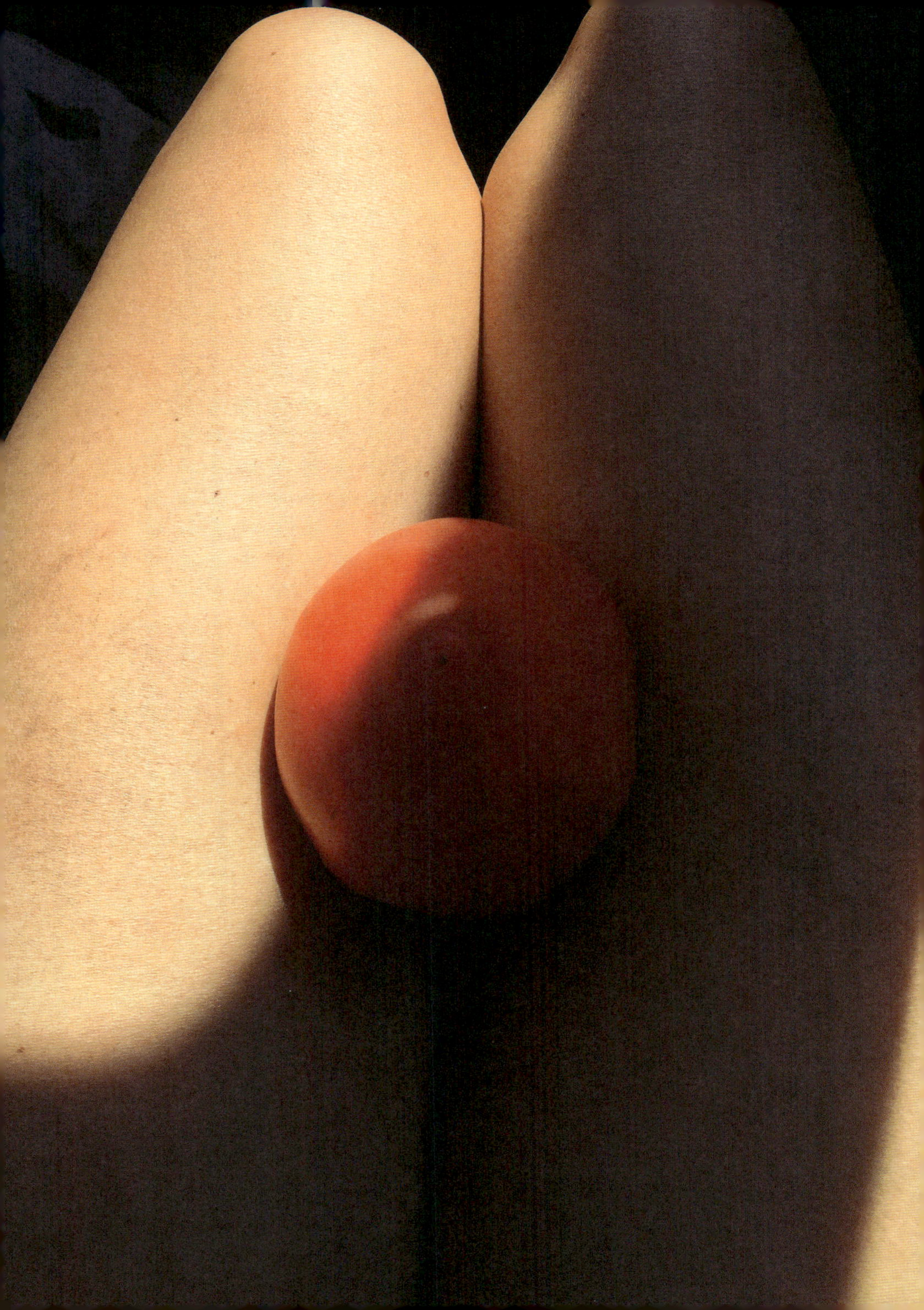

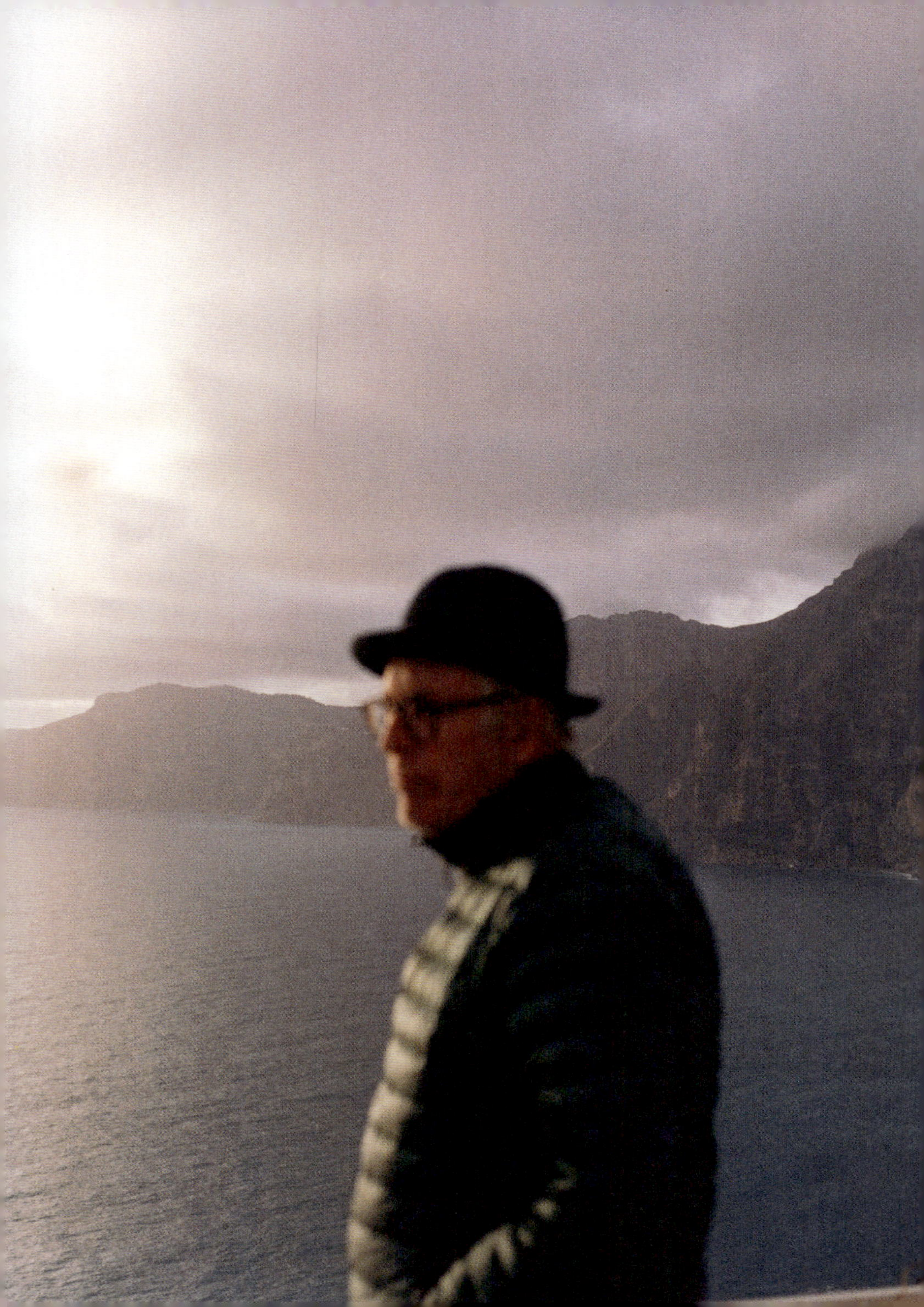

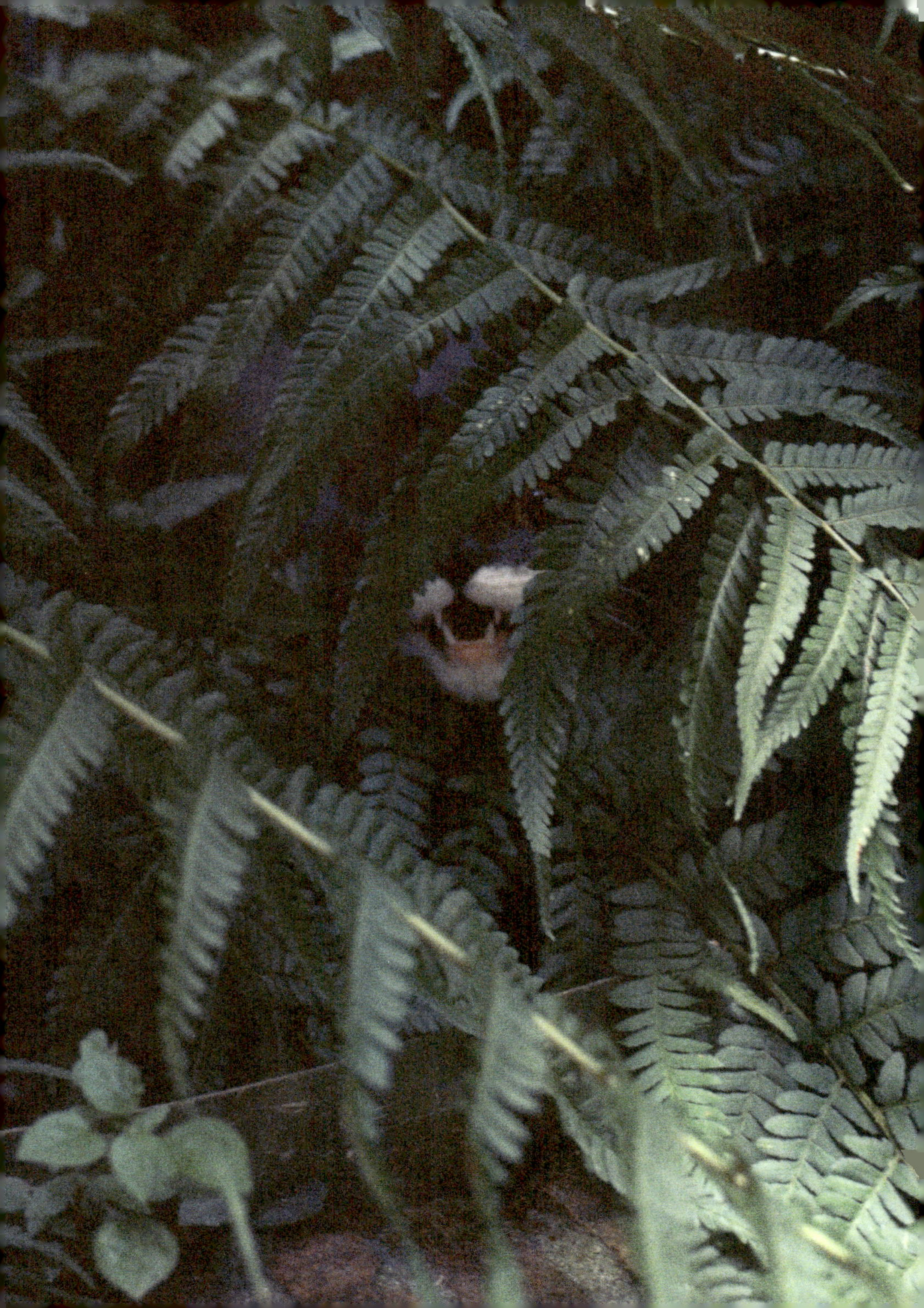

When I came back from work I found a colorful bunch of flowers in a red vase in the middle of the kitchen table. There was a paper bag with candies next to it and a note. It said 'good luck with your new home'. I had to step back and stare at the scene for a while. The orange ceiling lamp above it drew a soft, bright circle all around it. Everything else in the room looked very dark. The vase looked like the most lonesome, most fragile thing in the whole world.

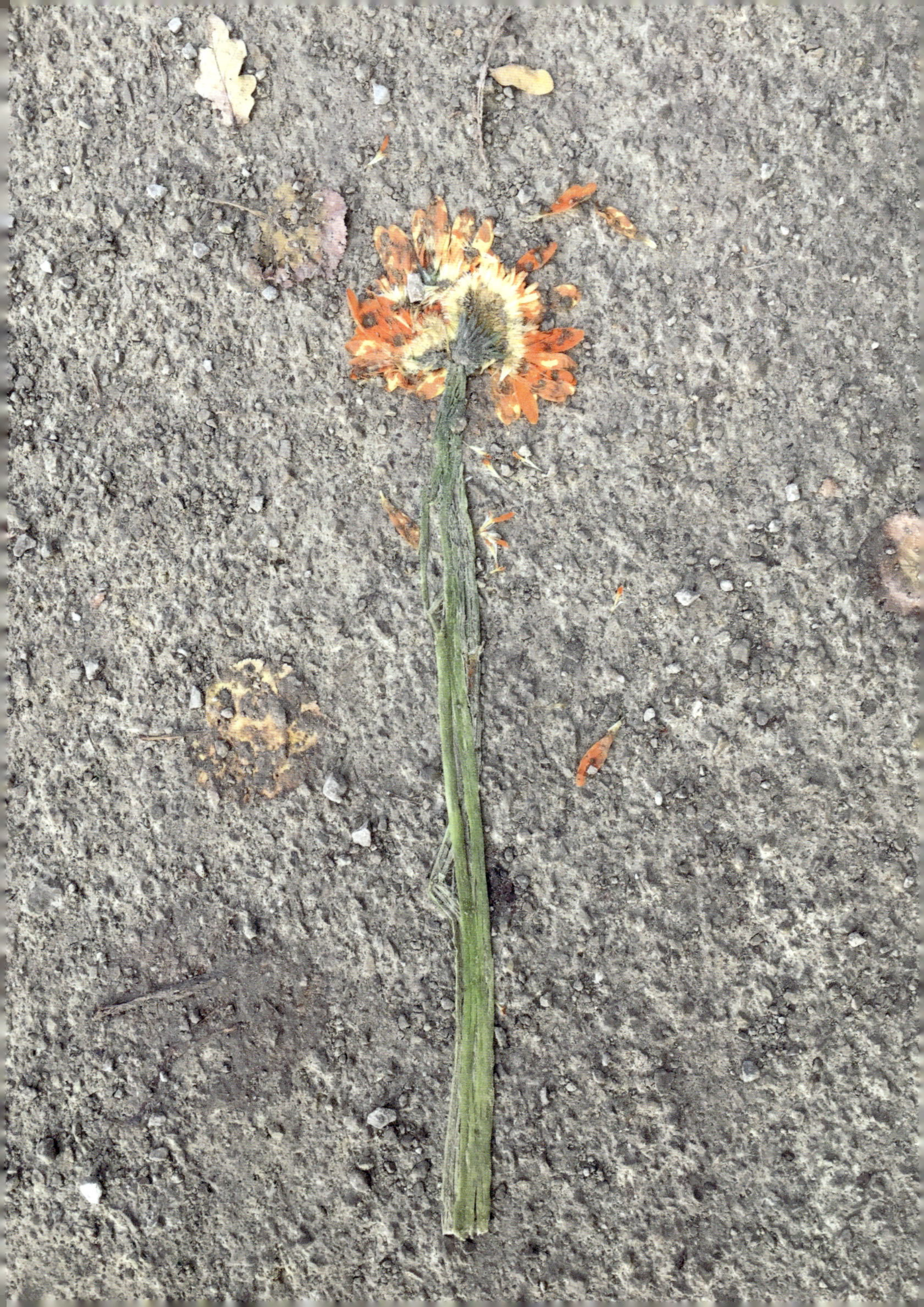

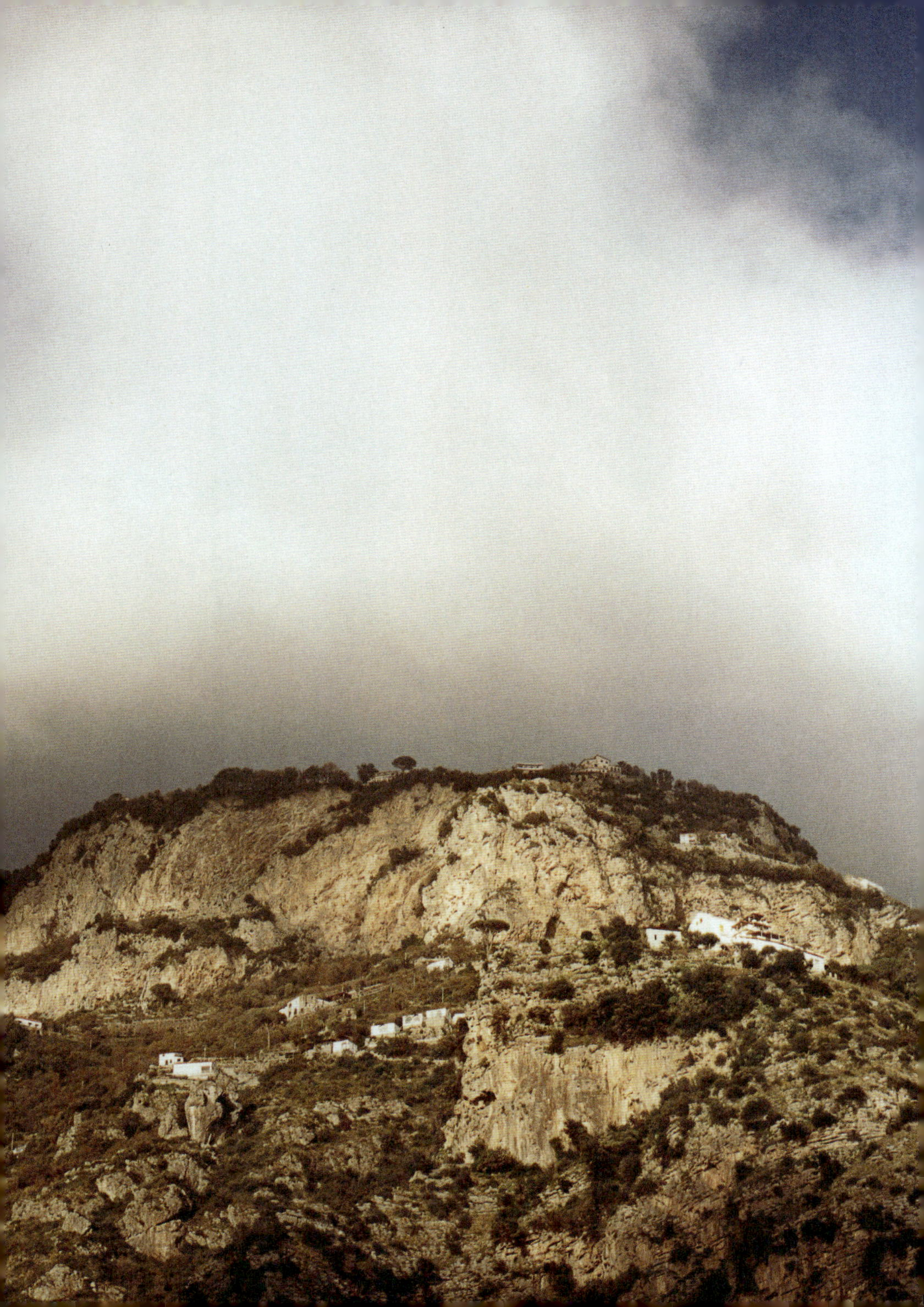

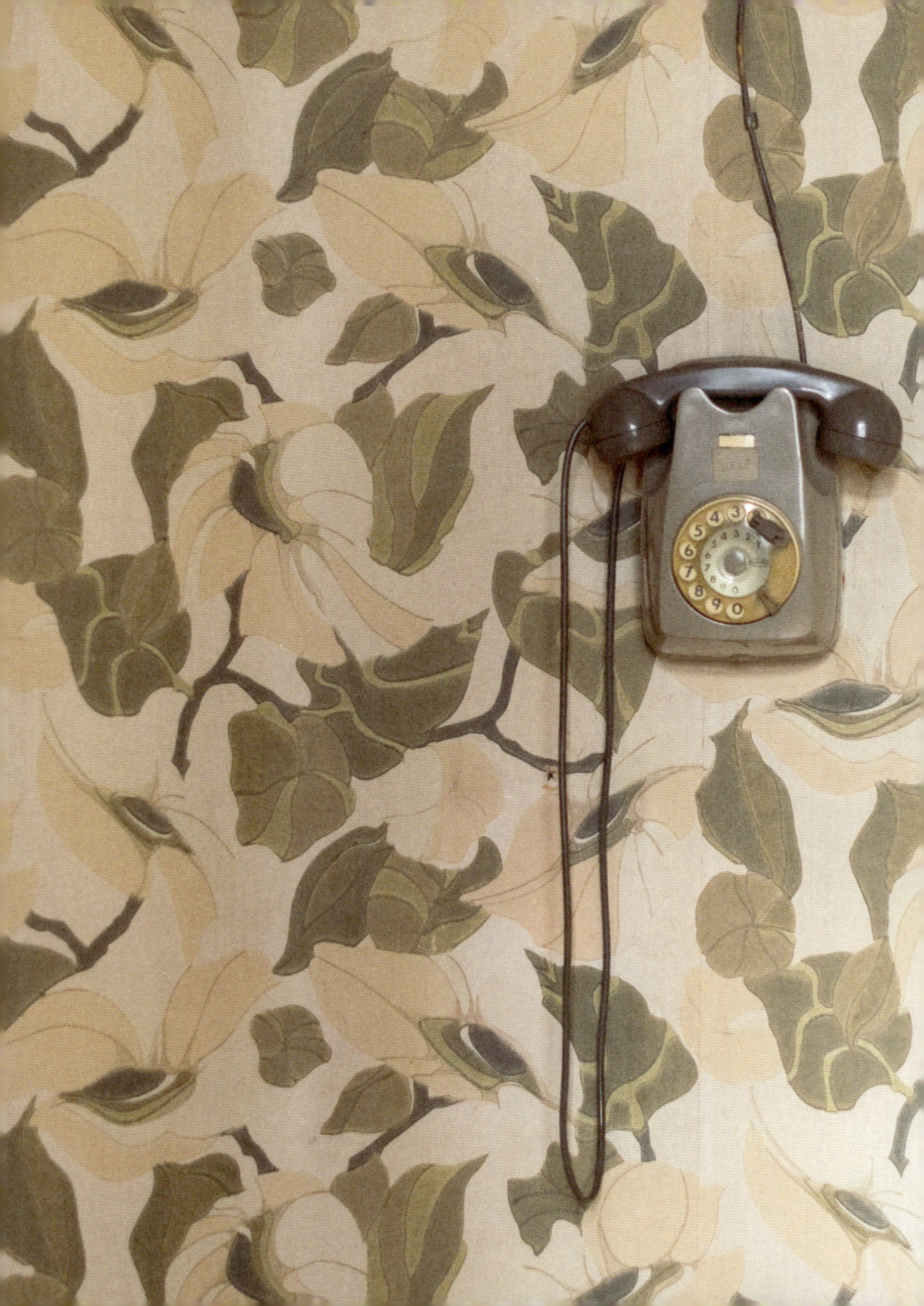

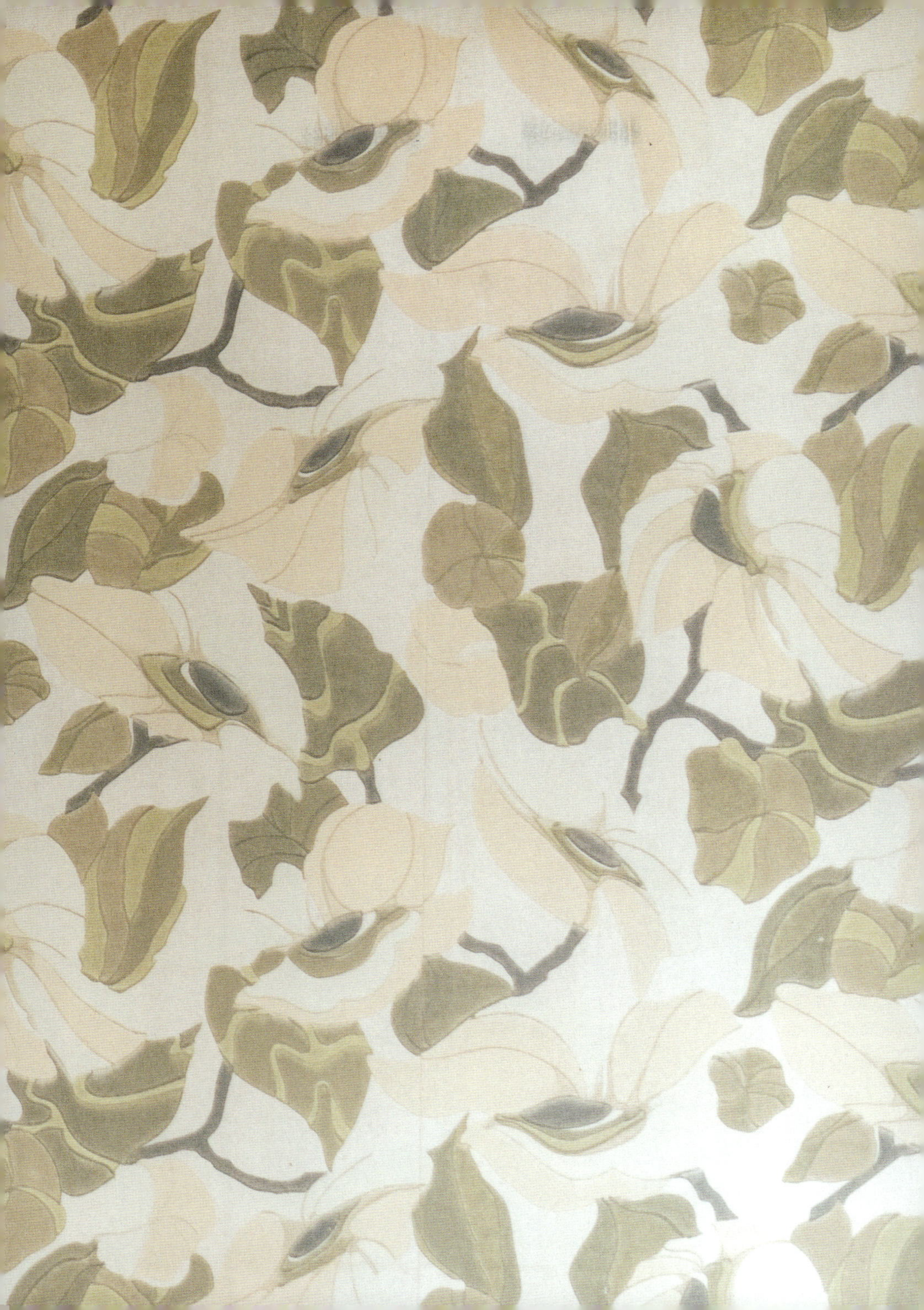

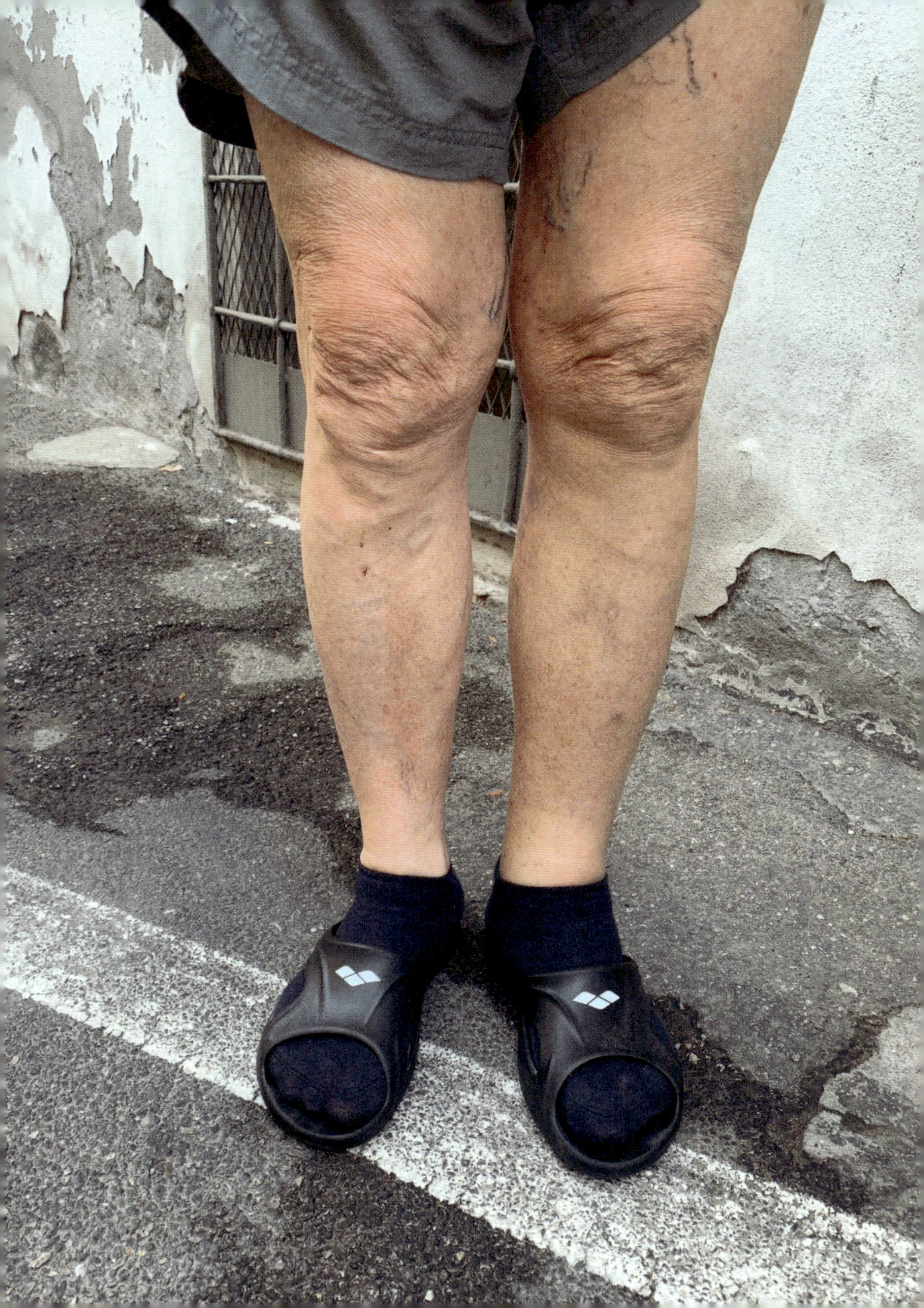

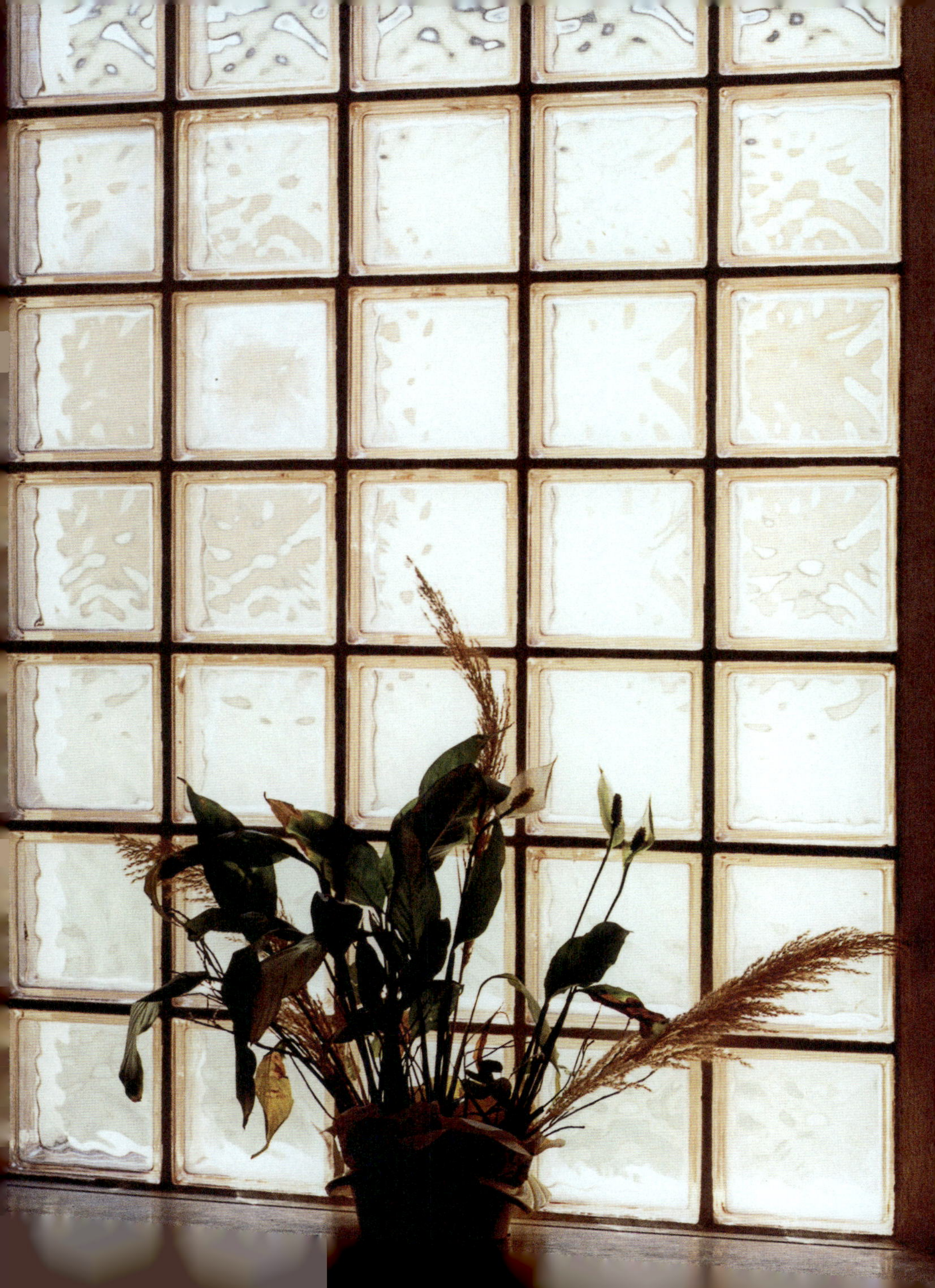

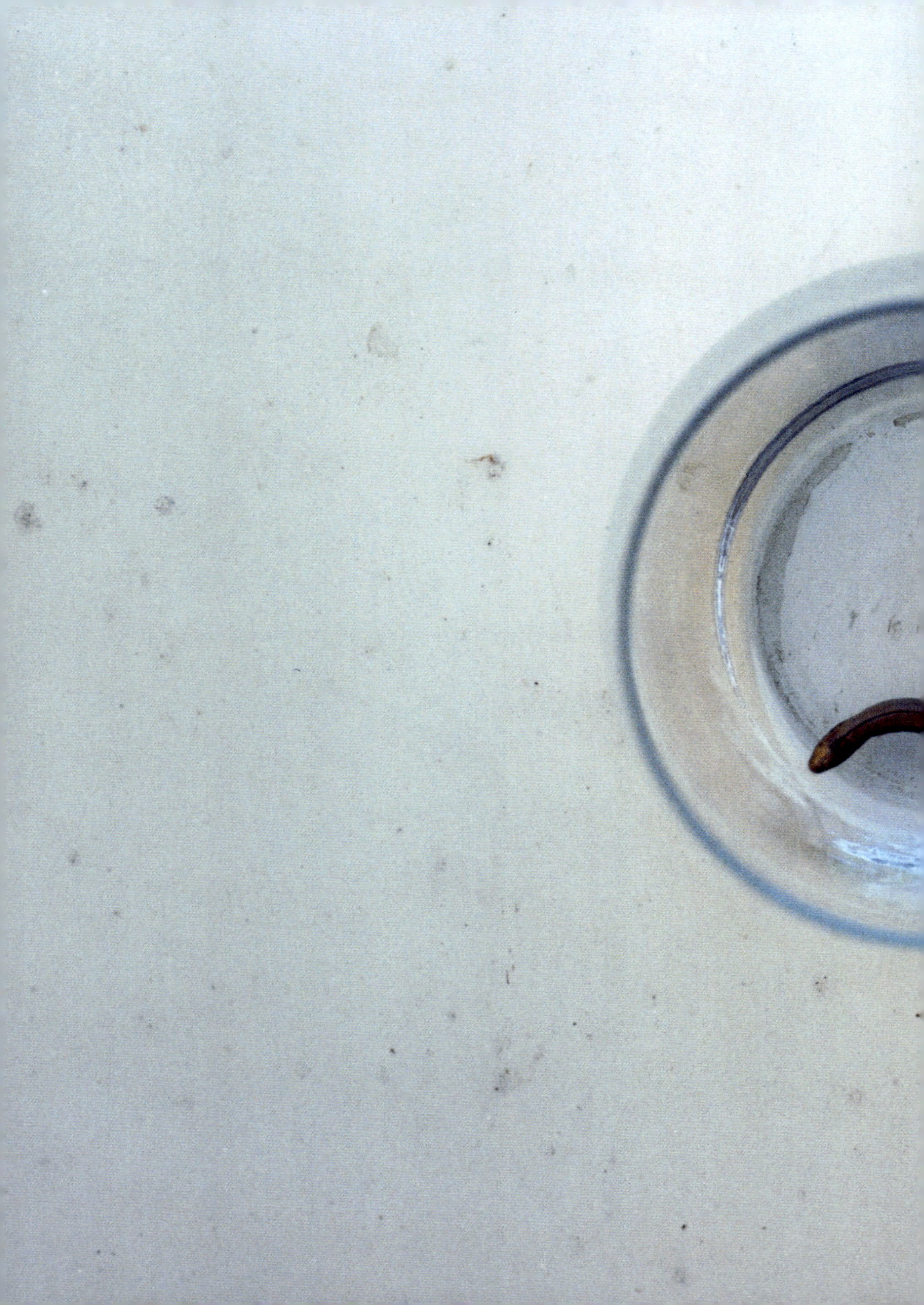

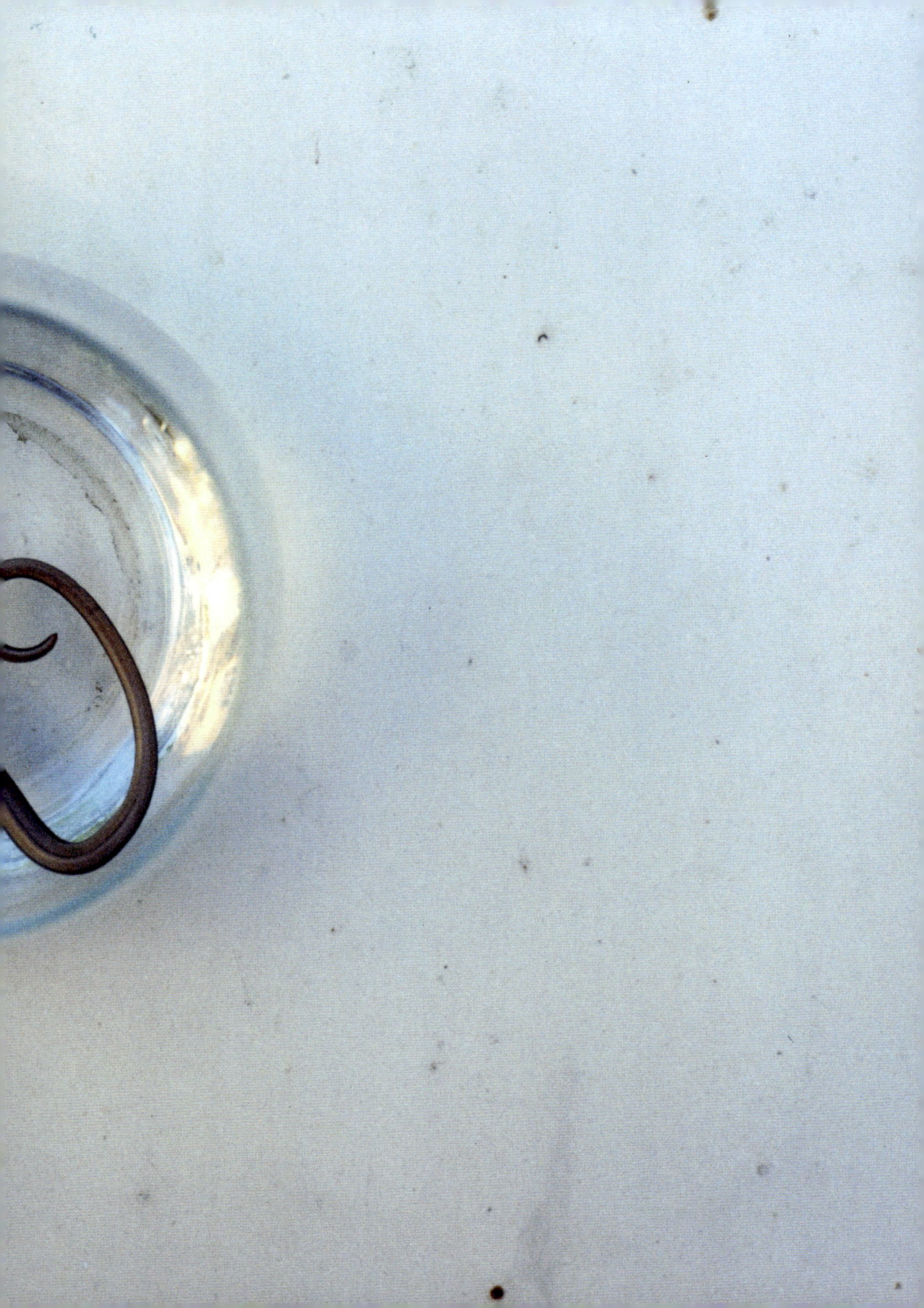

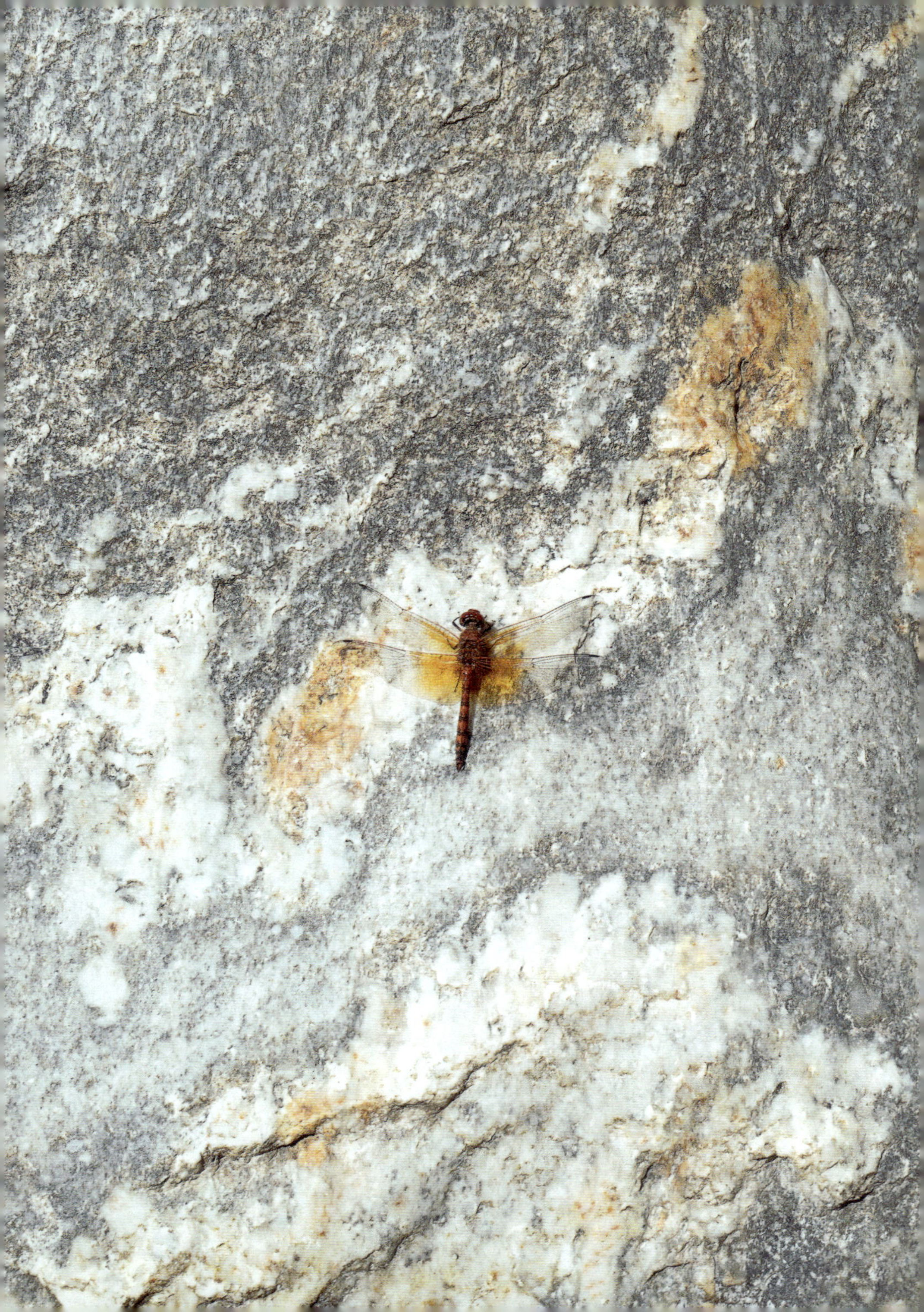

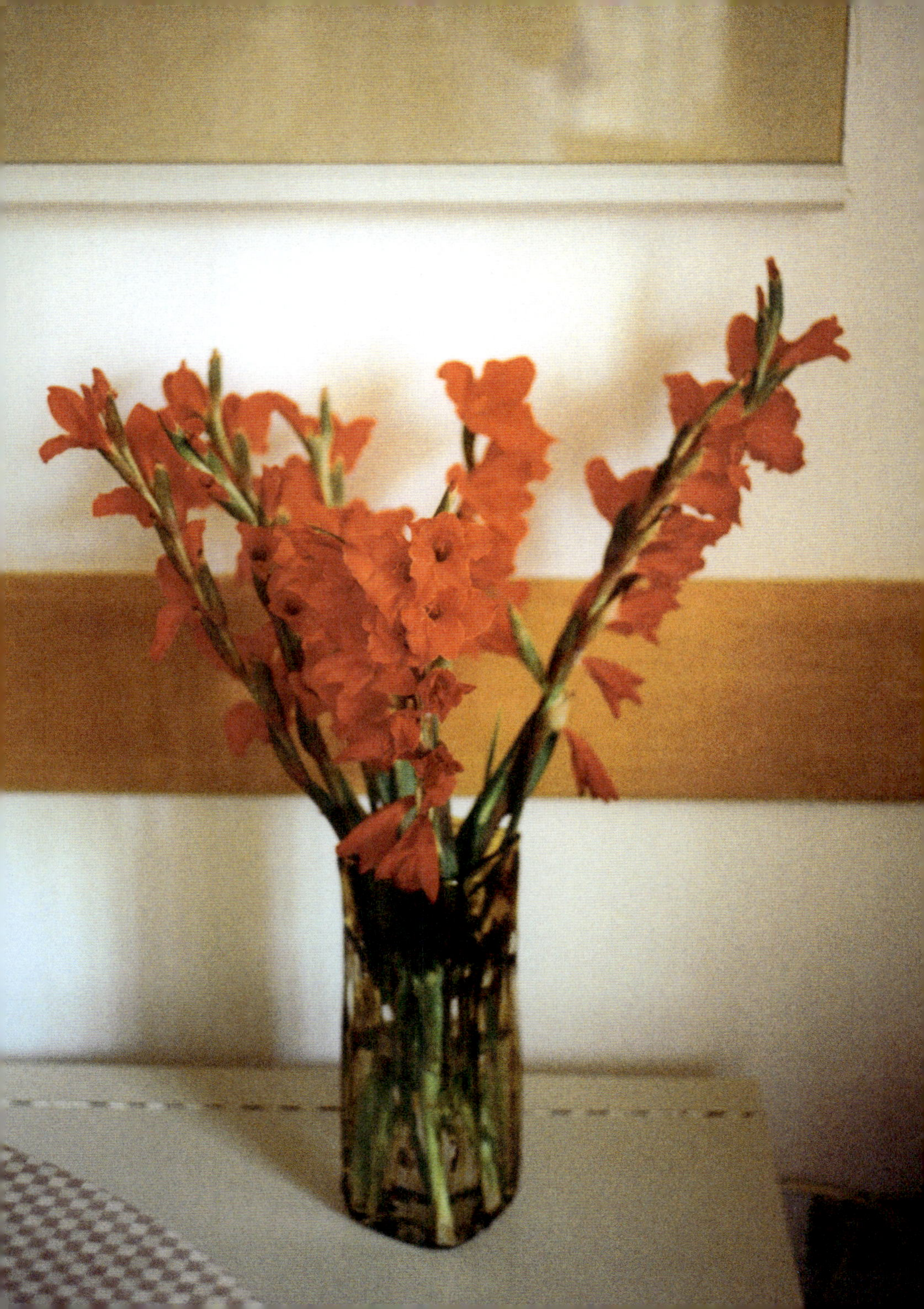

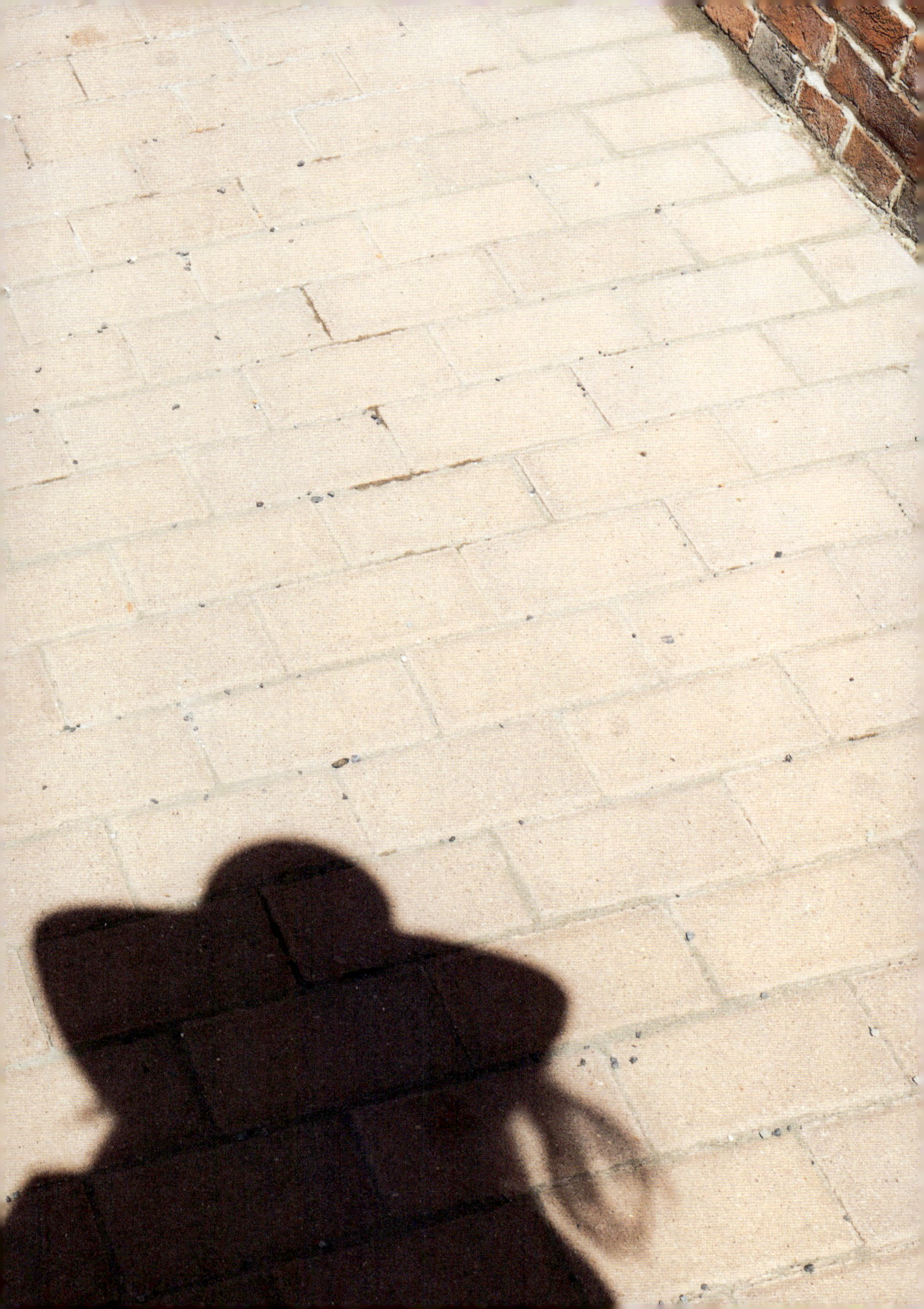

Sometimes I dream about a gigantic wave in front of me, bigger than the tallest buildings that are around. I am frightened, as it seems it is about to crash and destroy everything. But somebody tells not to worry as this happens all the time.
The underwater currents create it, but the wave just stands there for days and days, and then it goes away.

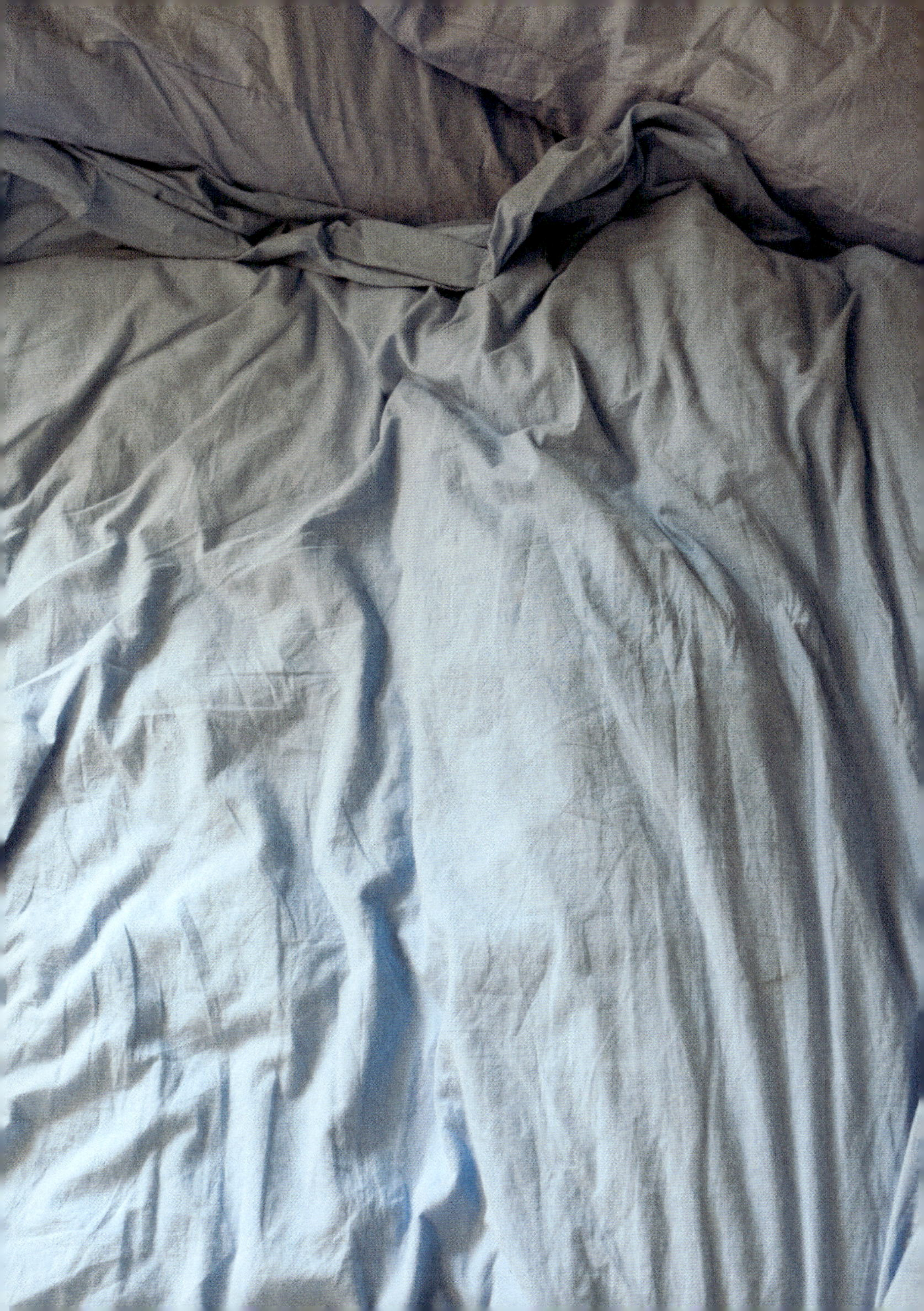

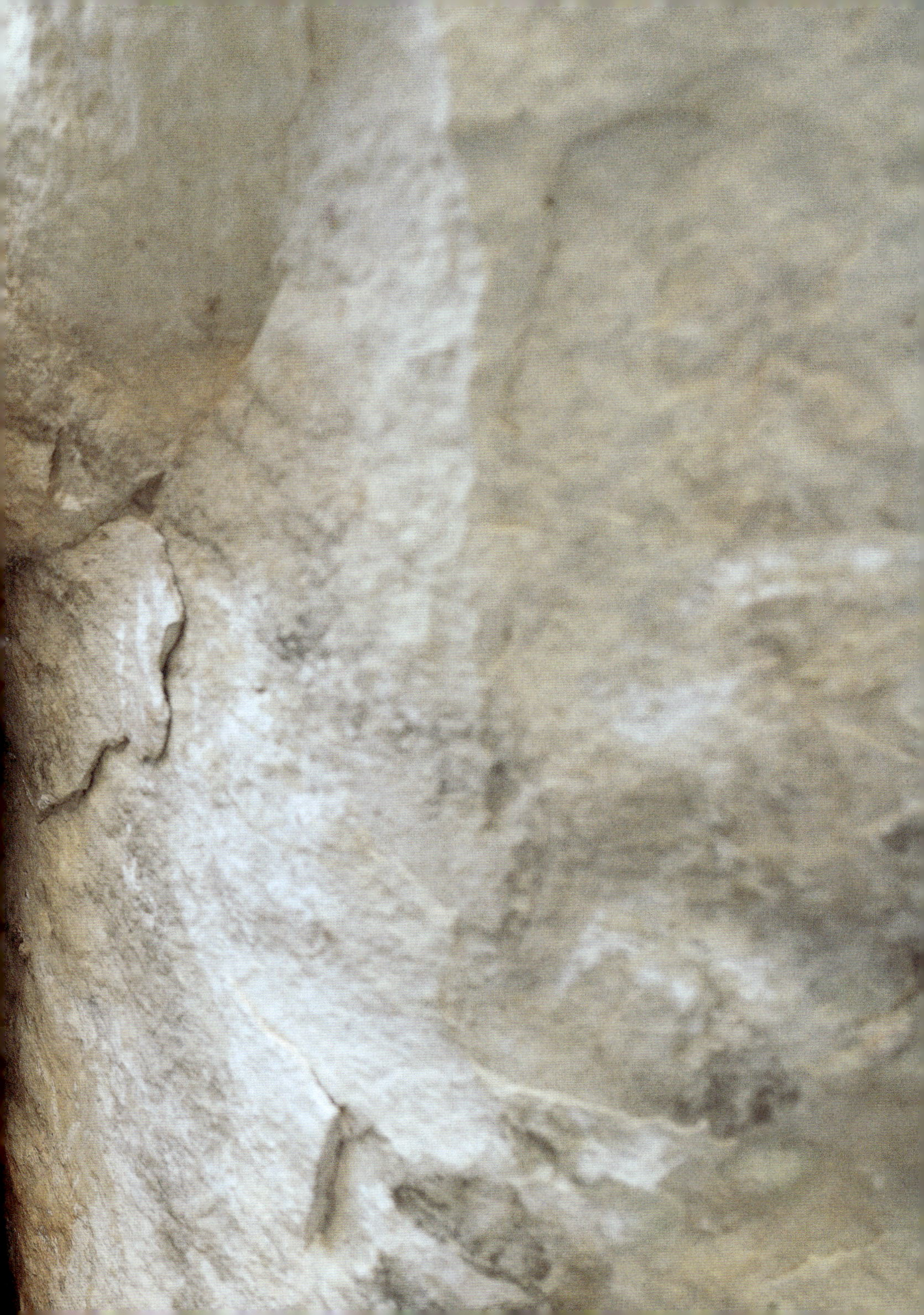

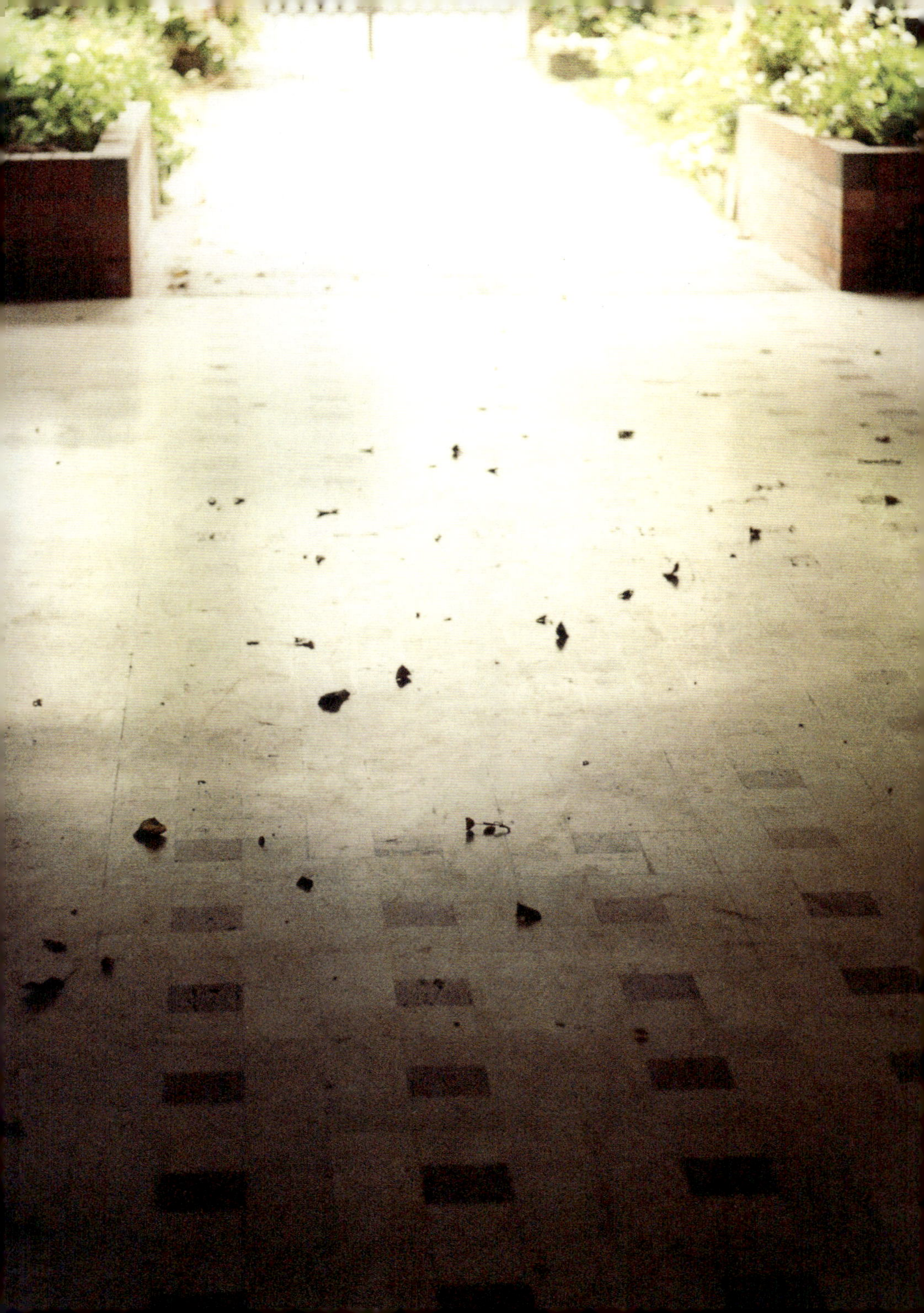

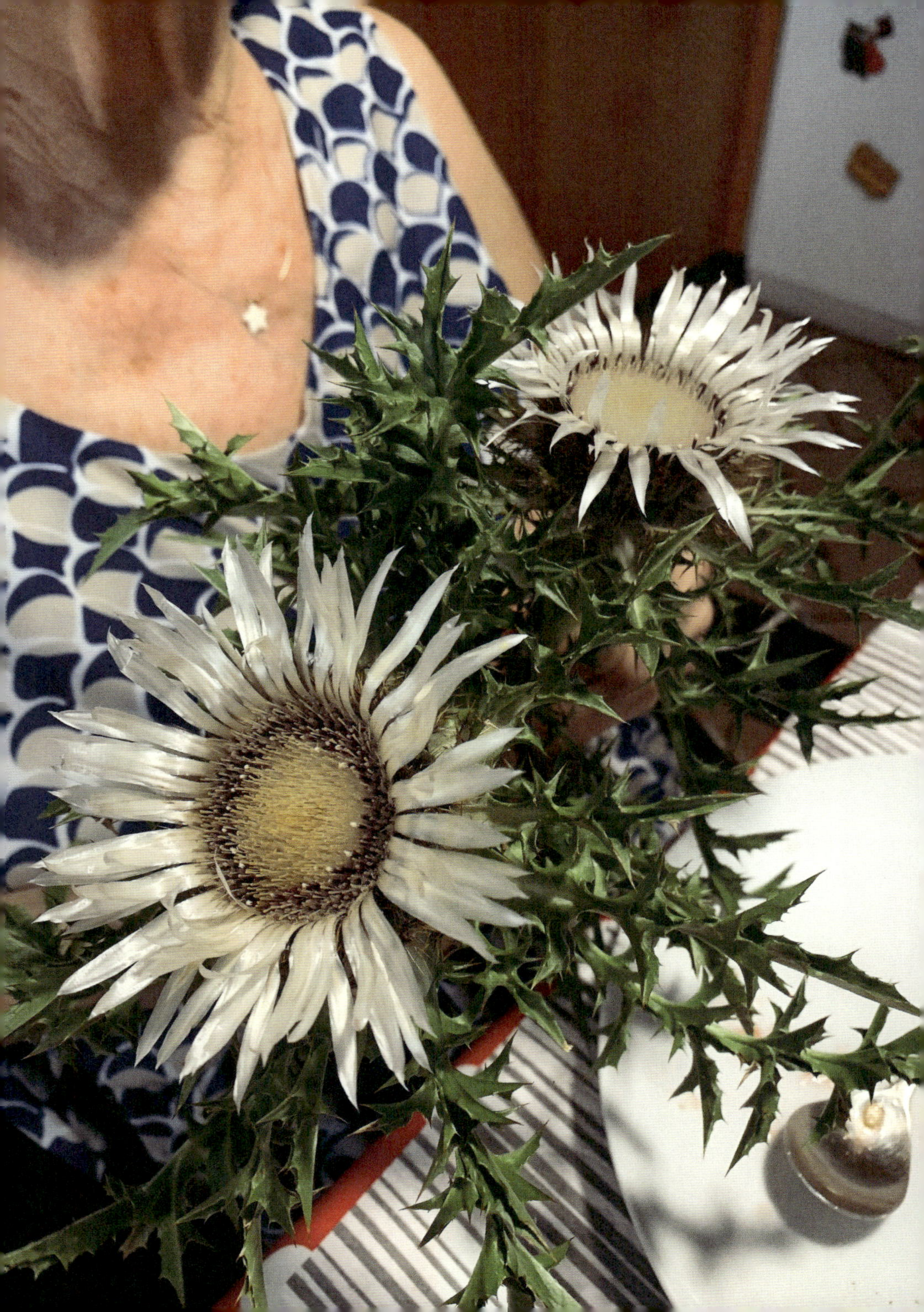

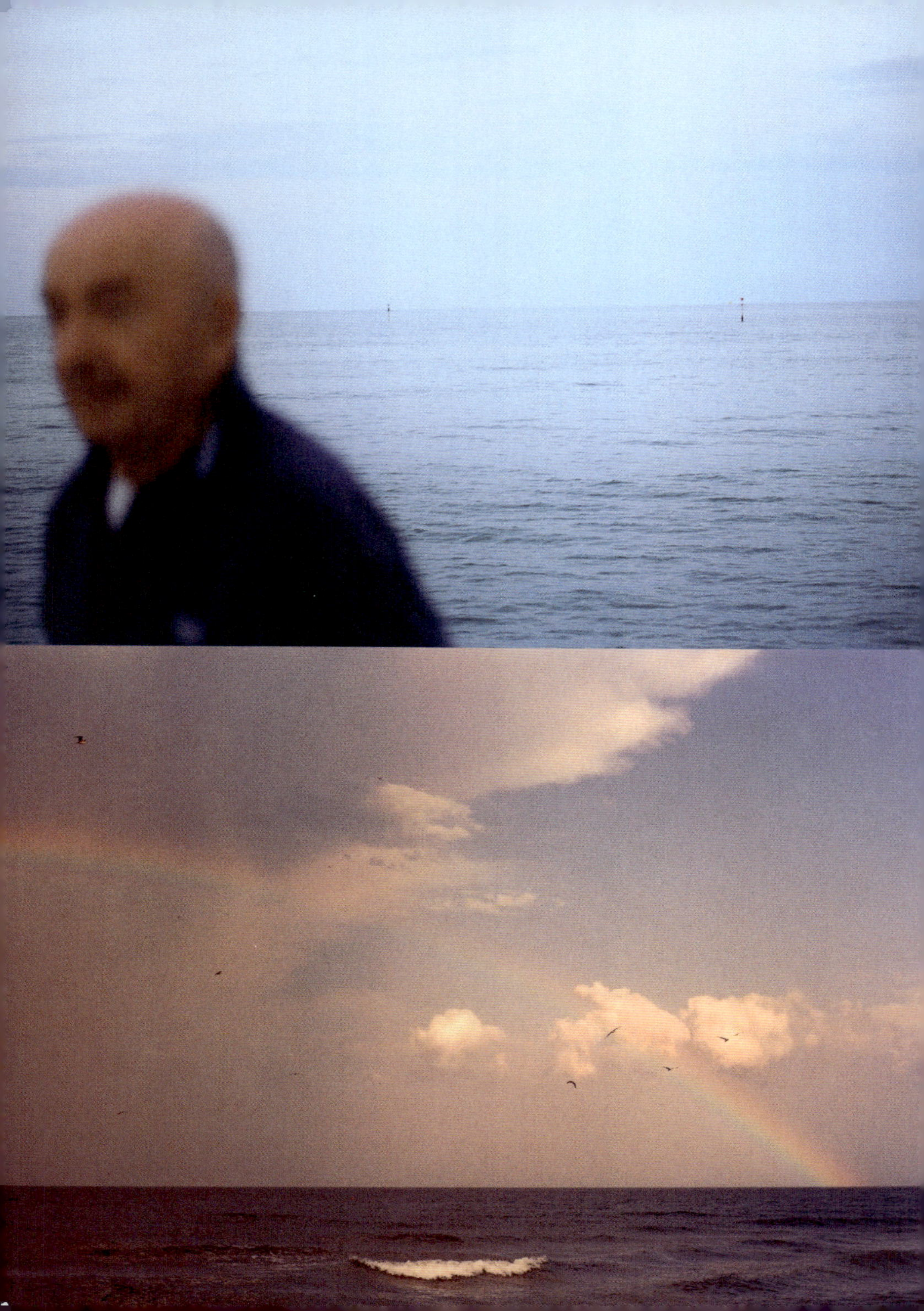

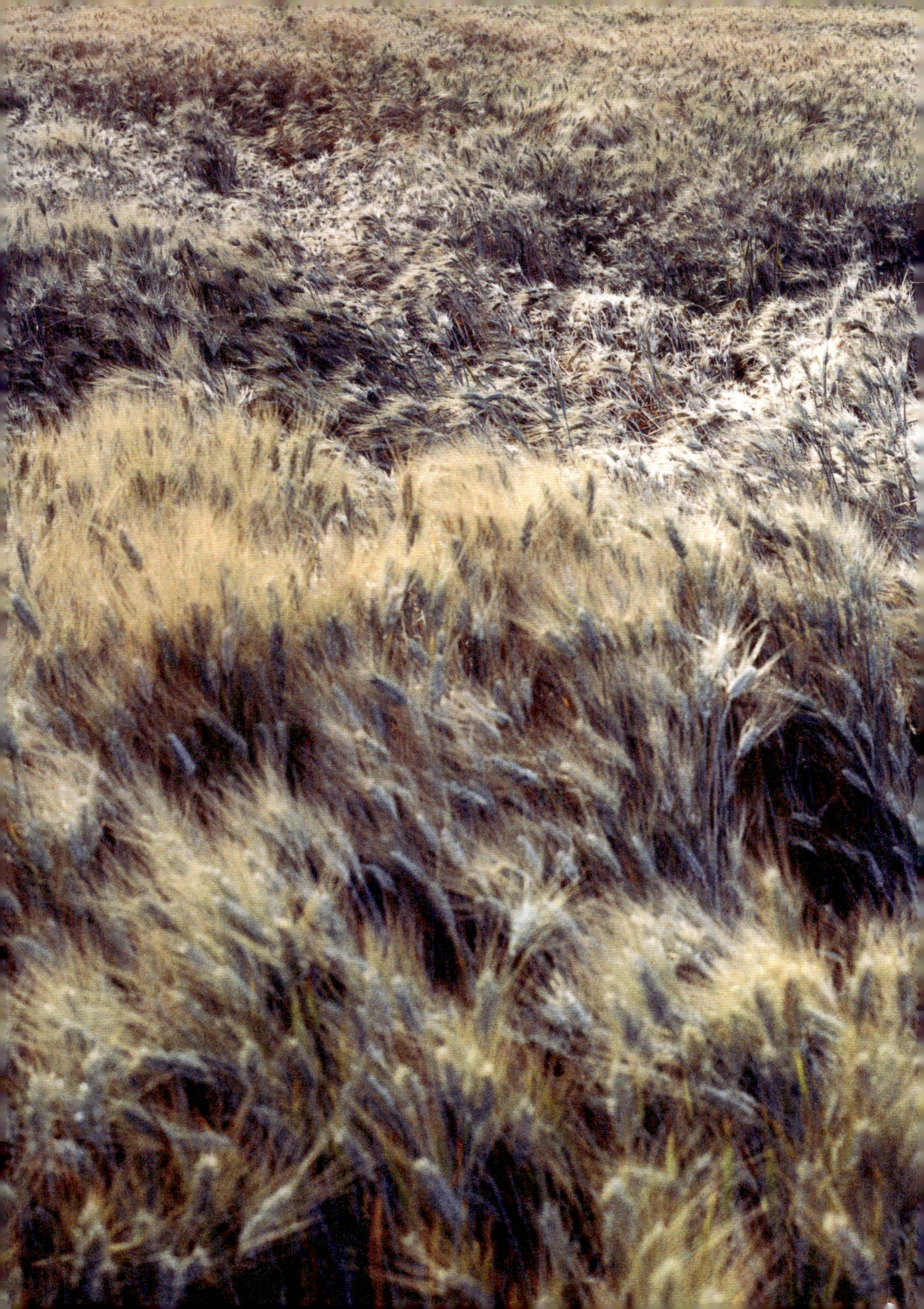

This morning I have decided to dress nicely. I wanted to look good. Now I am embarrassed by that thought. Like it'd be important while everything is falling apart. I think about the time we asked the hairdresser to visit my grandmother in the hospital, to help her feeling 'better'. Like you could feel better when you are dying.
The dress is light blue with a flimsy wide layered skirt. My mom bought it for me when we went on holiday to the south of Italy for a week, just the two of us. When my mind never stopped spinning and I felt I was ruining everything.

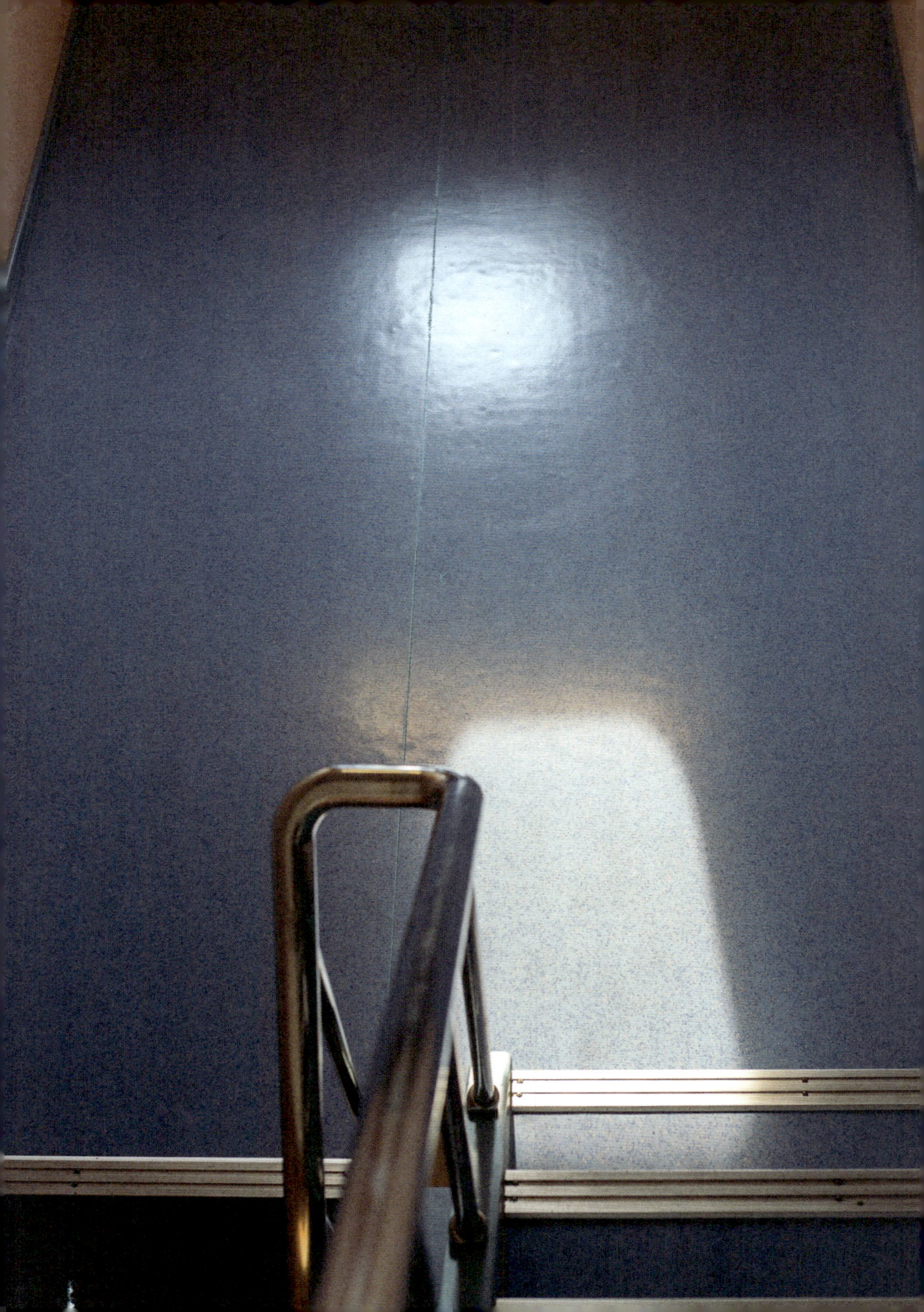

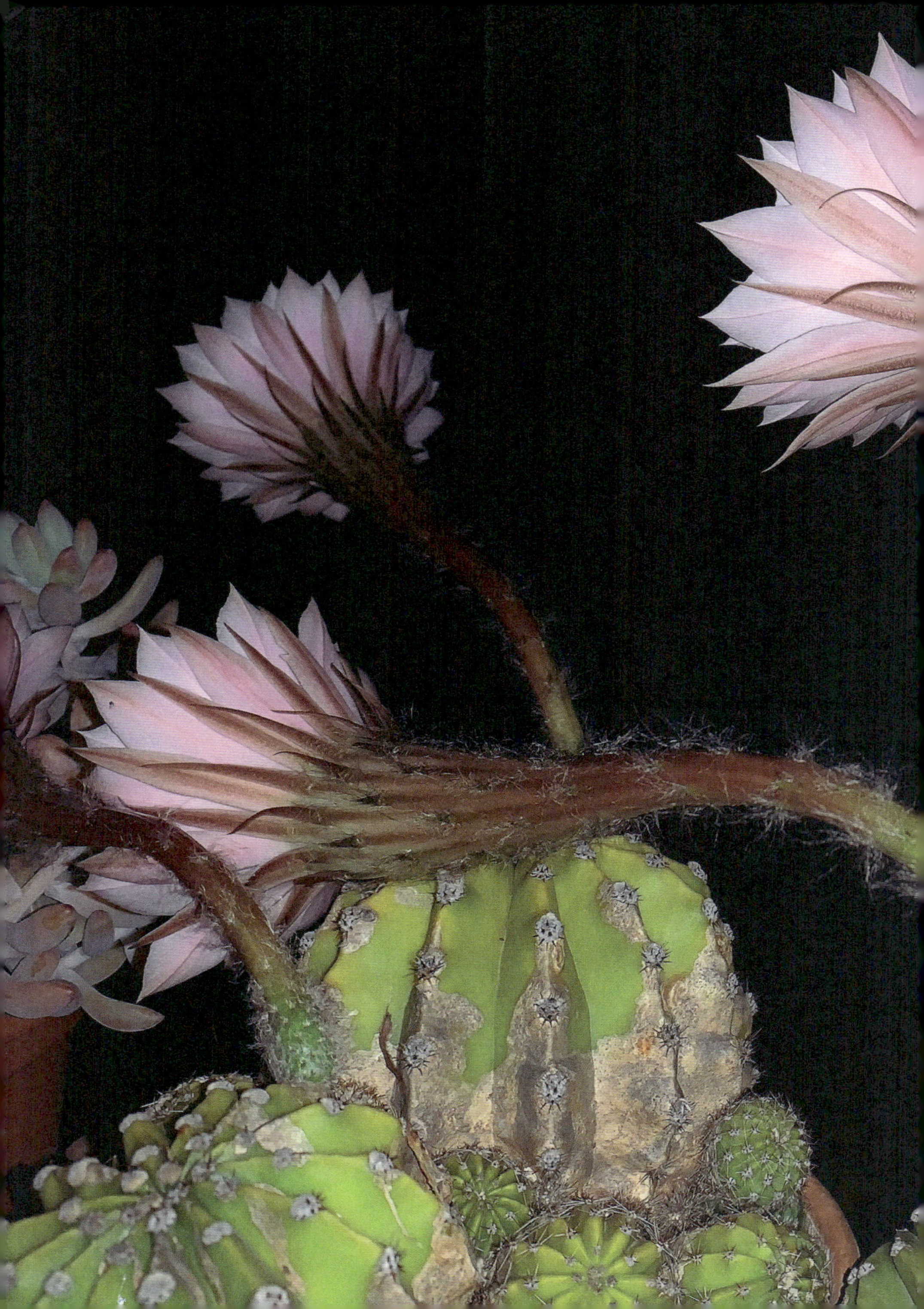

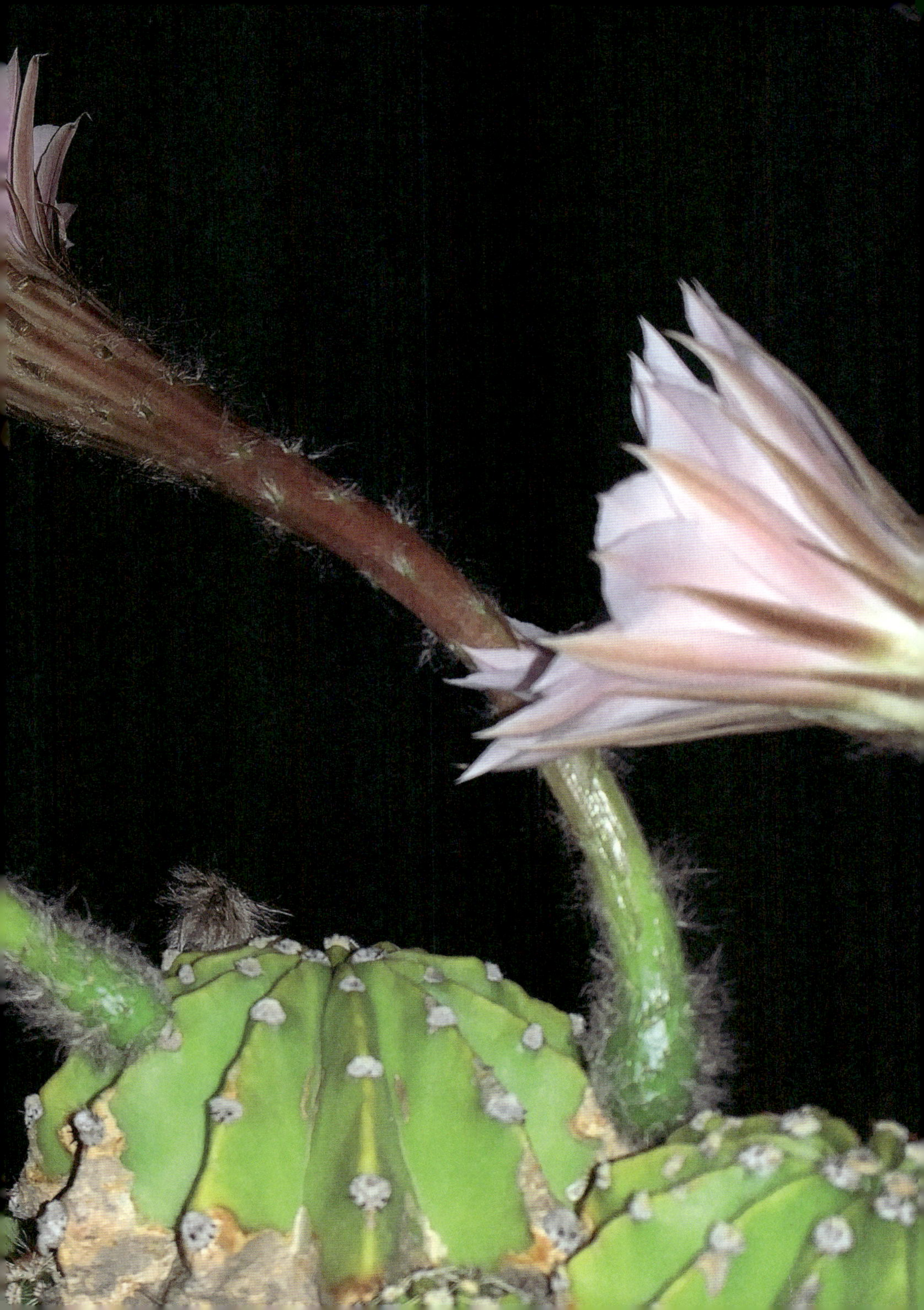

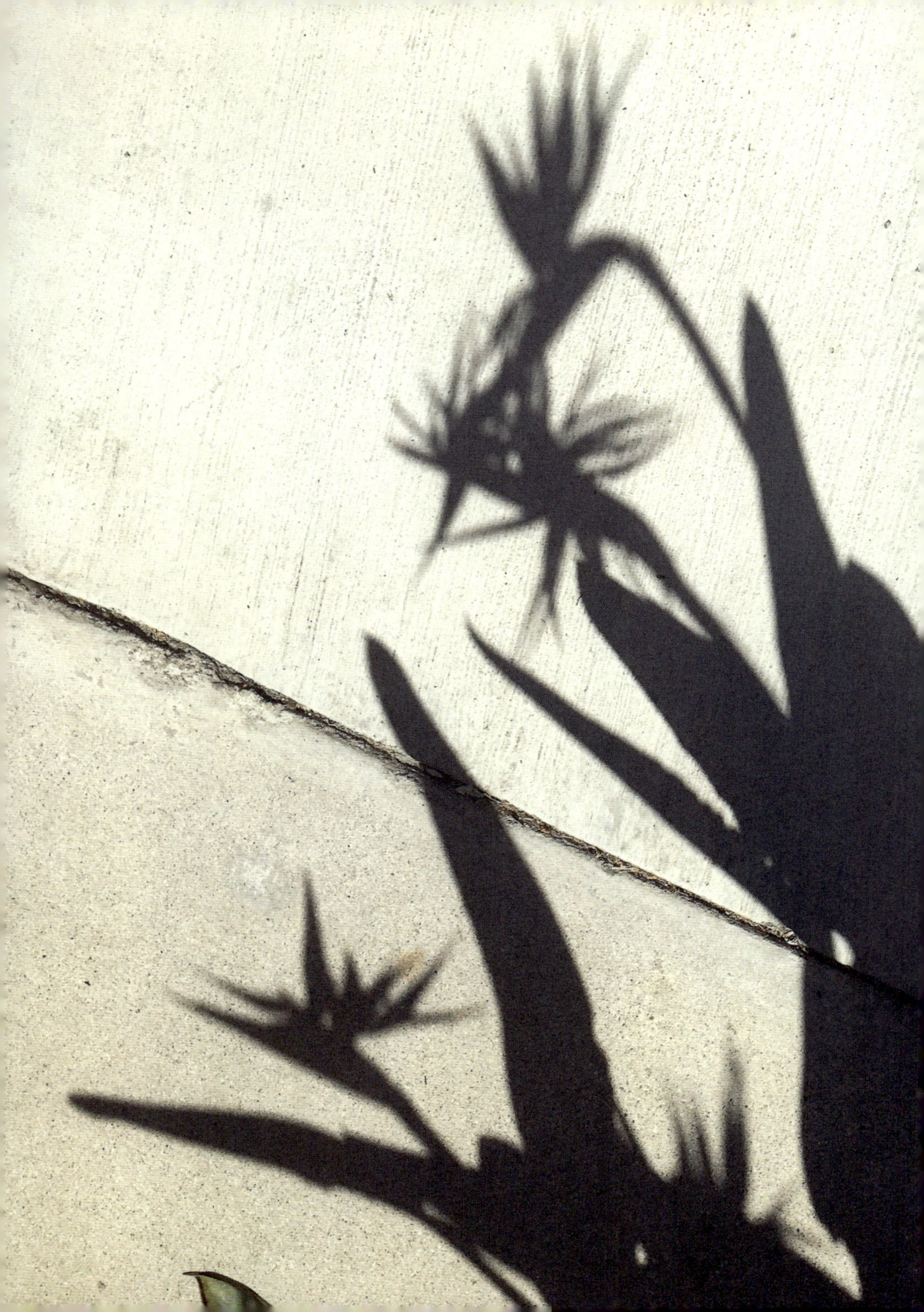

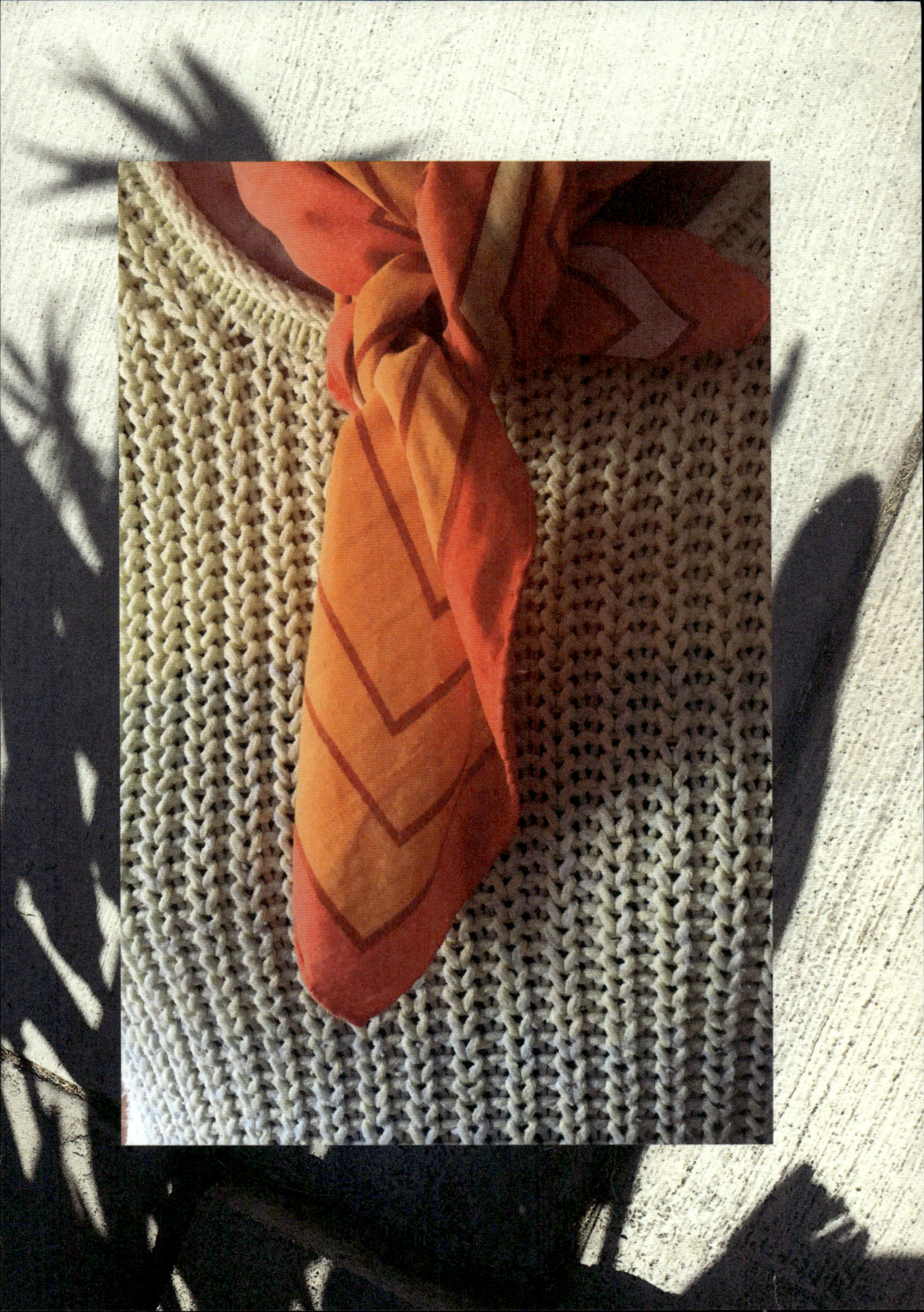

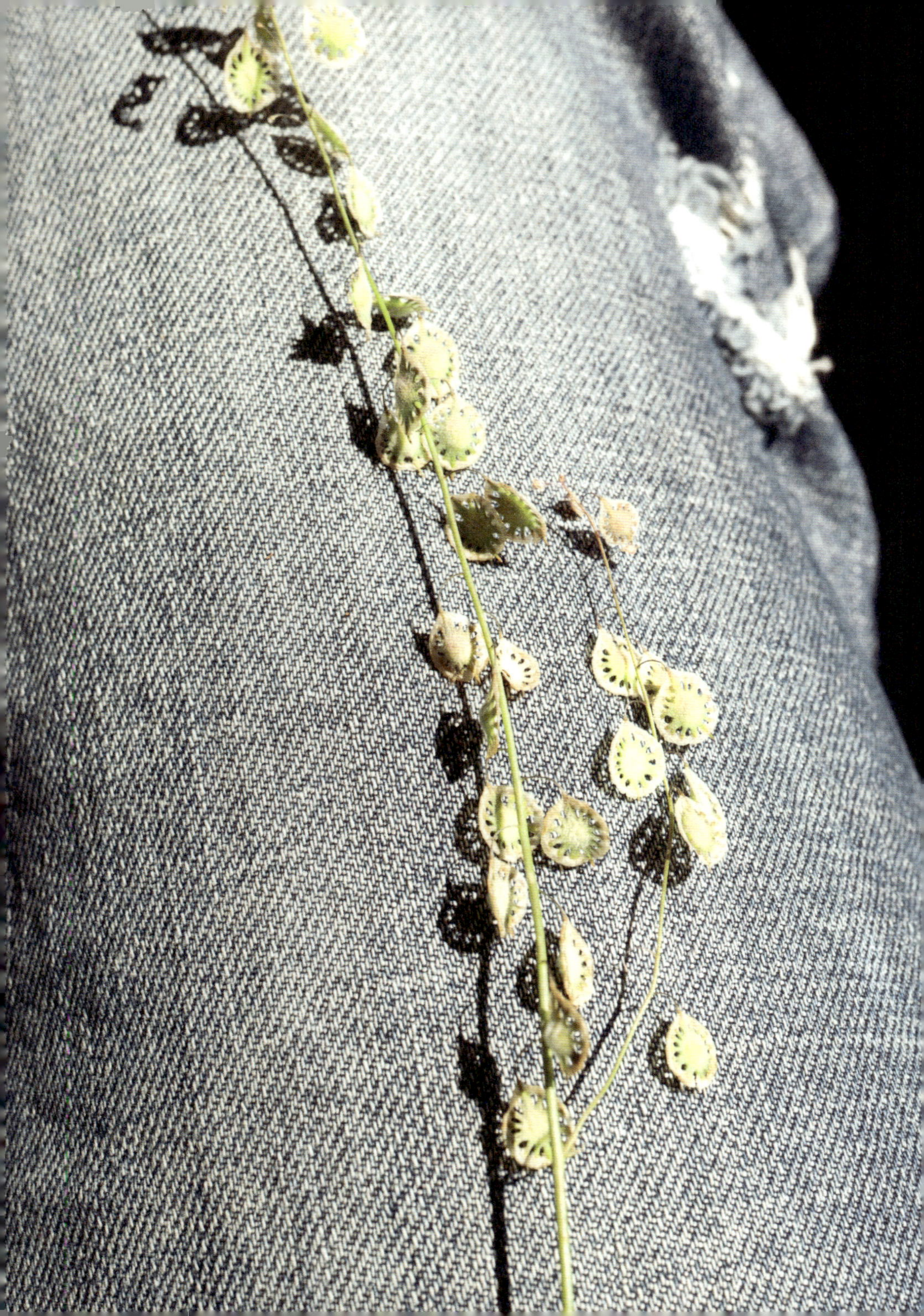

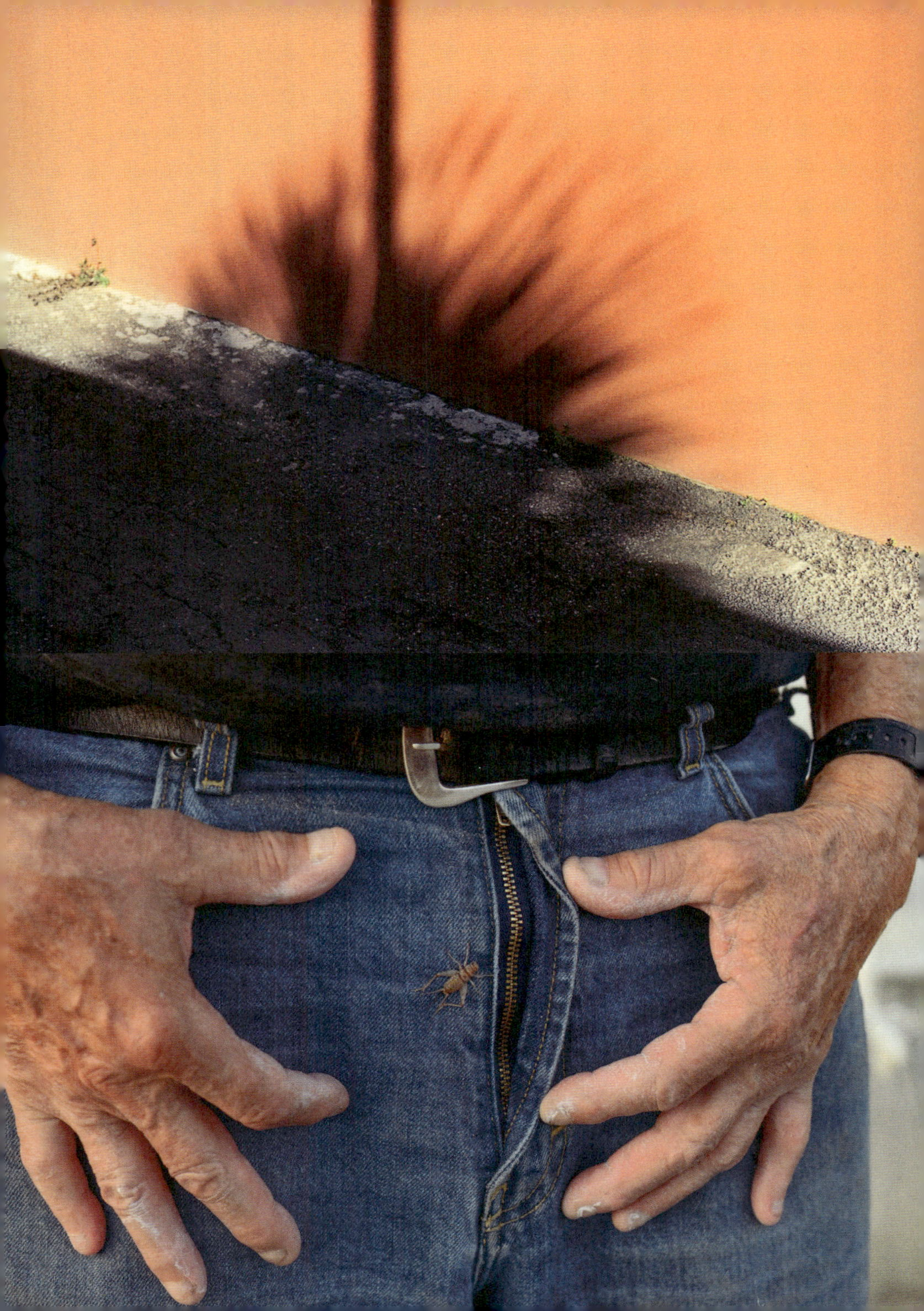

When my mom came back from the hospital, she had to spend a long period of time at home, often in bed.
One day my dad brought back a cricket from the countryside to cheer her up. My family has always had a thing for crickets. When I was little my dad taught me how to lure them out of their holes with a long blade of grass. He would put the cricket in the palm of his hand to show it to me. He wanted me to see things, especially nature.
They named the cricket Carletto and my mom fed him salad, cherries and canteloupe and a bunch of other things that he seemed to like. His chirping became really loud, so that they had to start putting him outside the window at night, to be able to sleep.
The neighbors started complaining about the constant sound, but they didn't know it was coming from our balcony.
I met Carletto over FaceTime, then later on, in person. It wasn't until later that I realized, surprisingly for the first time, that our names were pretty similar.

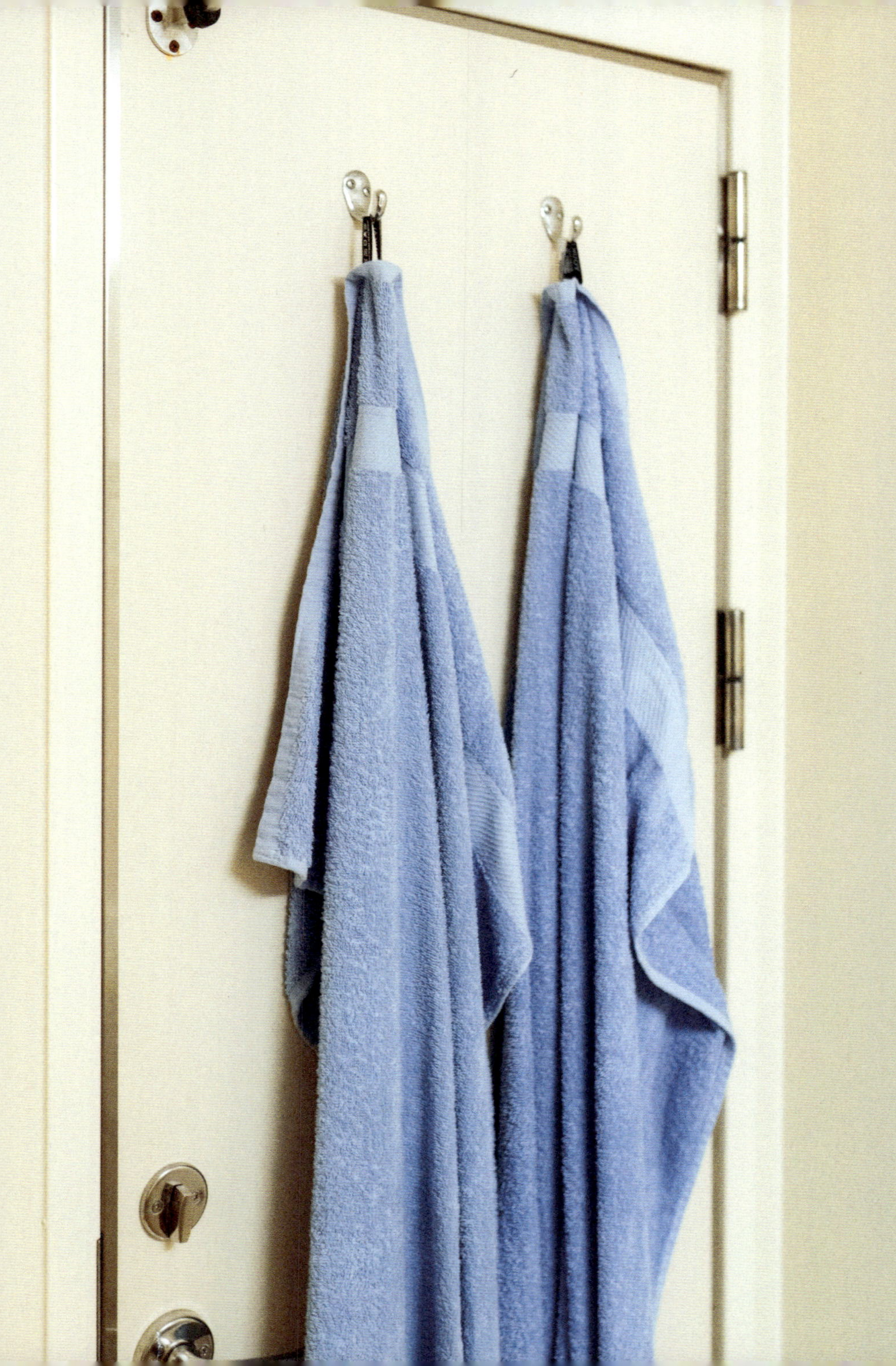

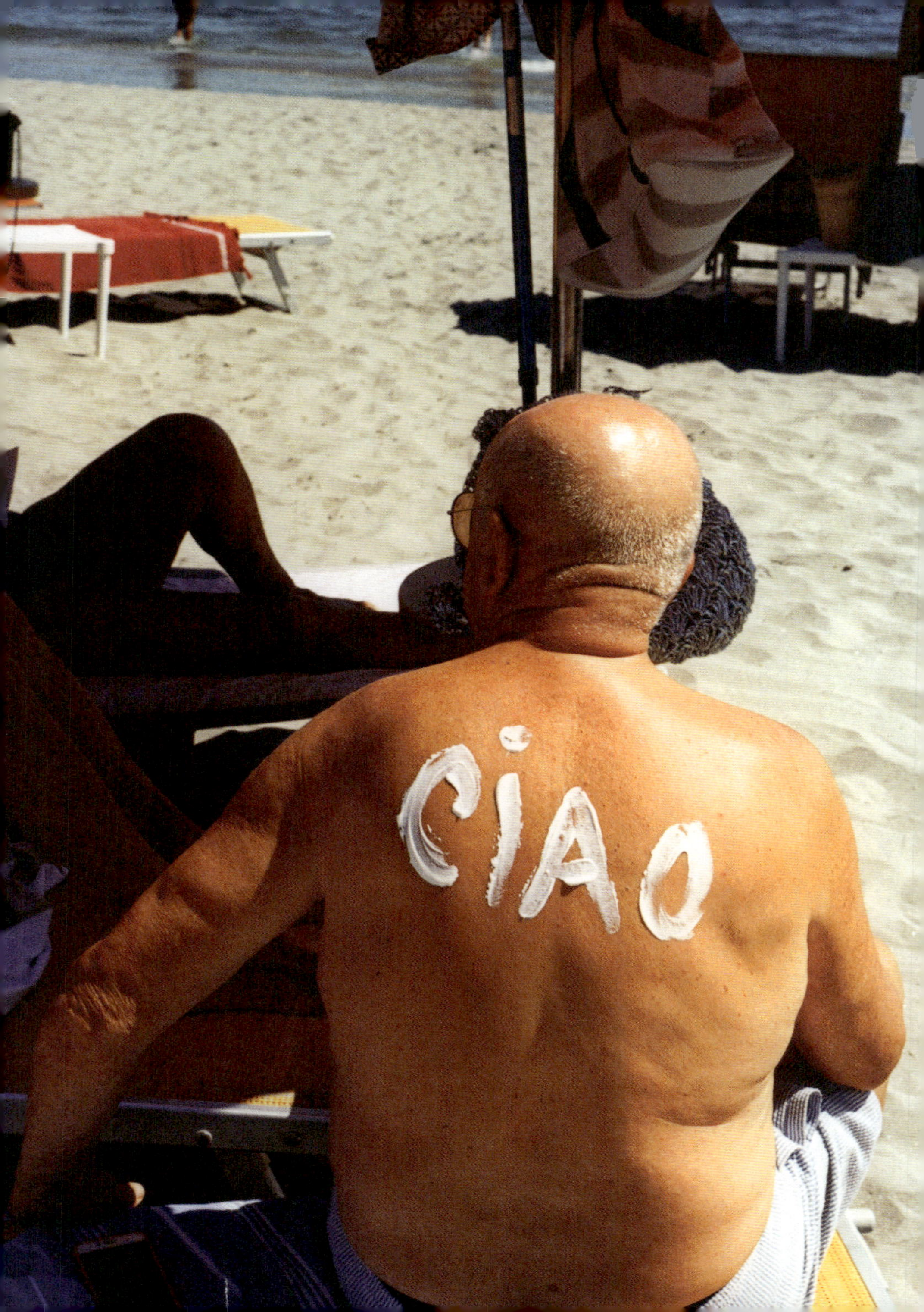
CiAO

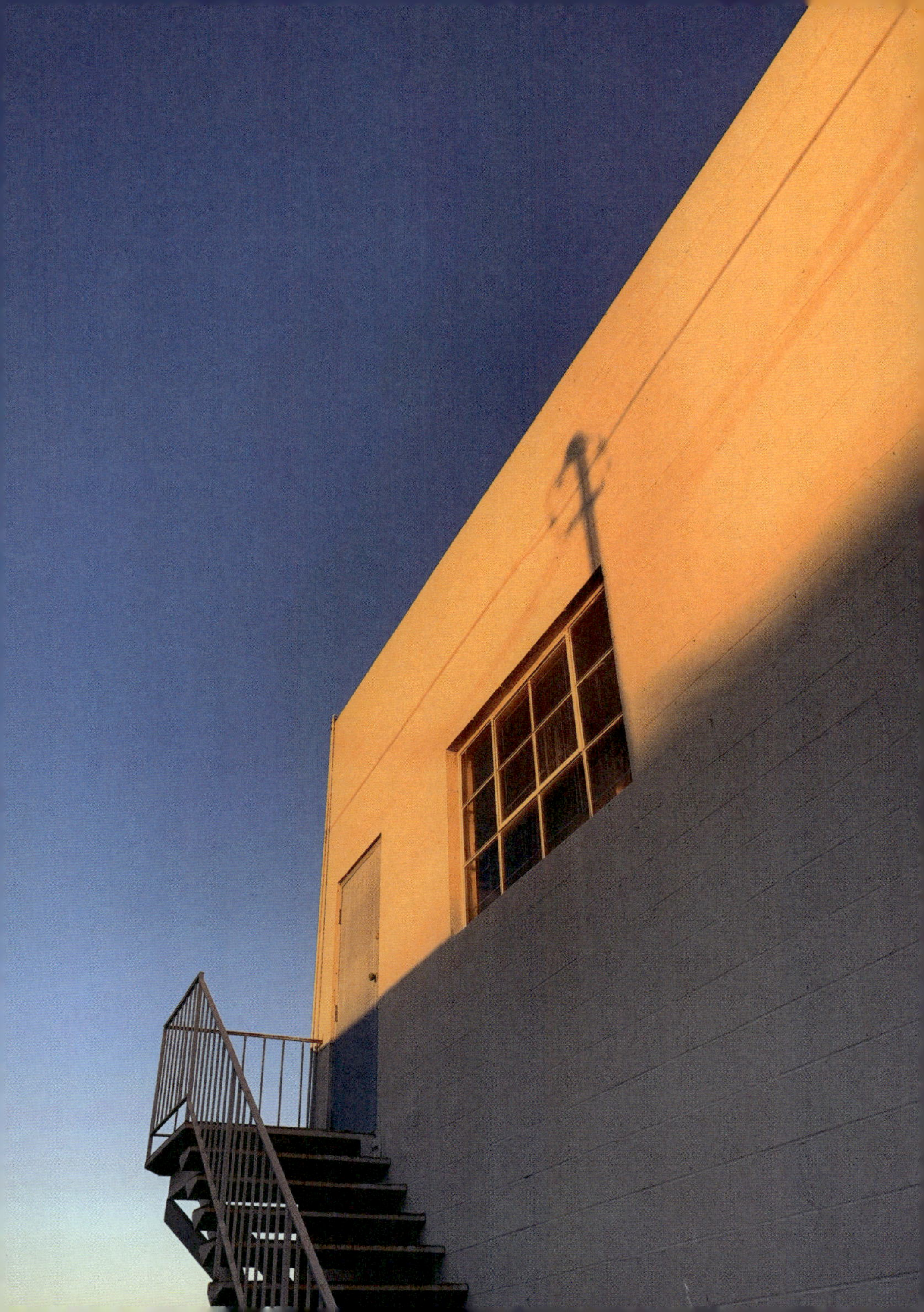

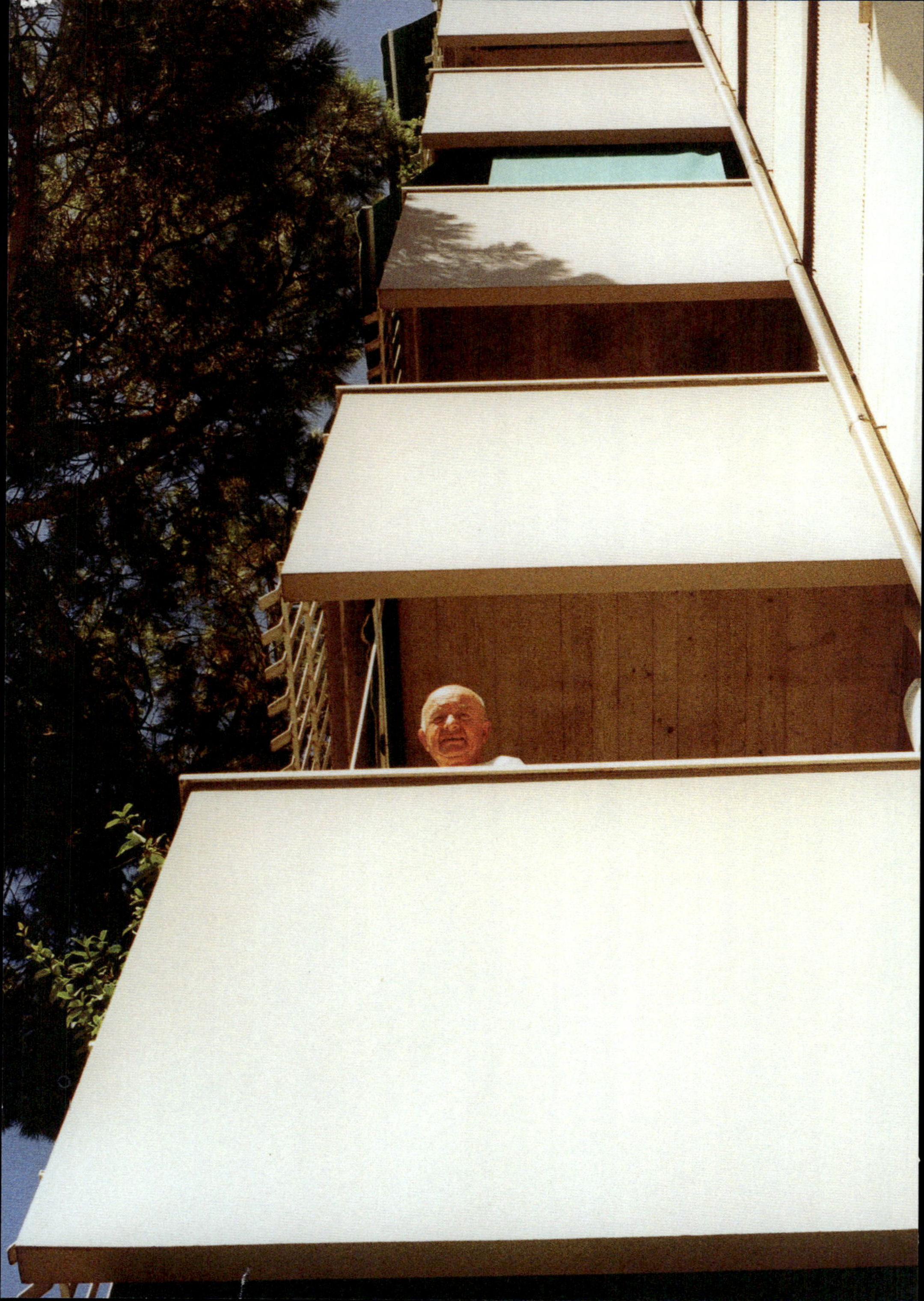

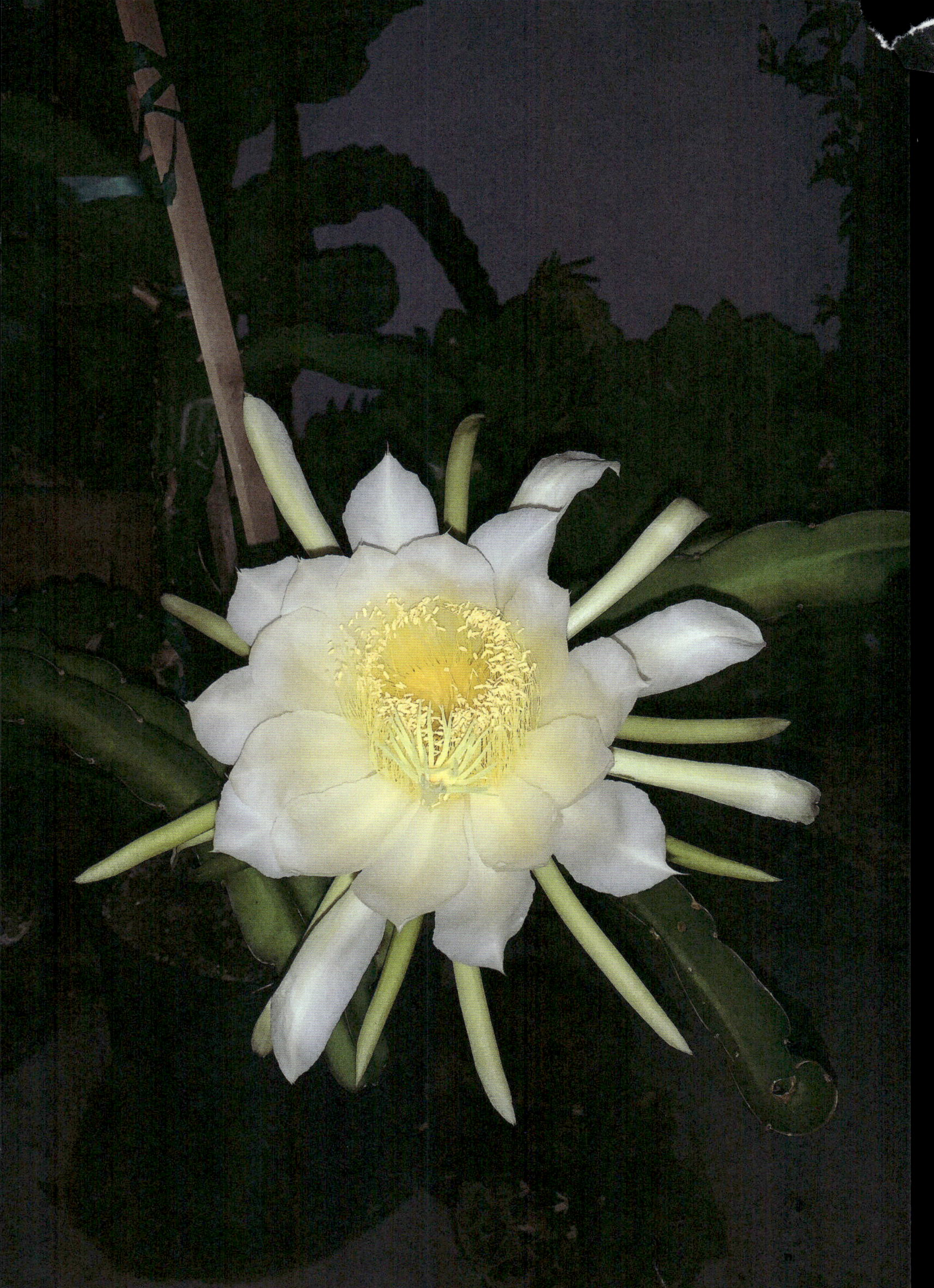

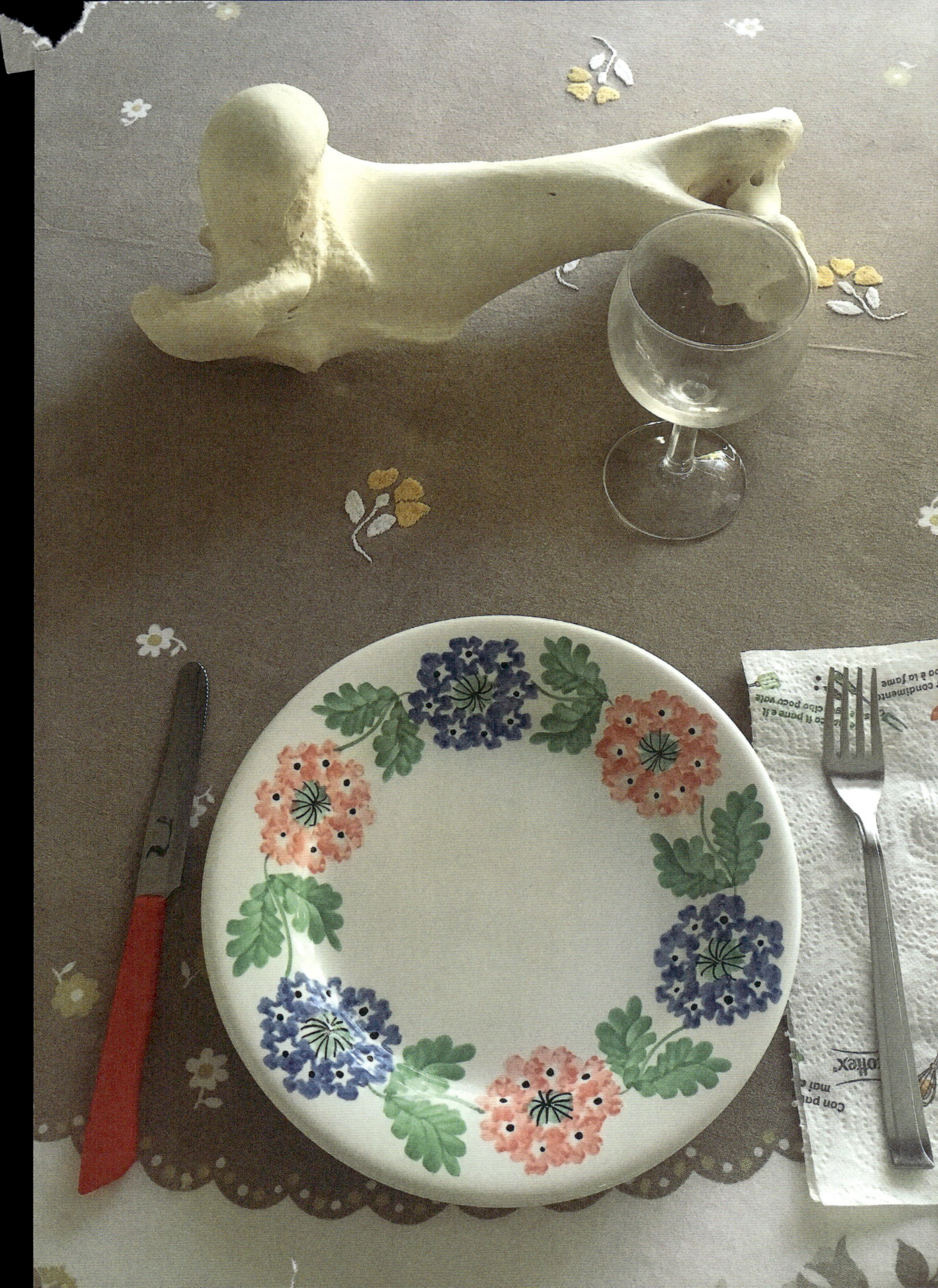

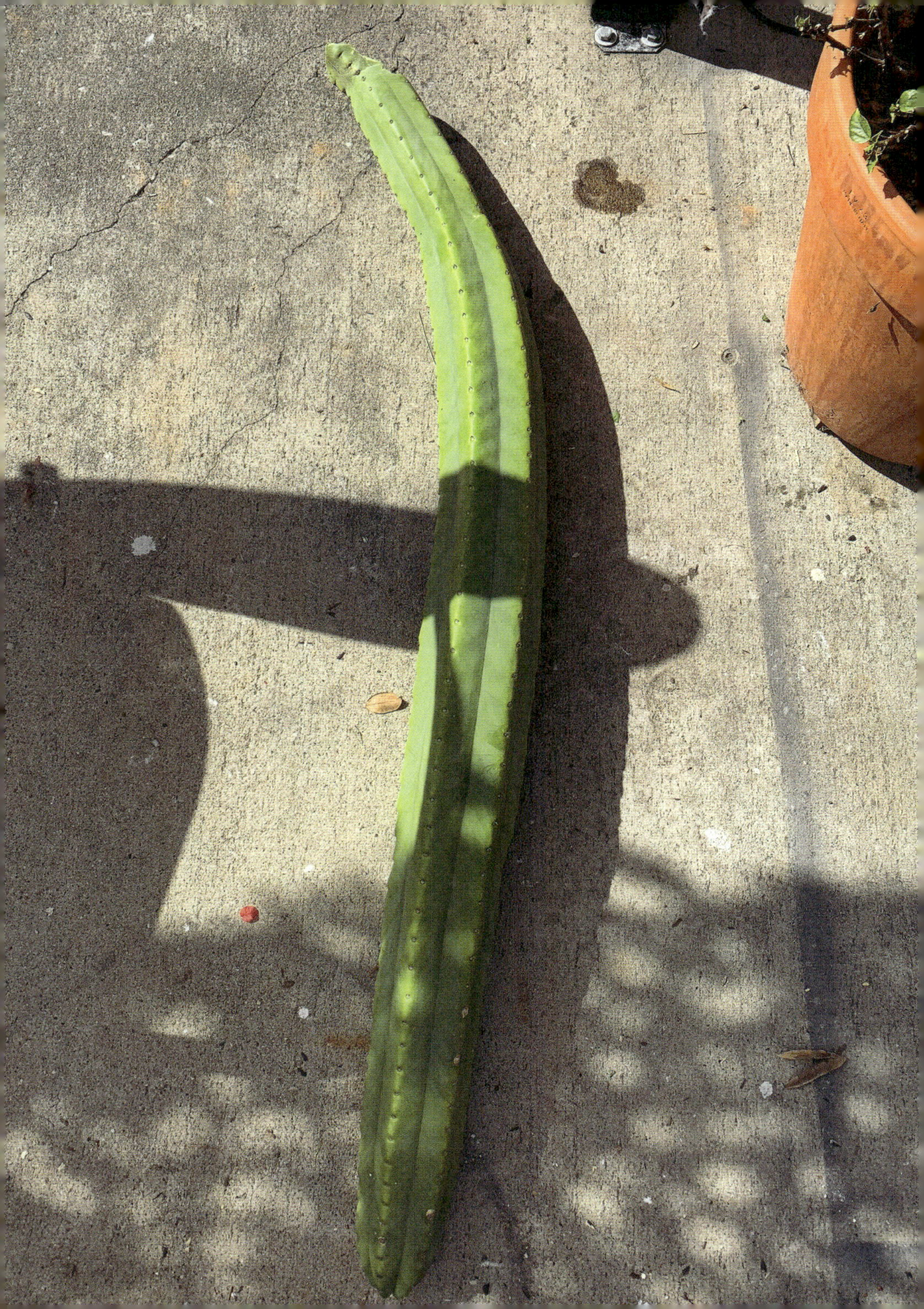

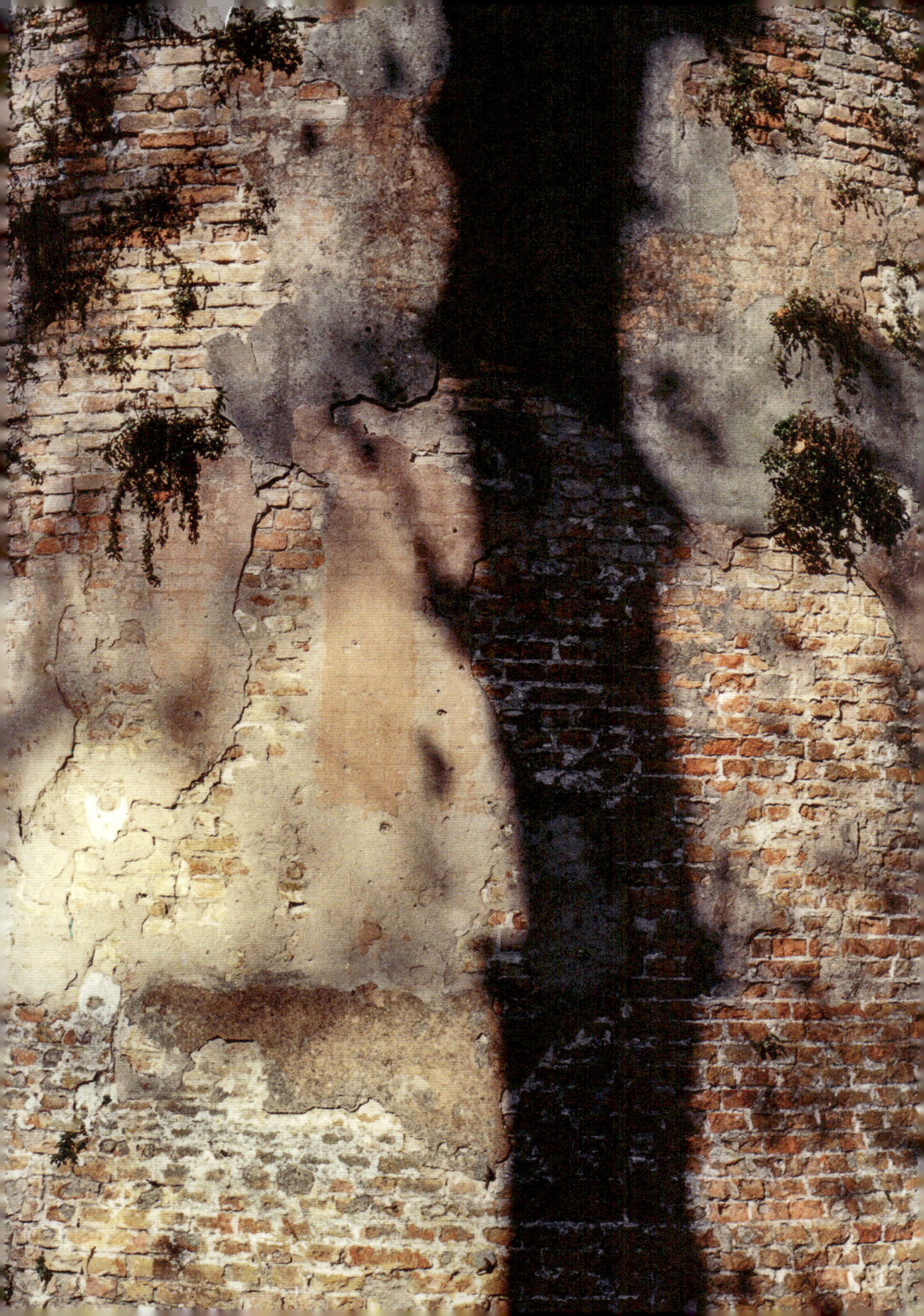

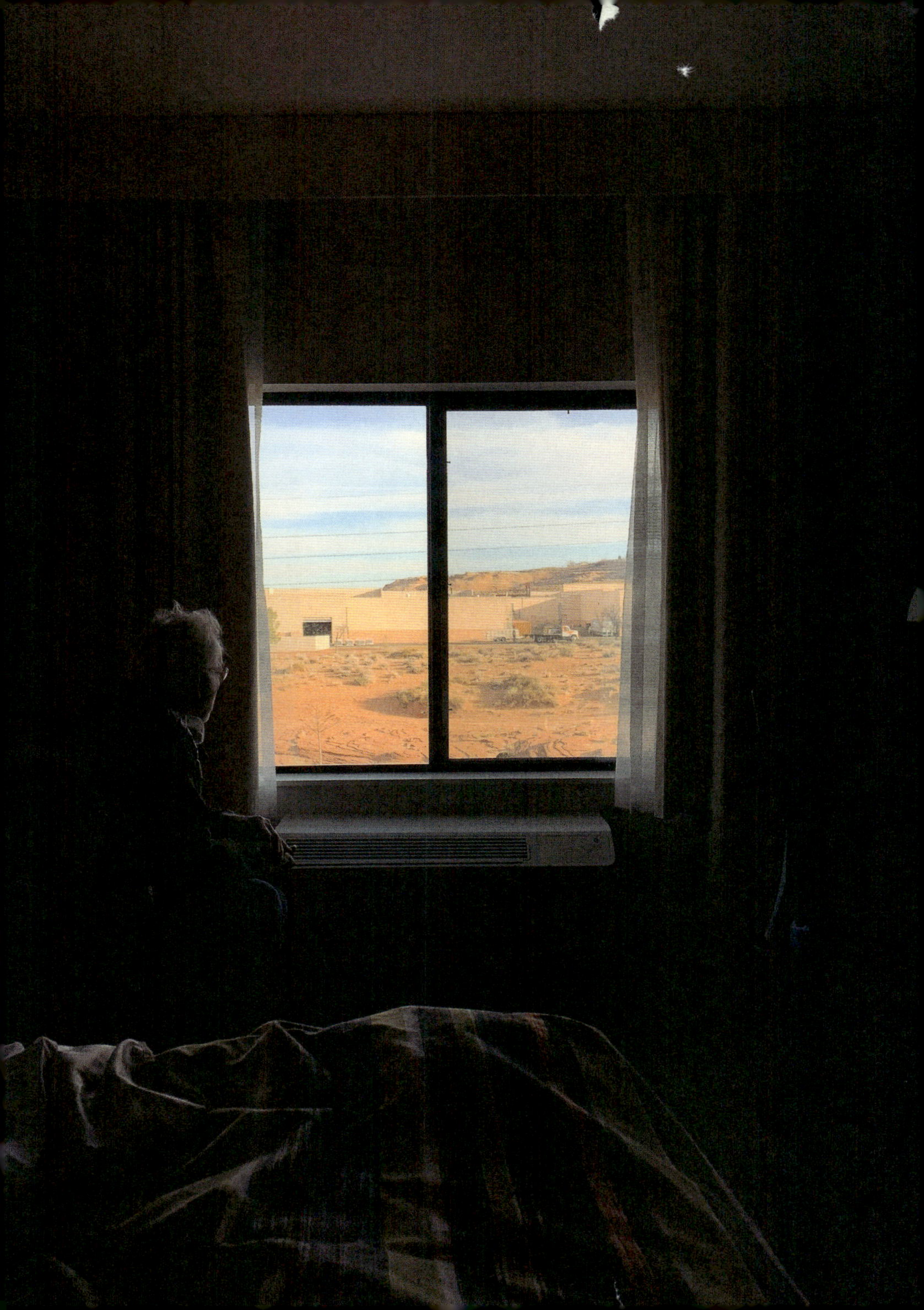

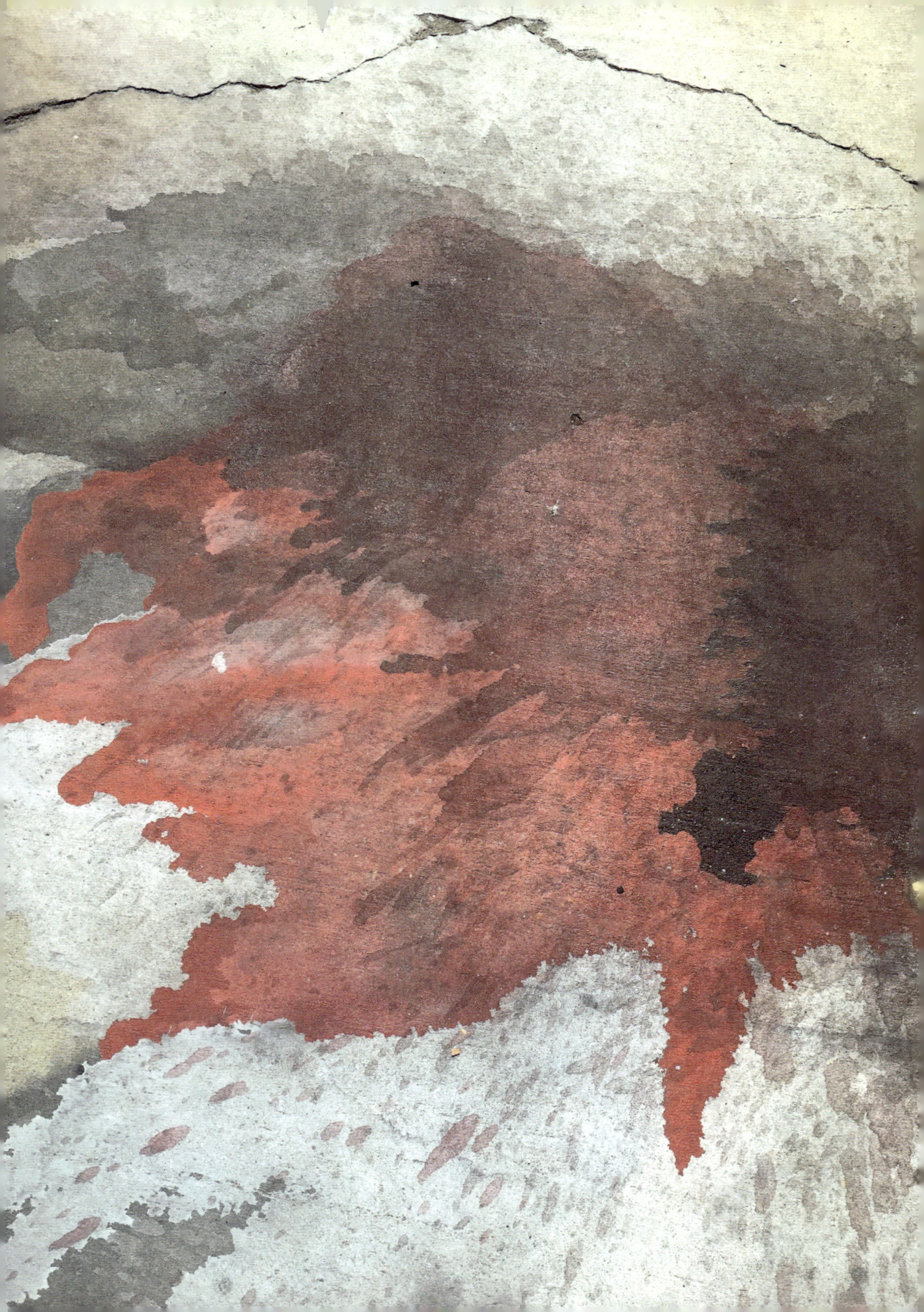

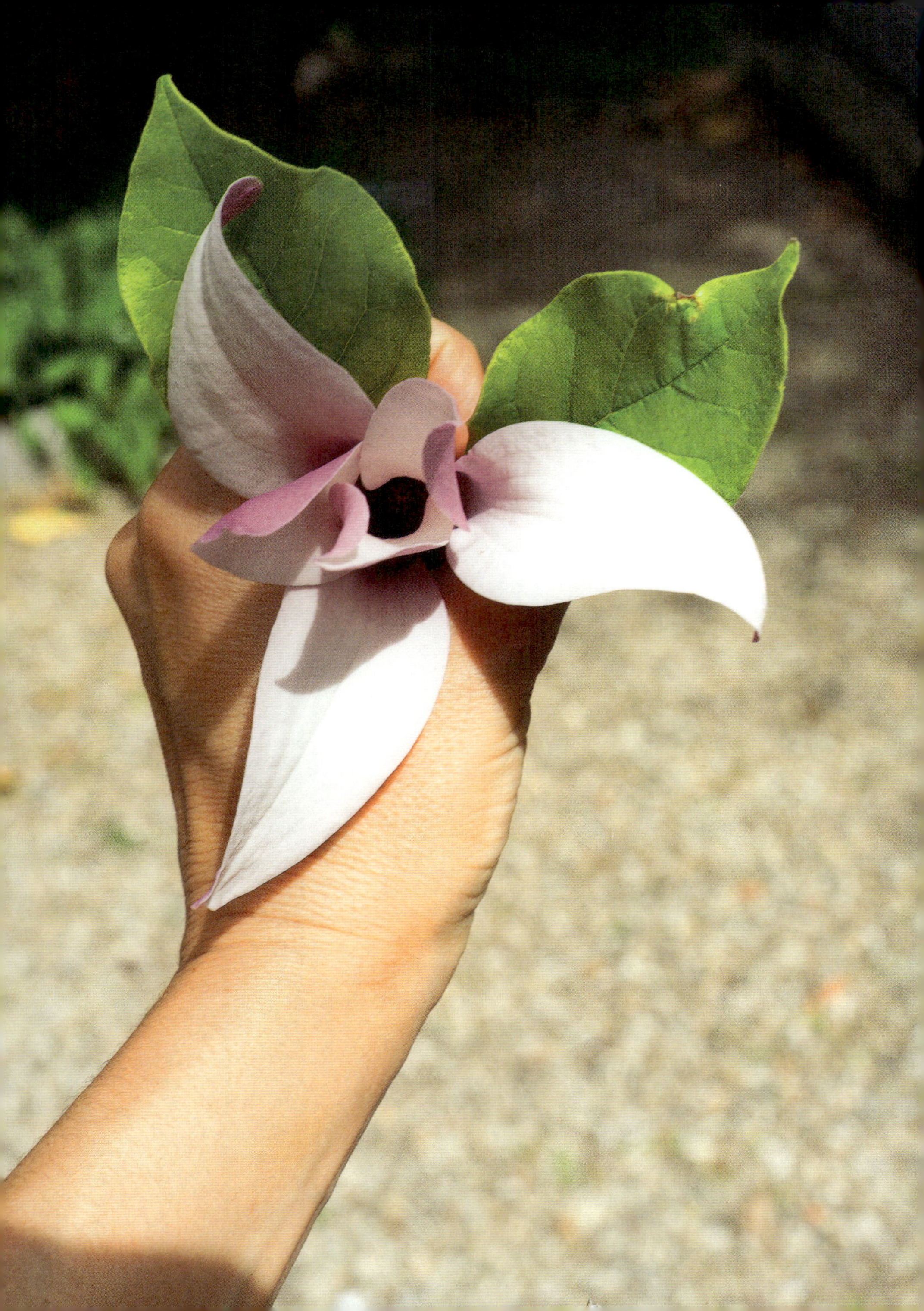

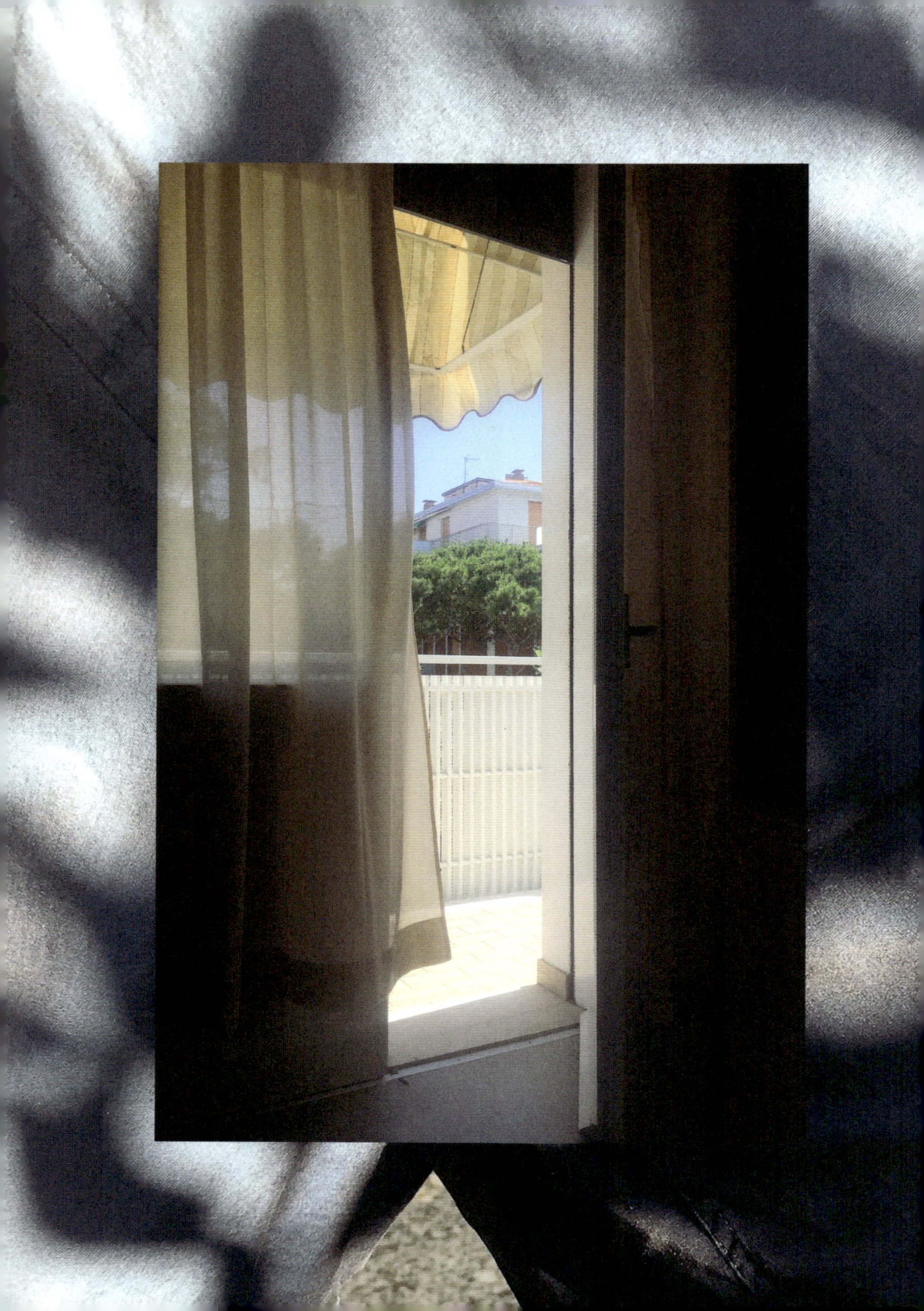

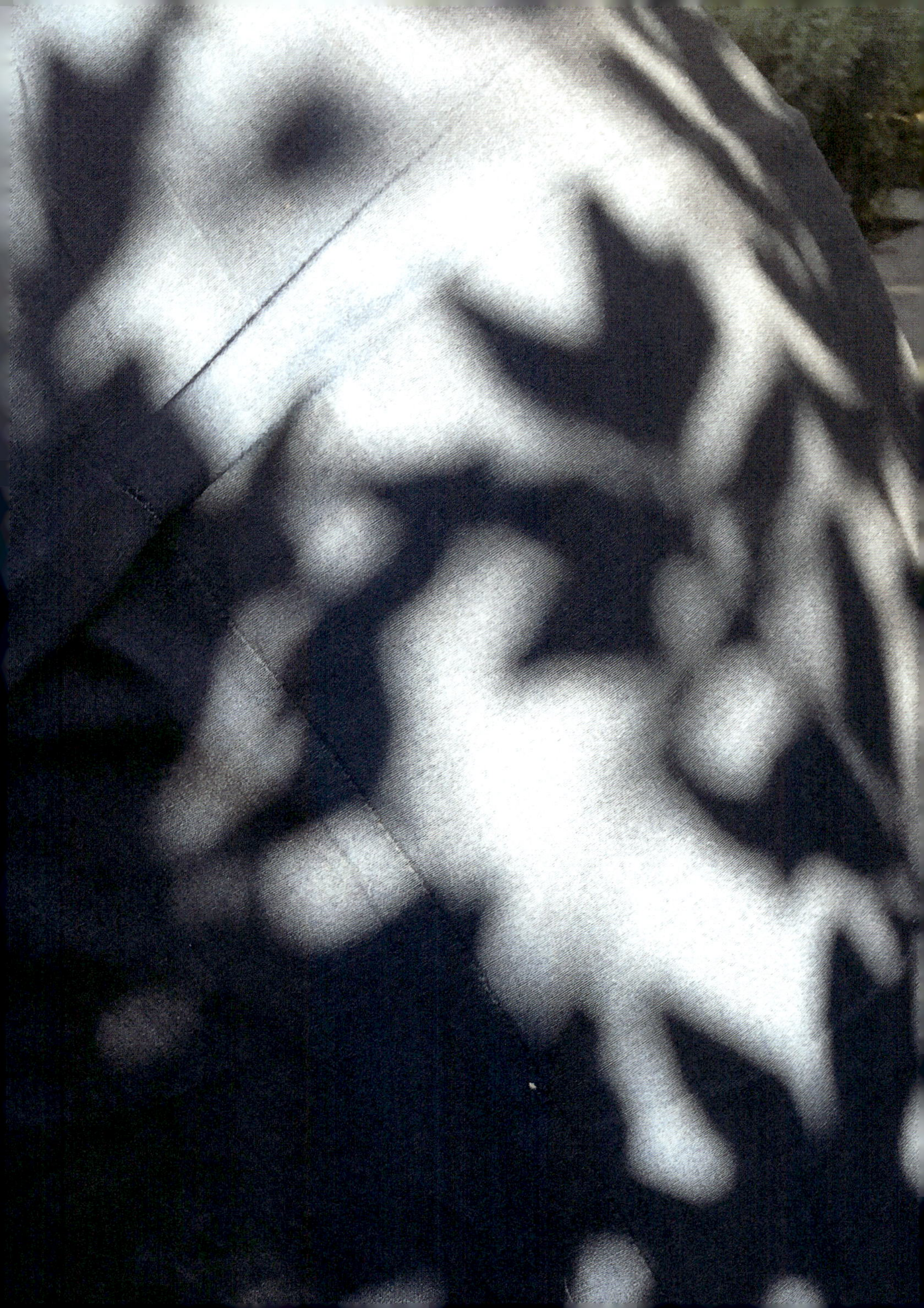

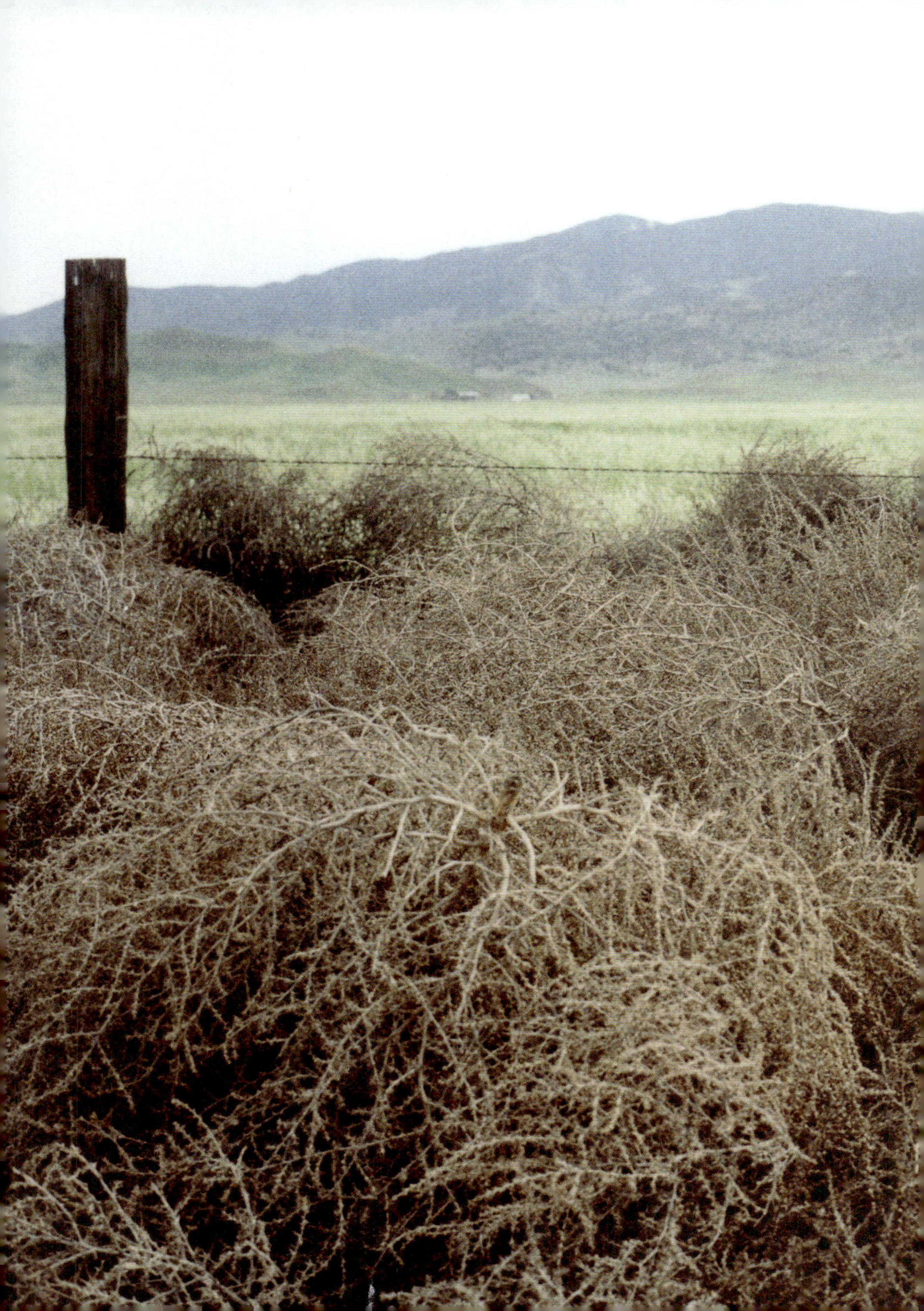

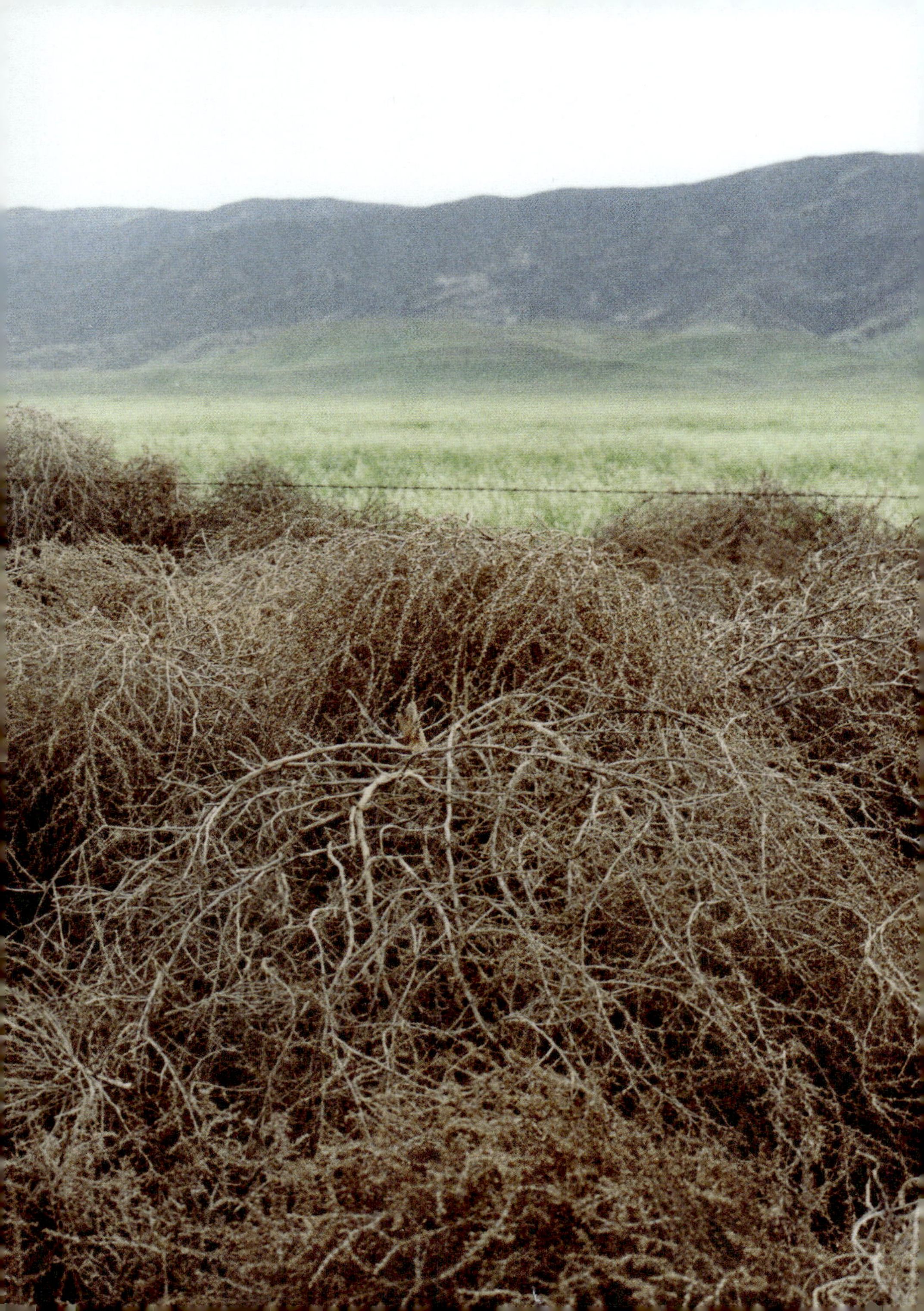

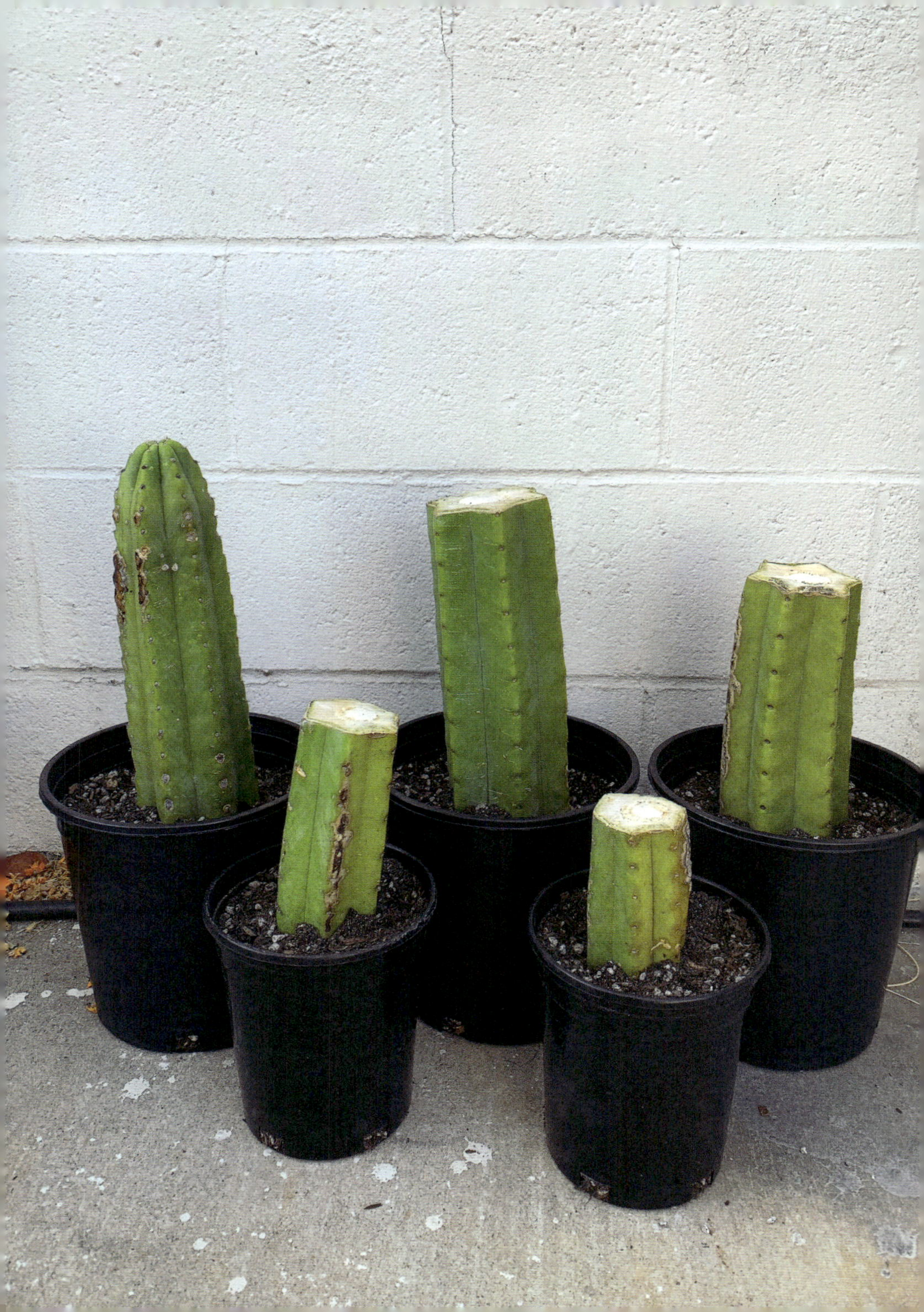

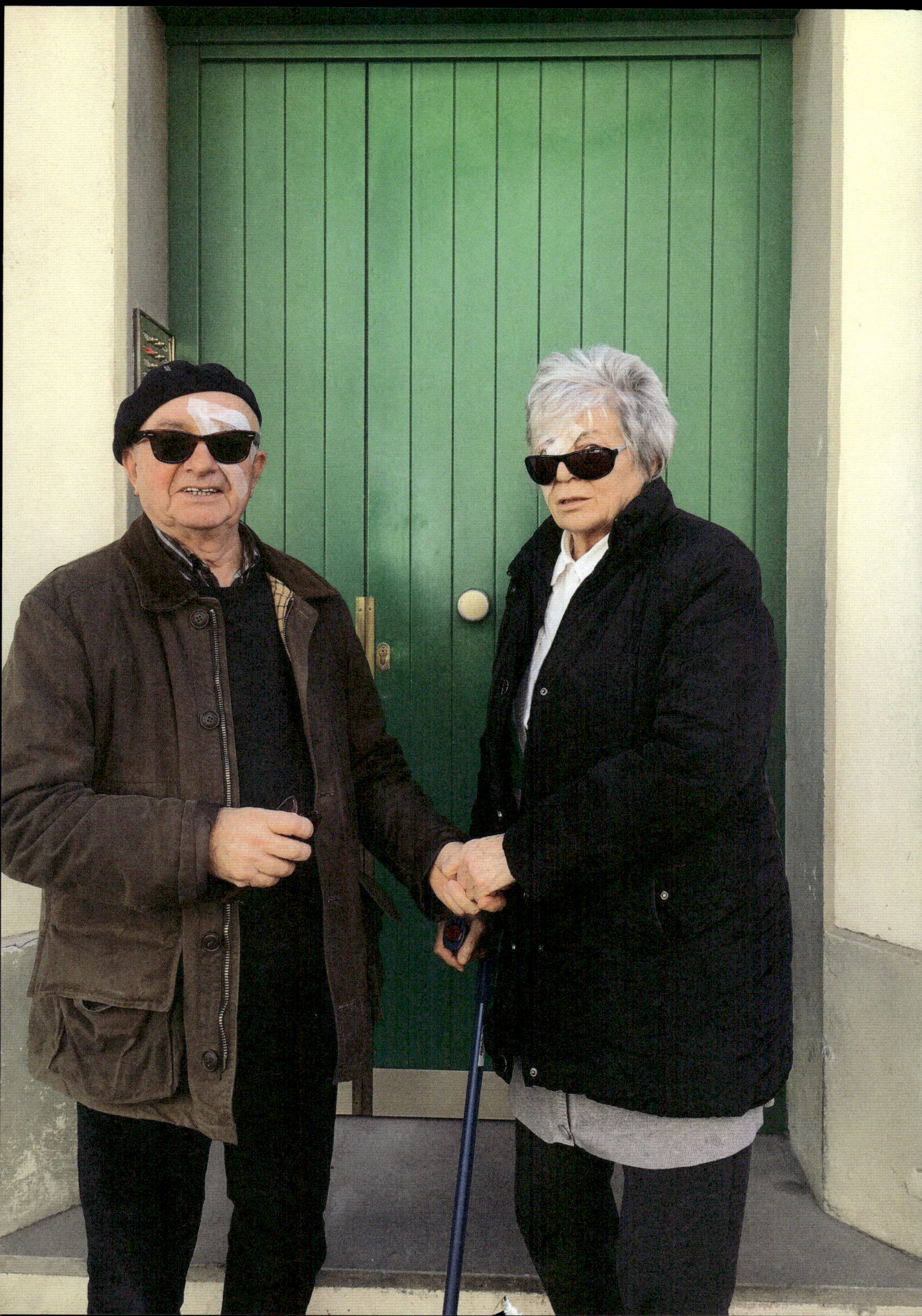

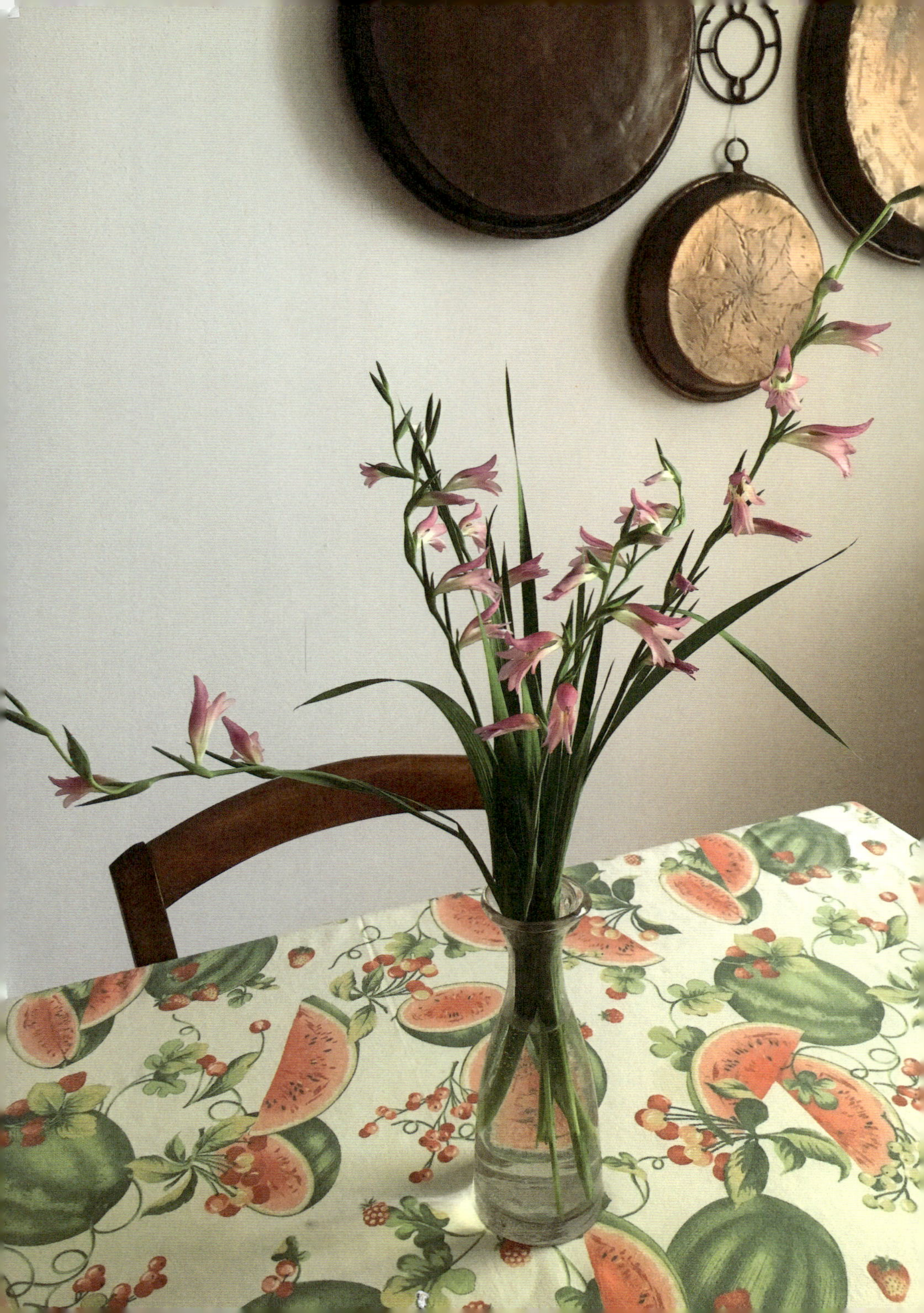

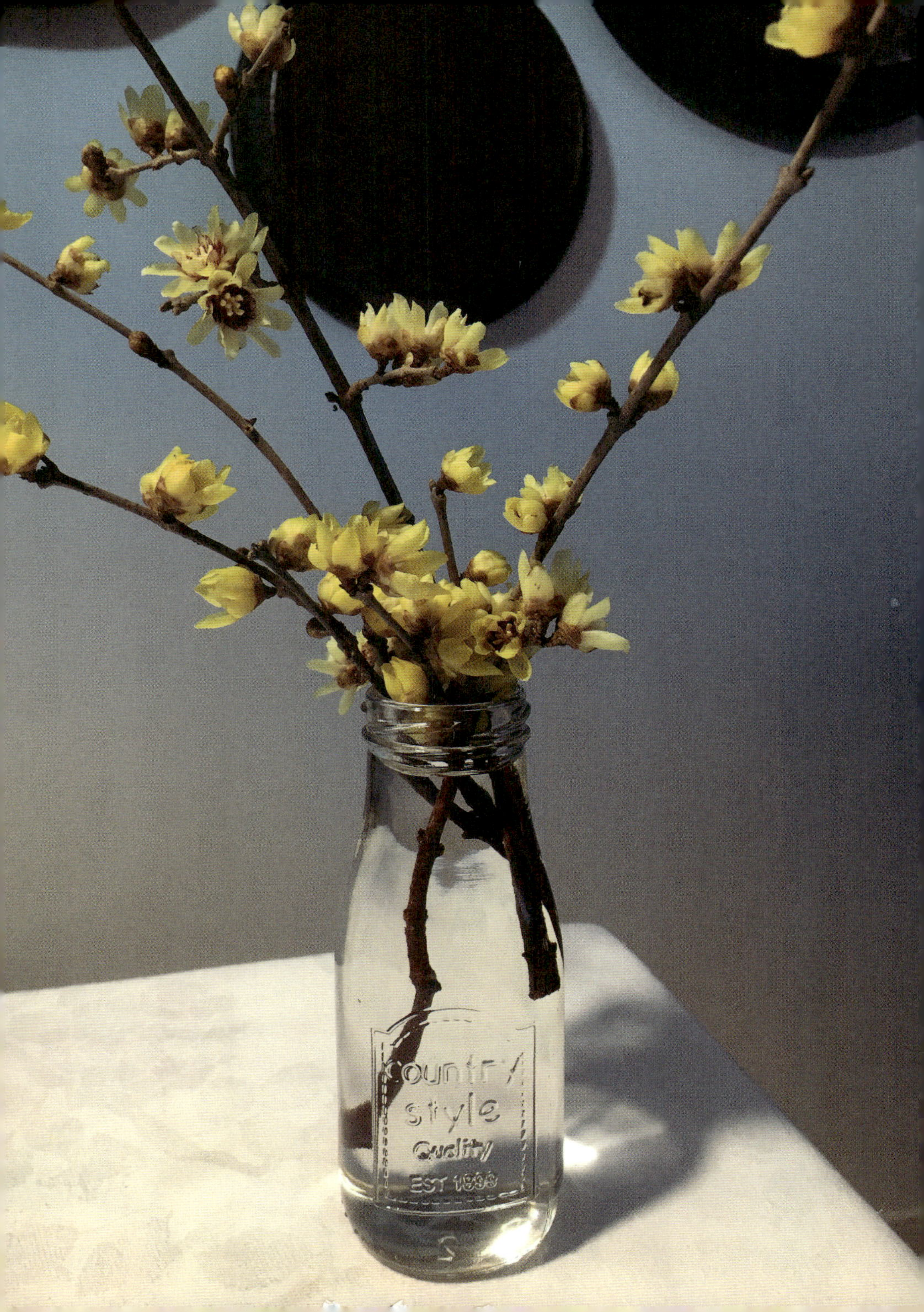
country
style
Quality
EST 1899

My dad woke up at 6 am and waited for me to get ready to leave. He put a little package of cookies on the table for me, he really cared about giving me something that morning. He wanted me to take some oranges as well, but I don't really like oranges. The kitchen had the same old smell as ever, a combination of the food from the dinner of the night before and something else I can't ever put my finger on. Comforting and suffocating at the same time because I know it won't be there forever.

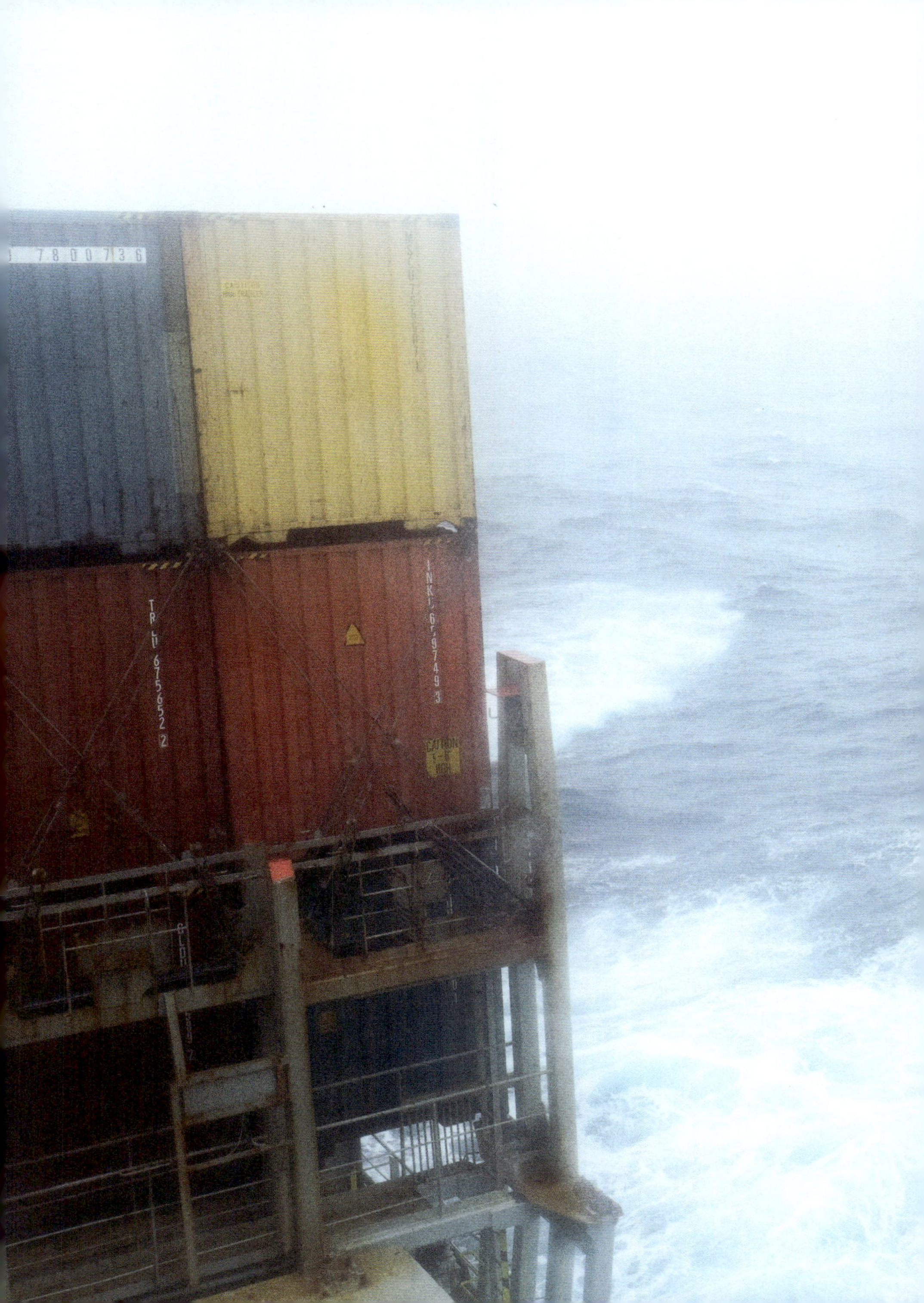

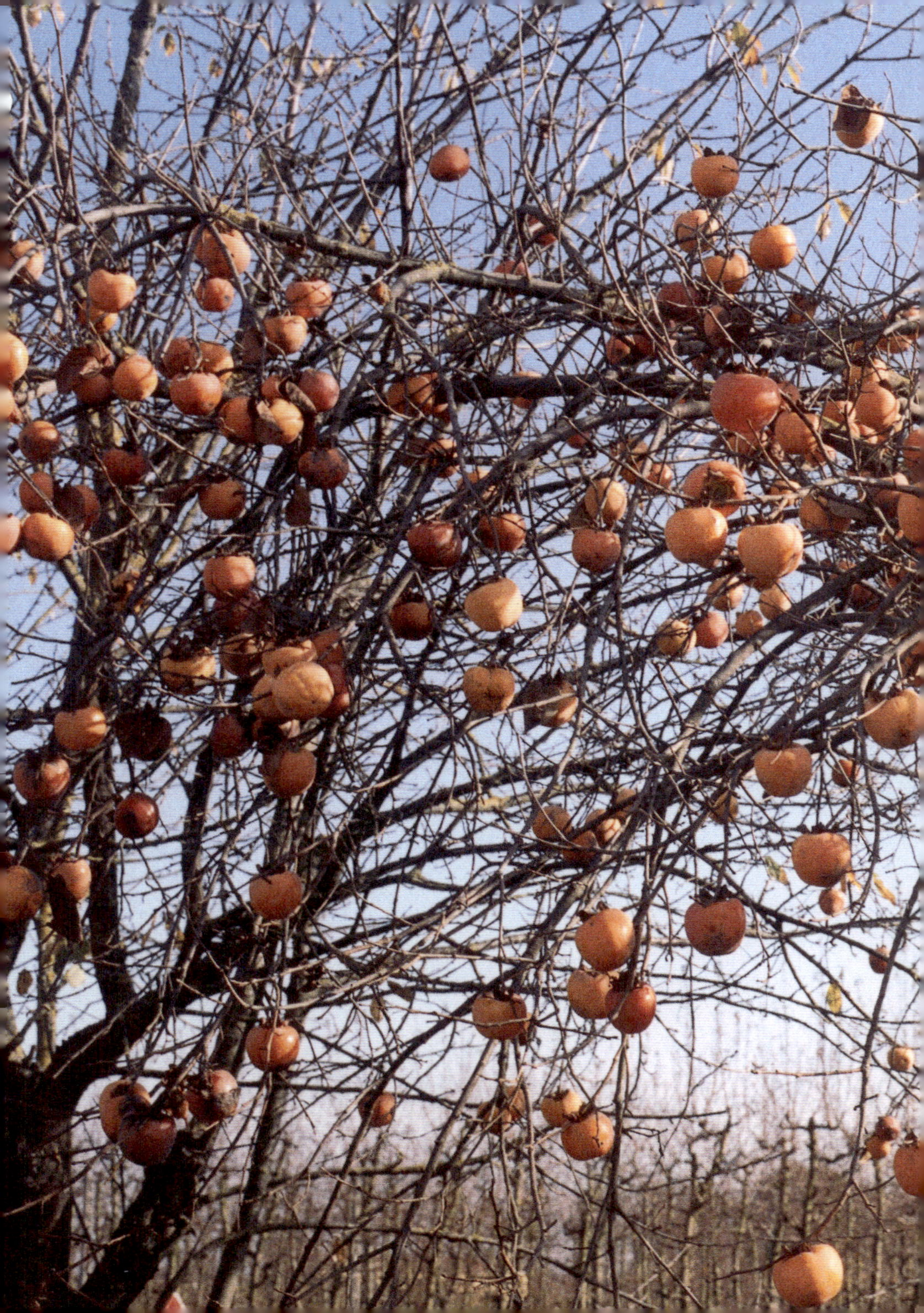

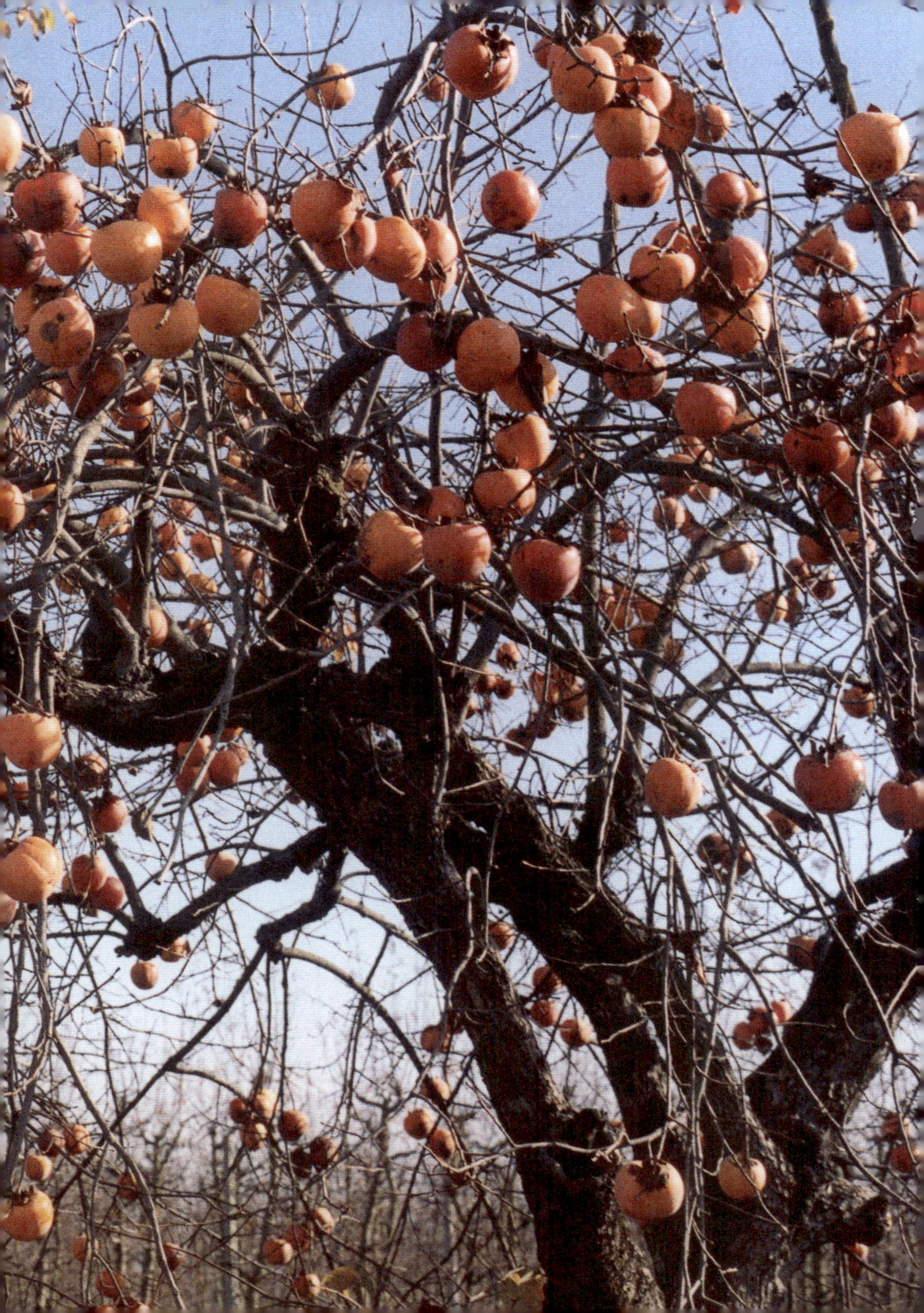

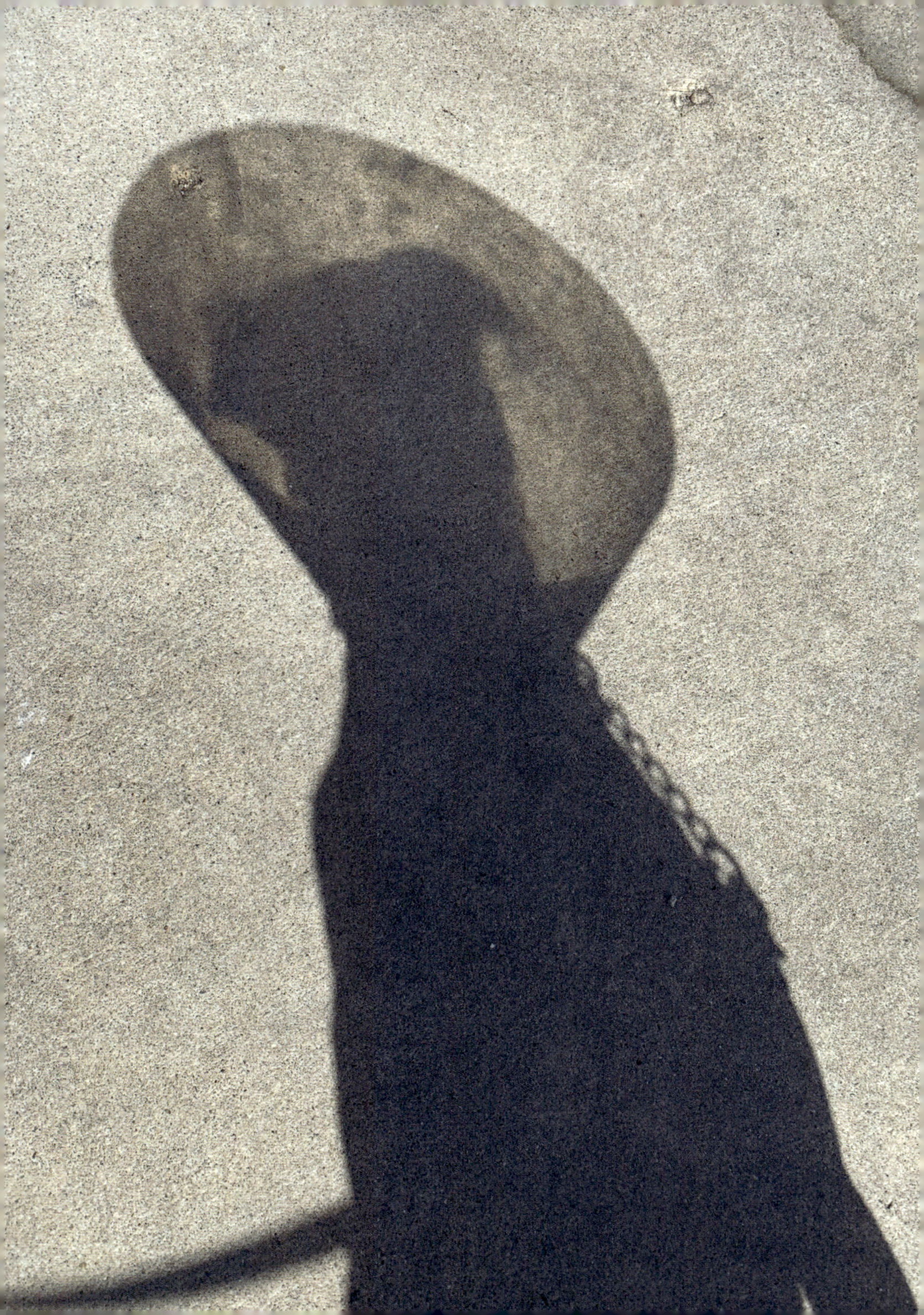

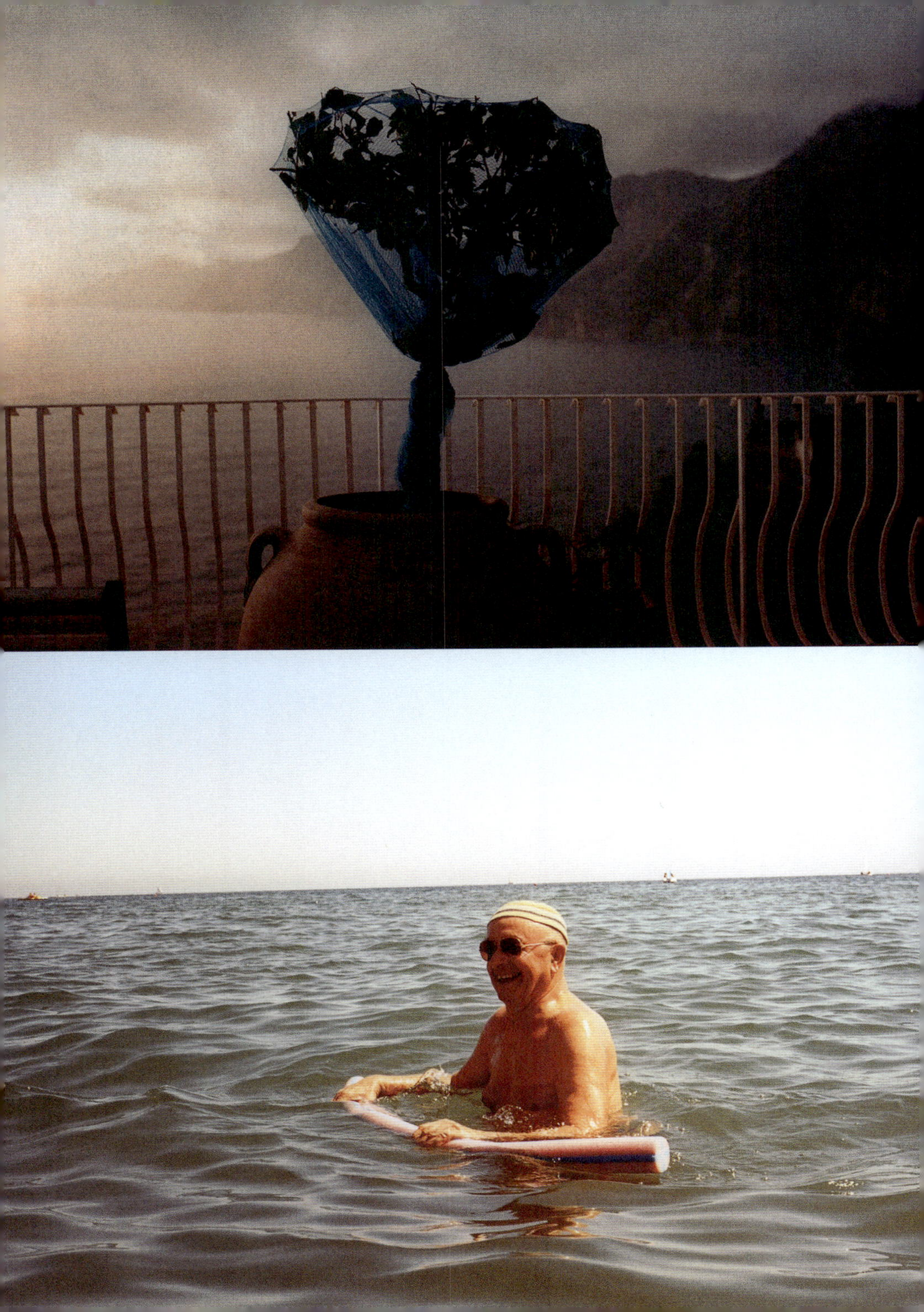

Yesterday Eric died. Eric was Paola's giant dog. She lives alone in her house on the hill. My dad goes to visit her sometimes, and also to look for mushrooms and fruit. Eric had grown a swollen, big stomach, so my dad suggested to Paola to have him checked out because it was a bad sign. She told him Eric didn't want to go to the vet and that he was old anyway.

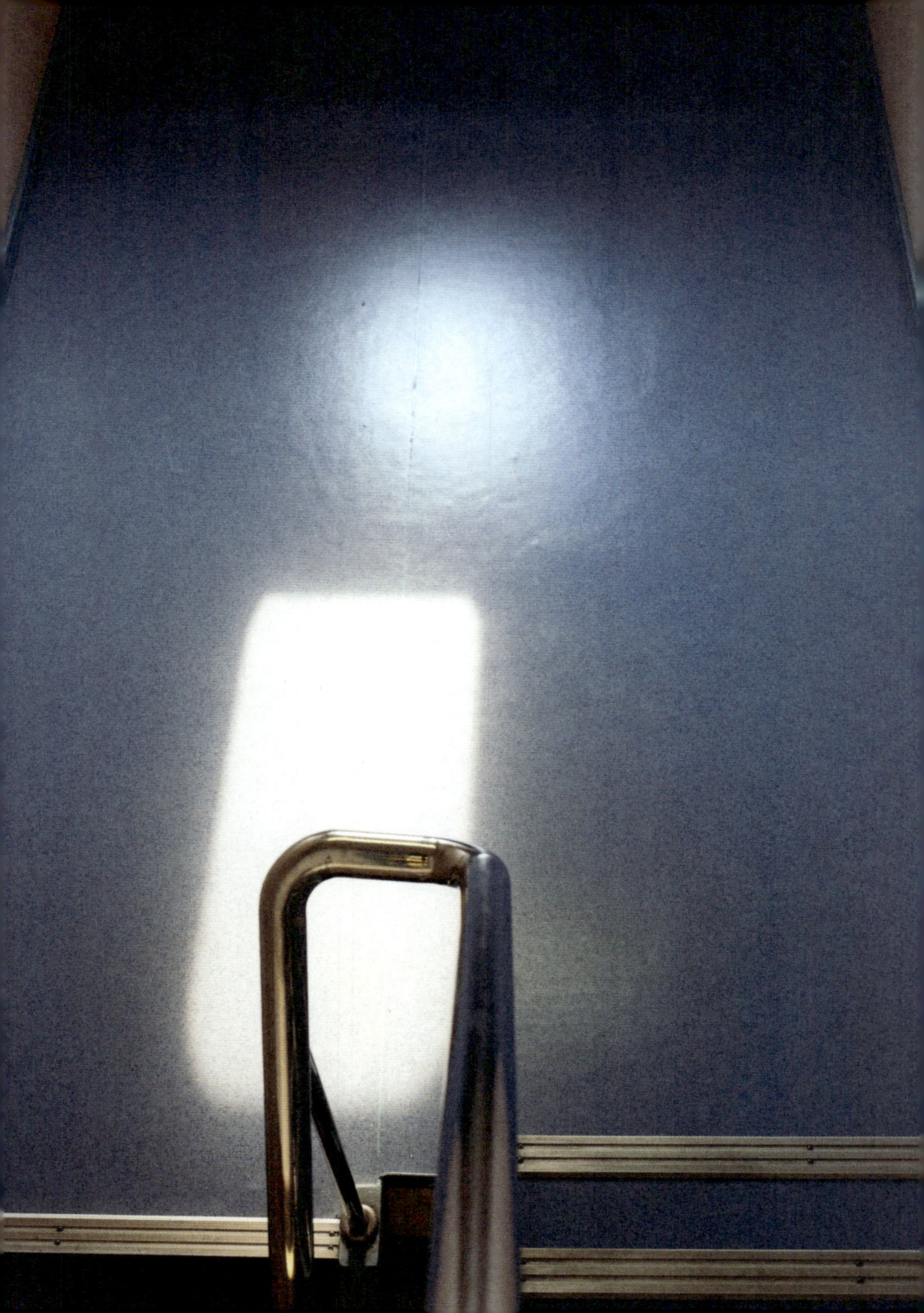

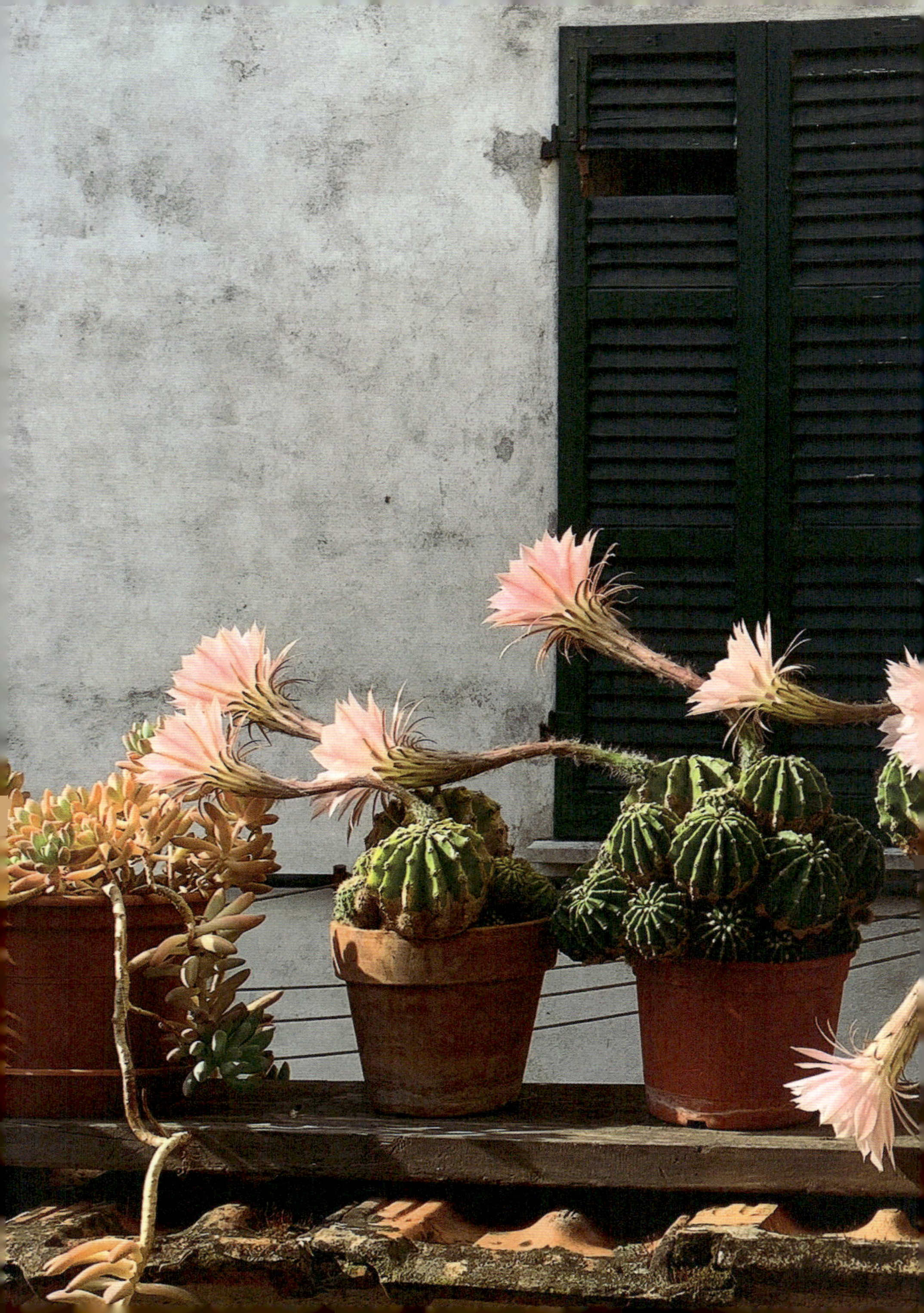

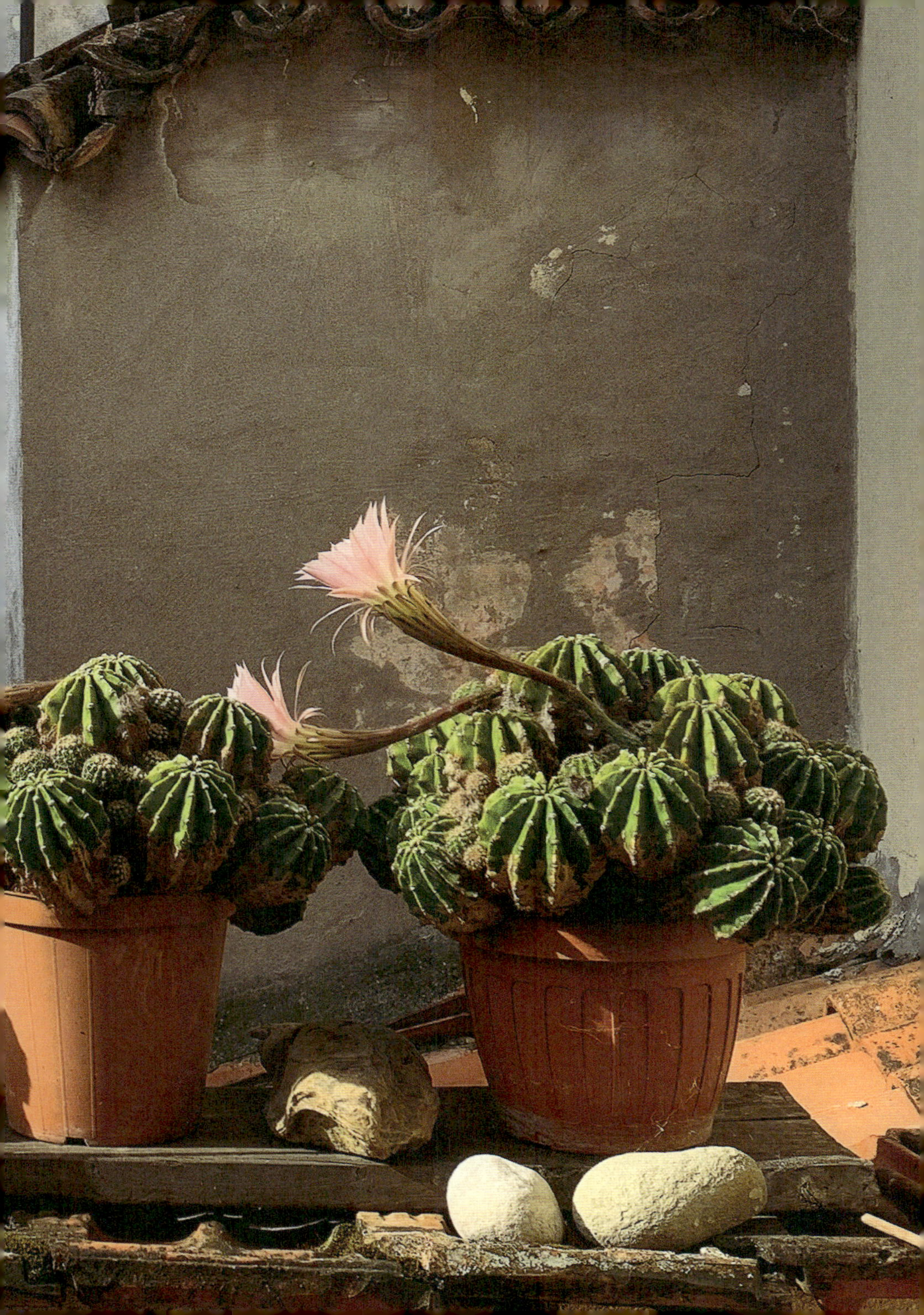

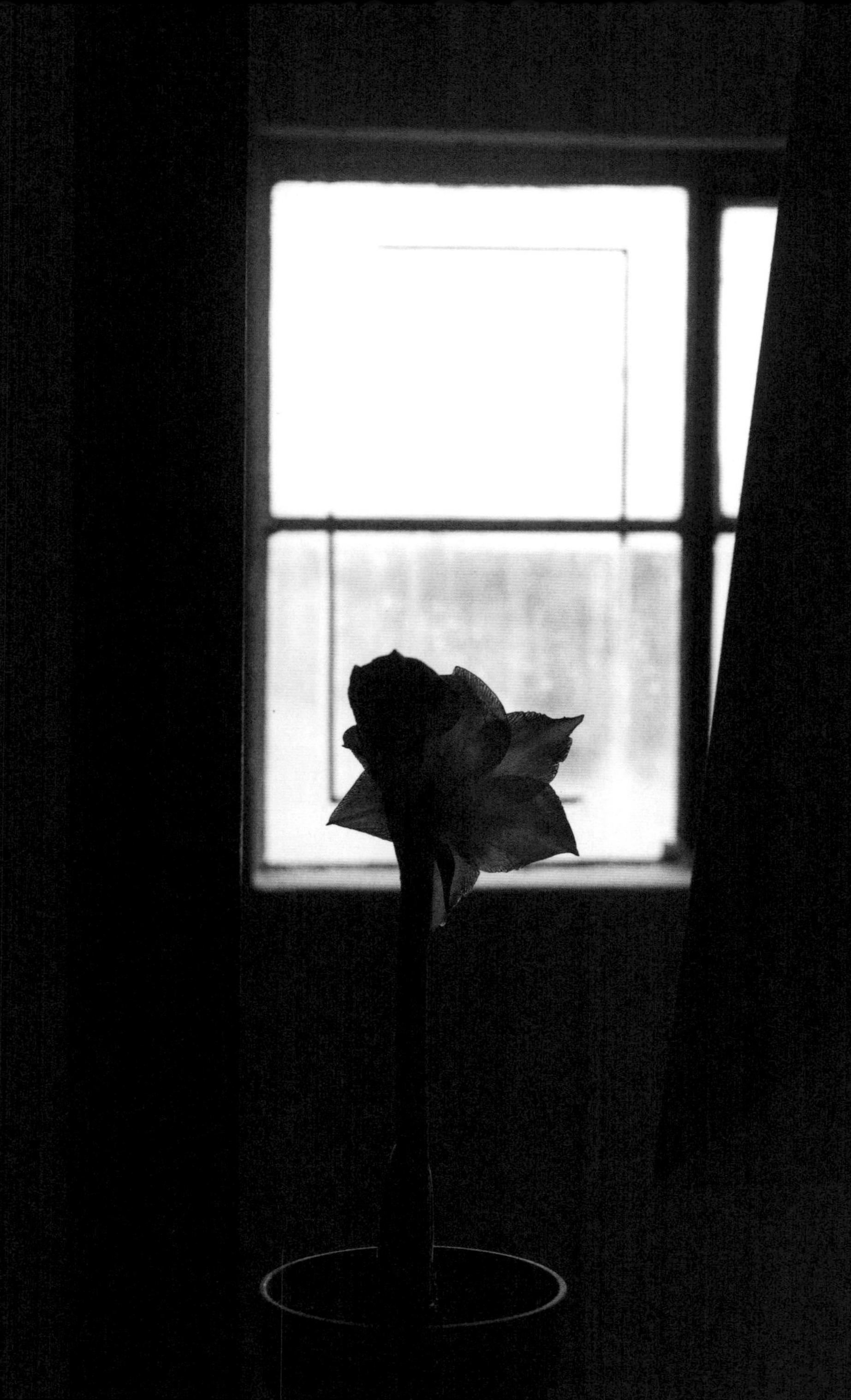

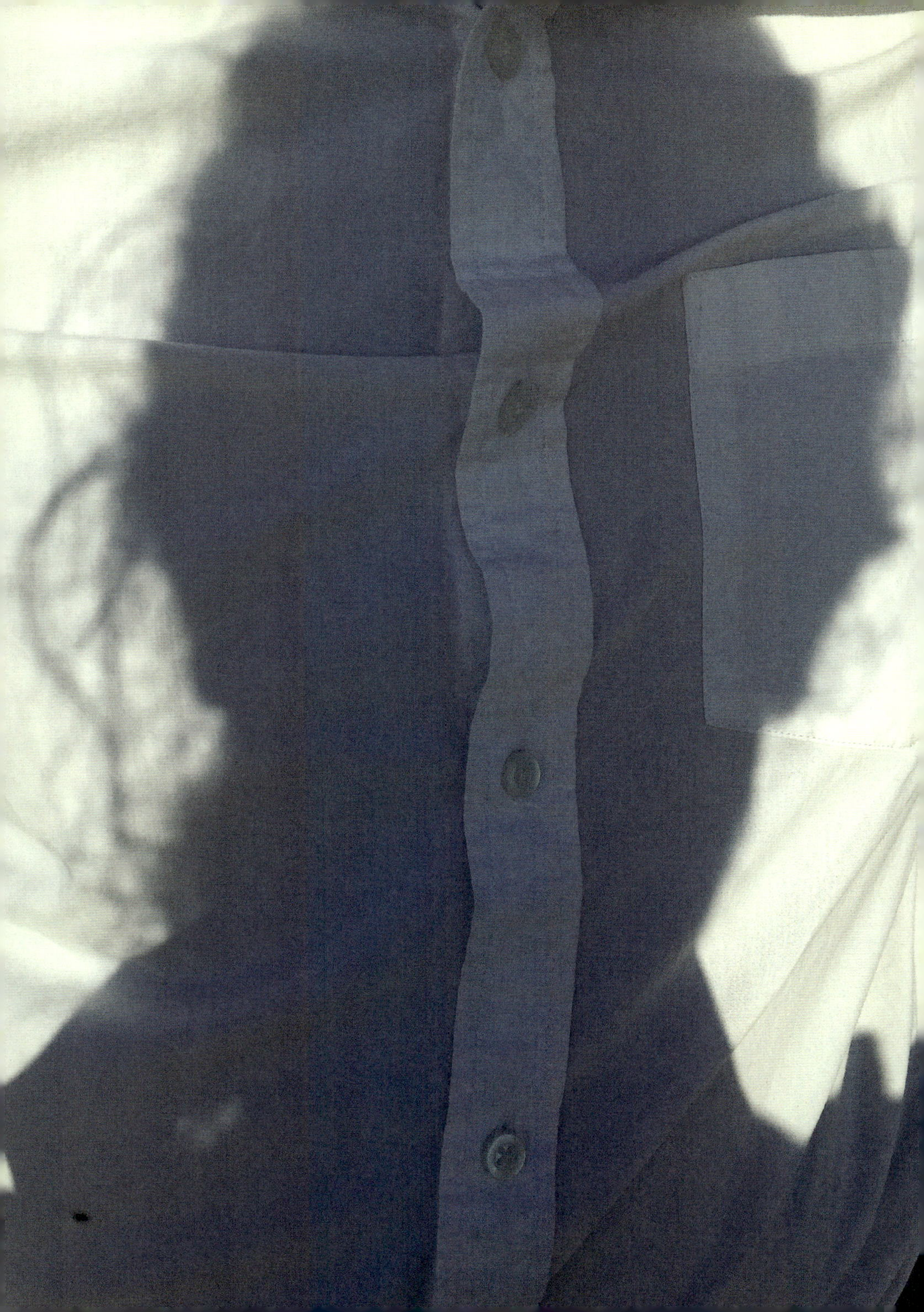

I was on the floor, belly down with so many images running through my mind. What the heck was I doing? Why was everything getting so messed up? If I think about it now, it seems to me that being immobile is one of the things I have always liked the most. I felt safer that way.

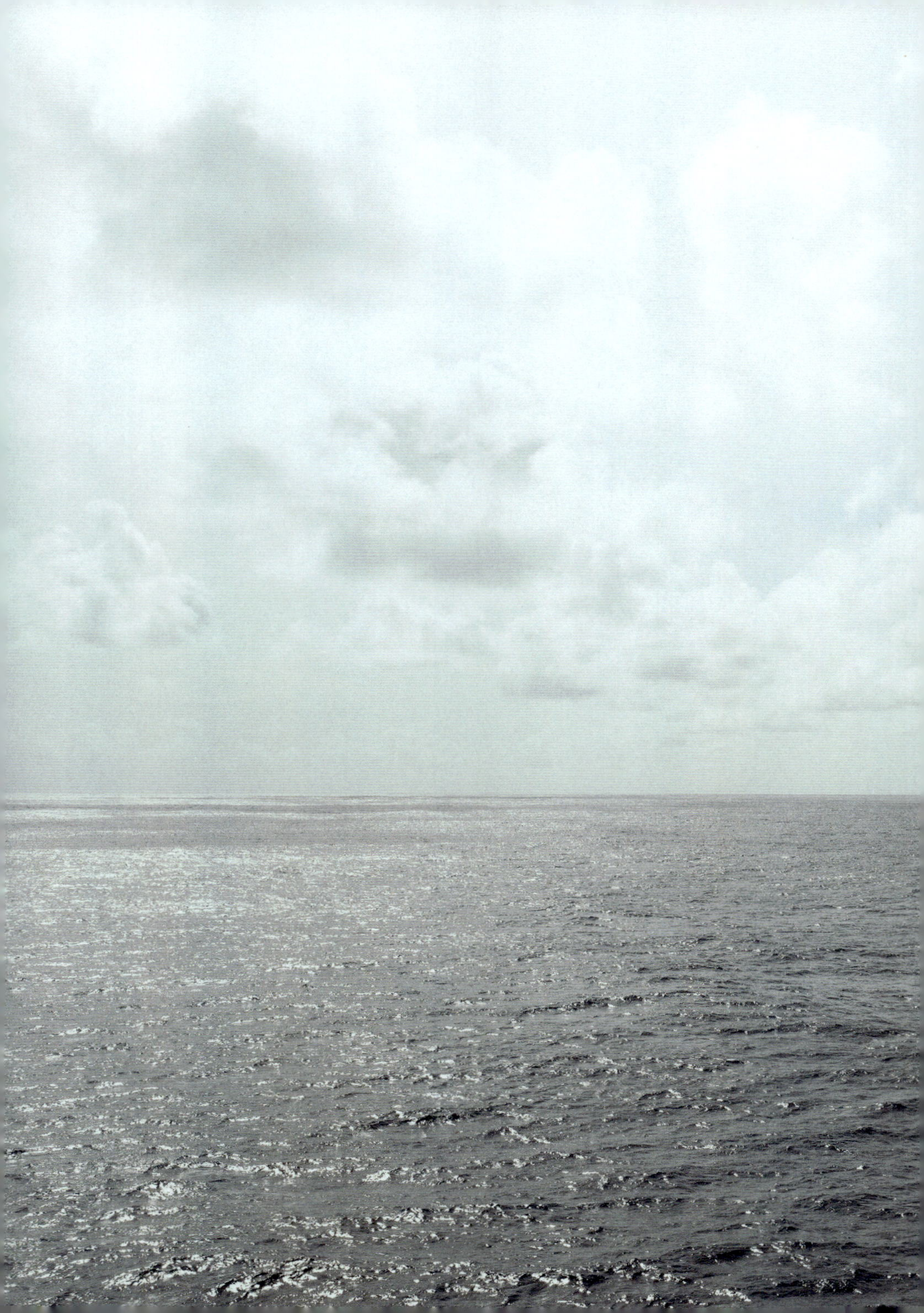

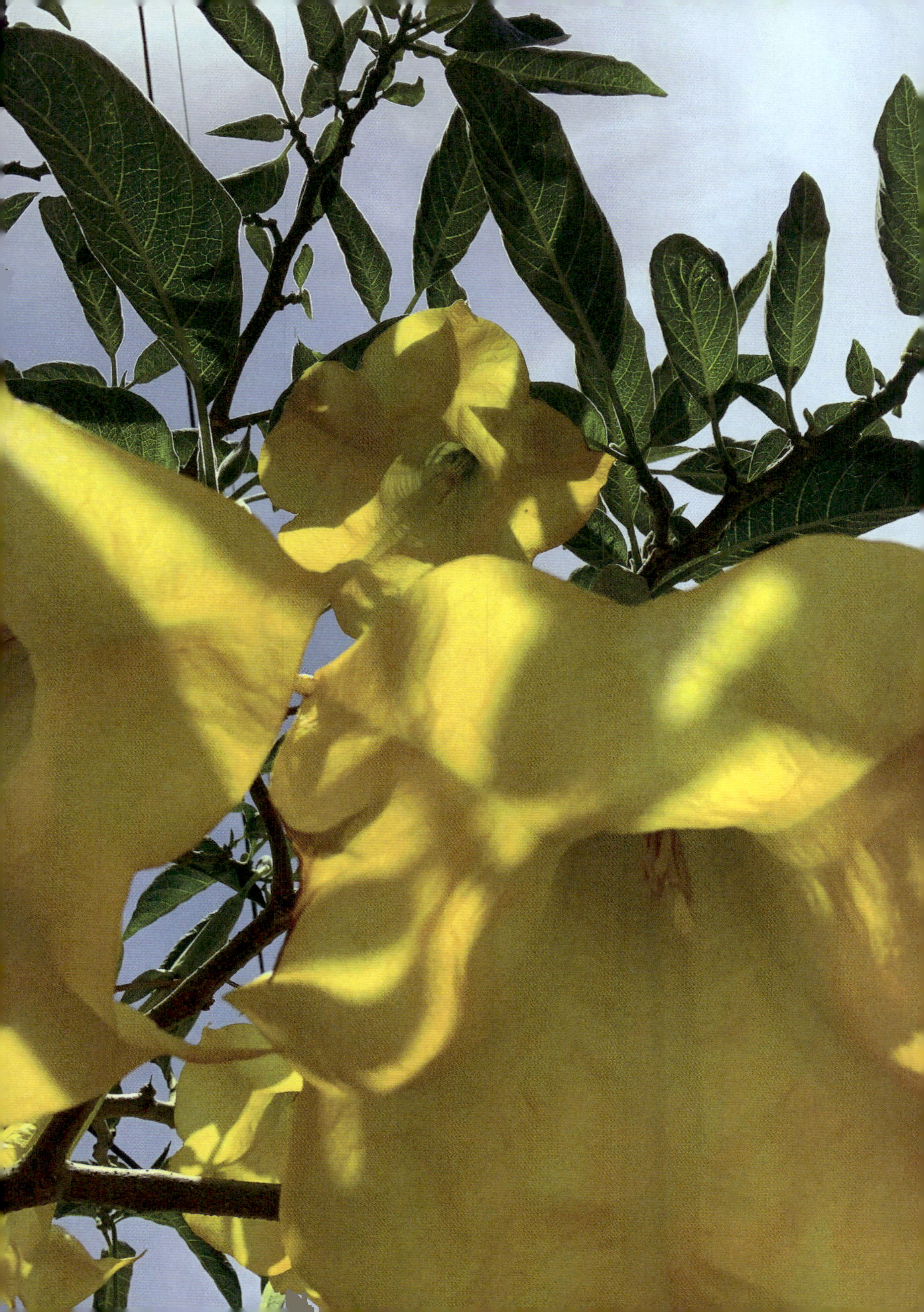

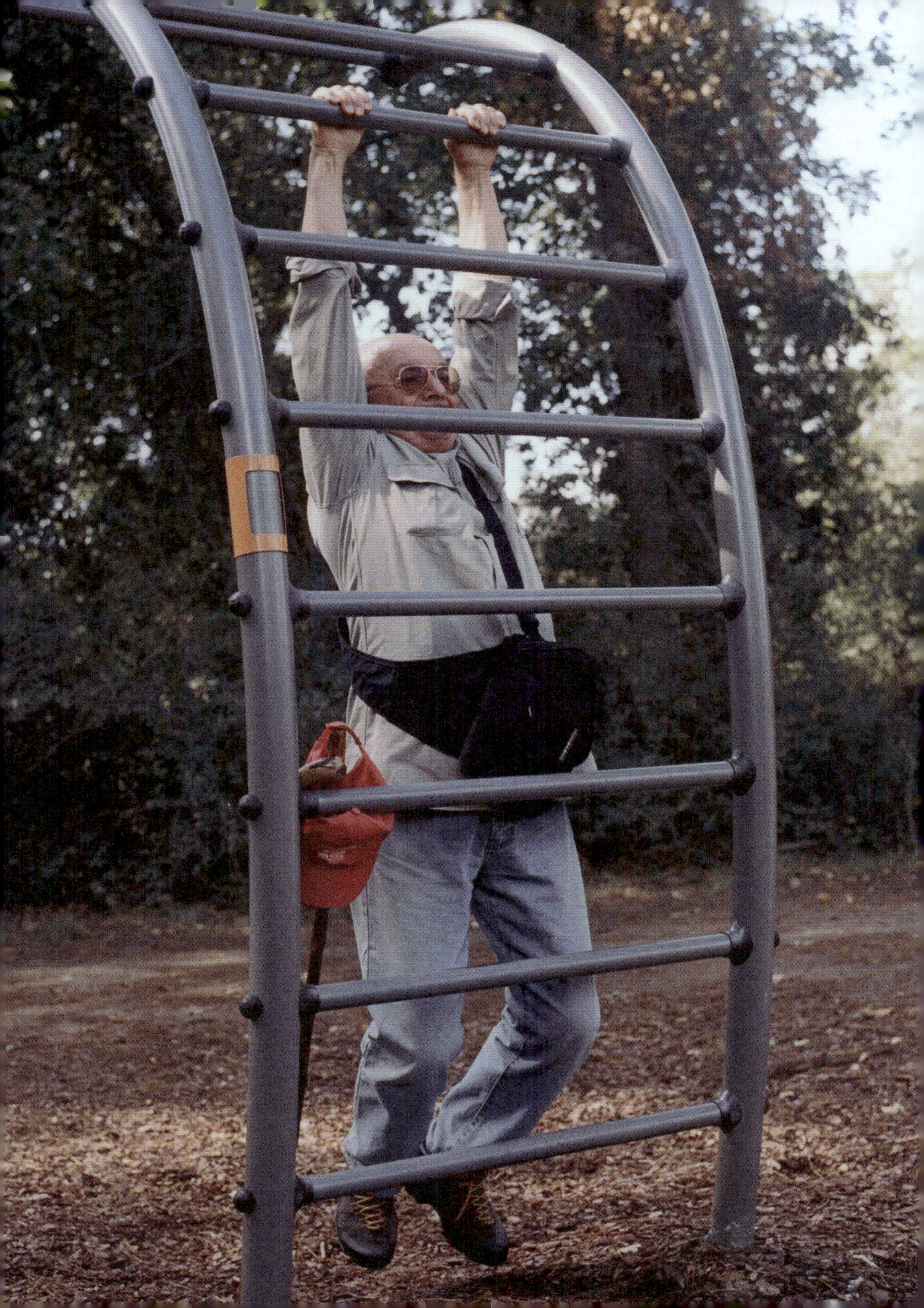

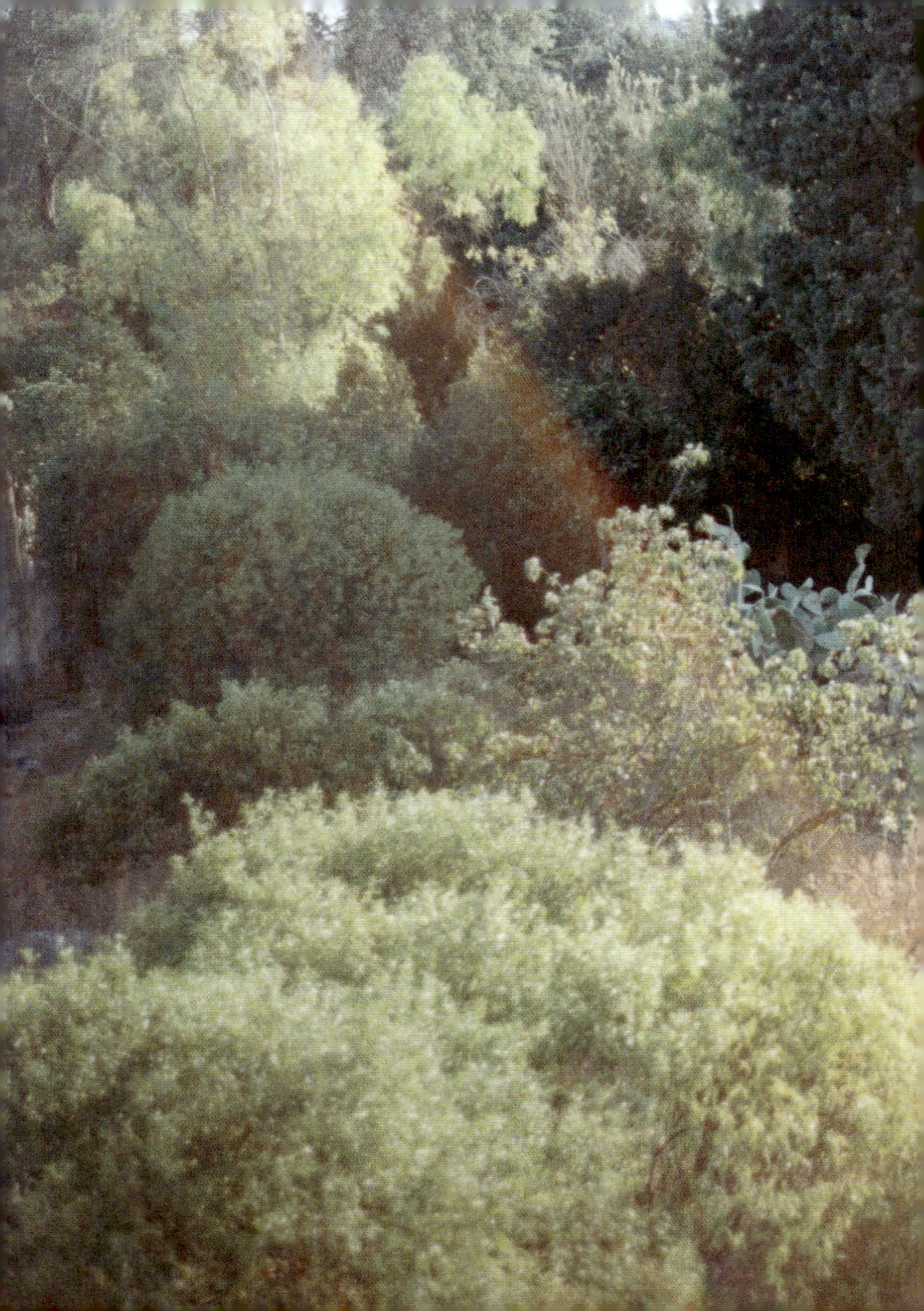

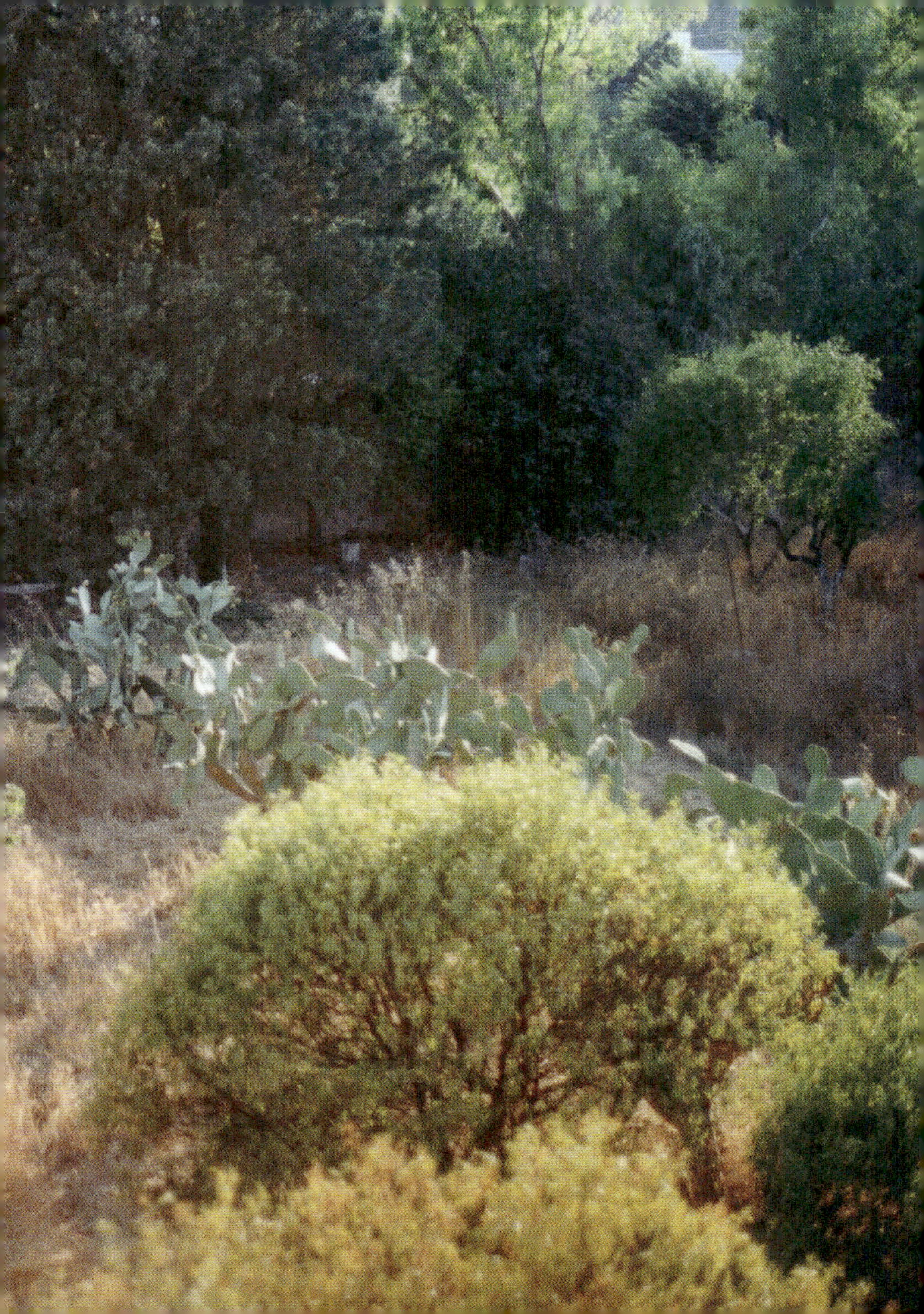

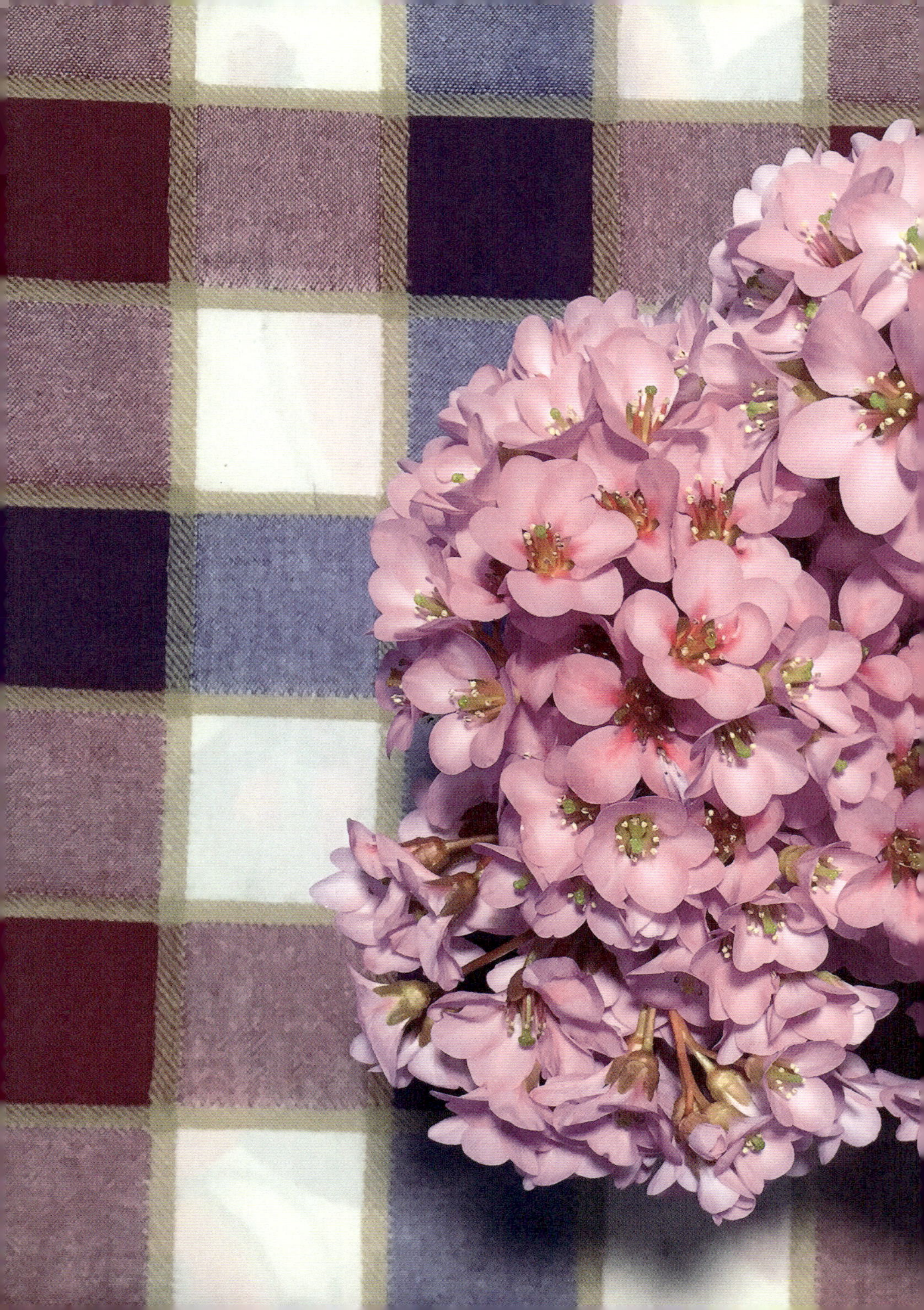

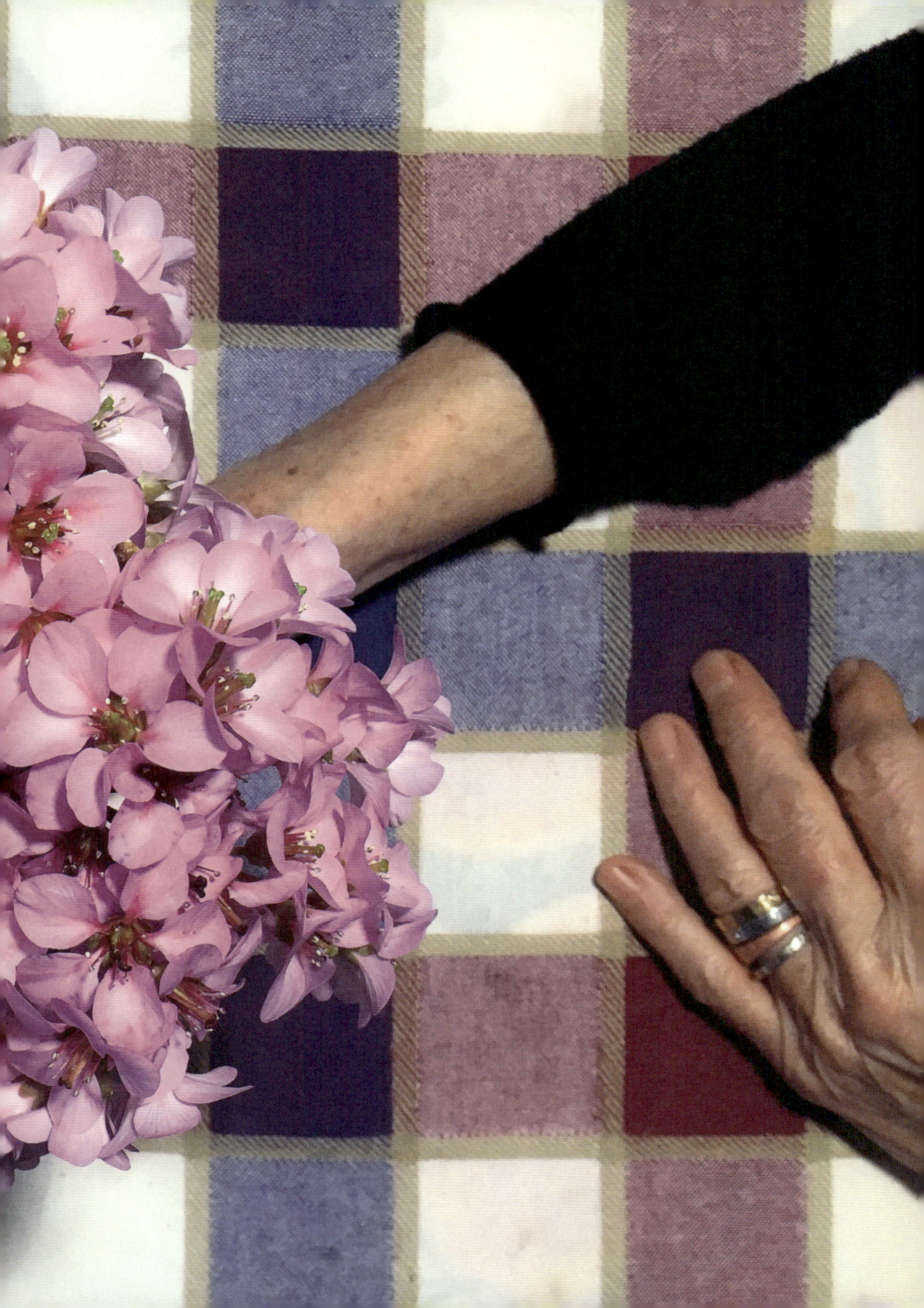

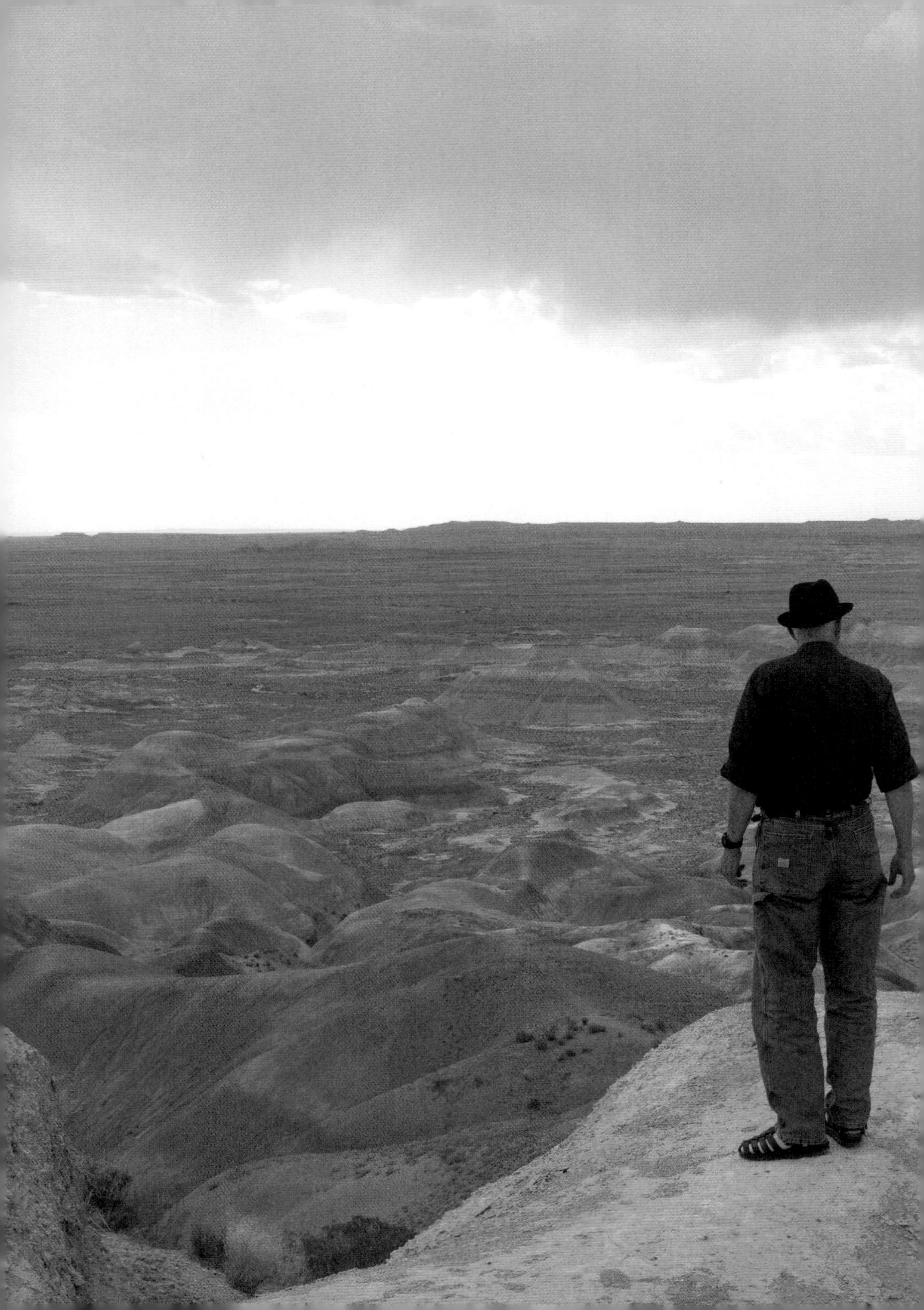

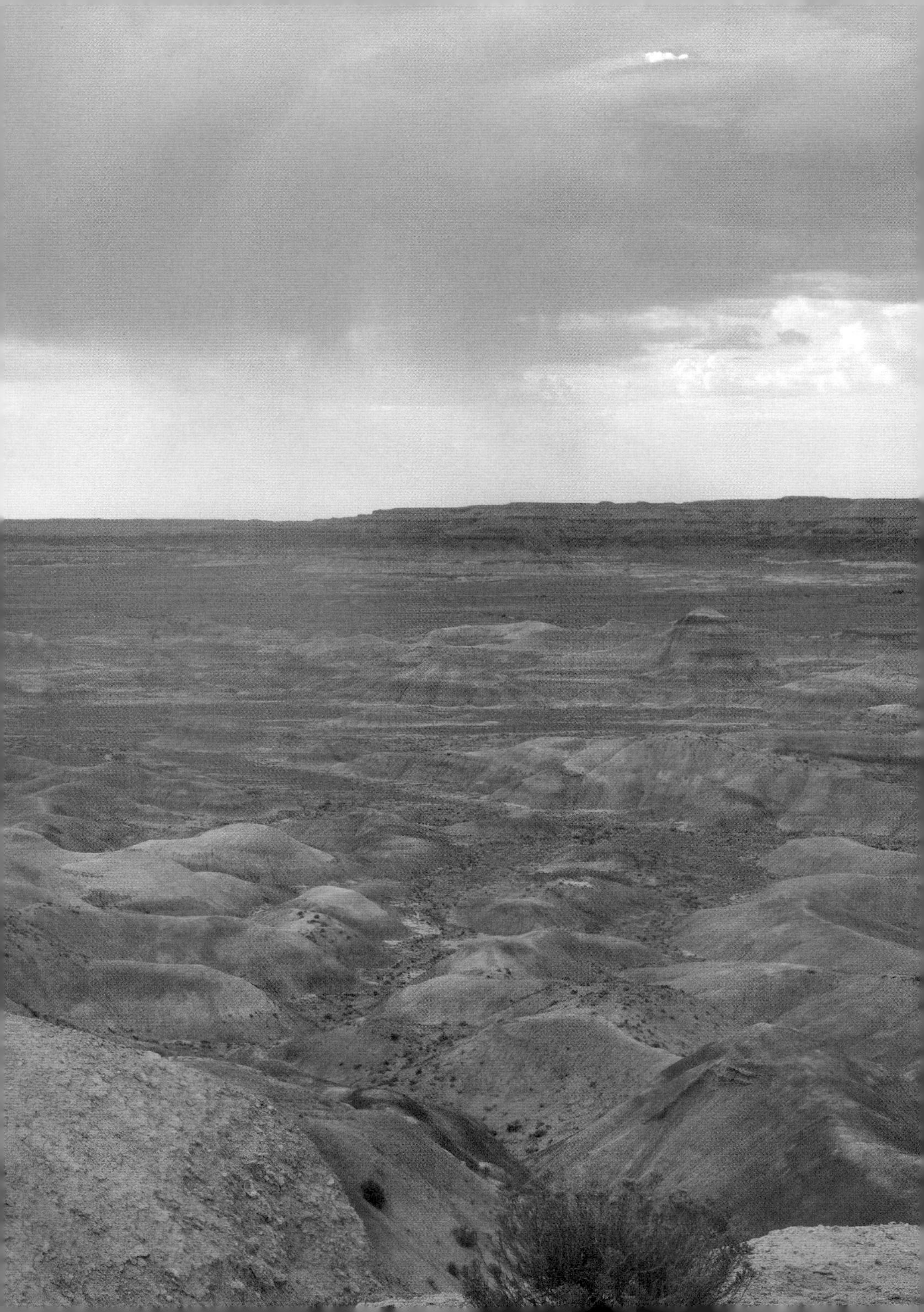

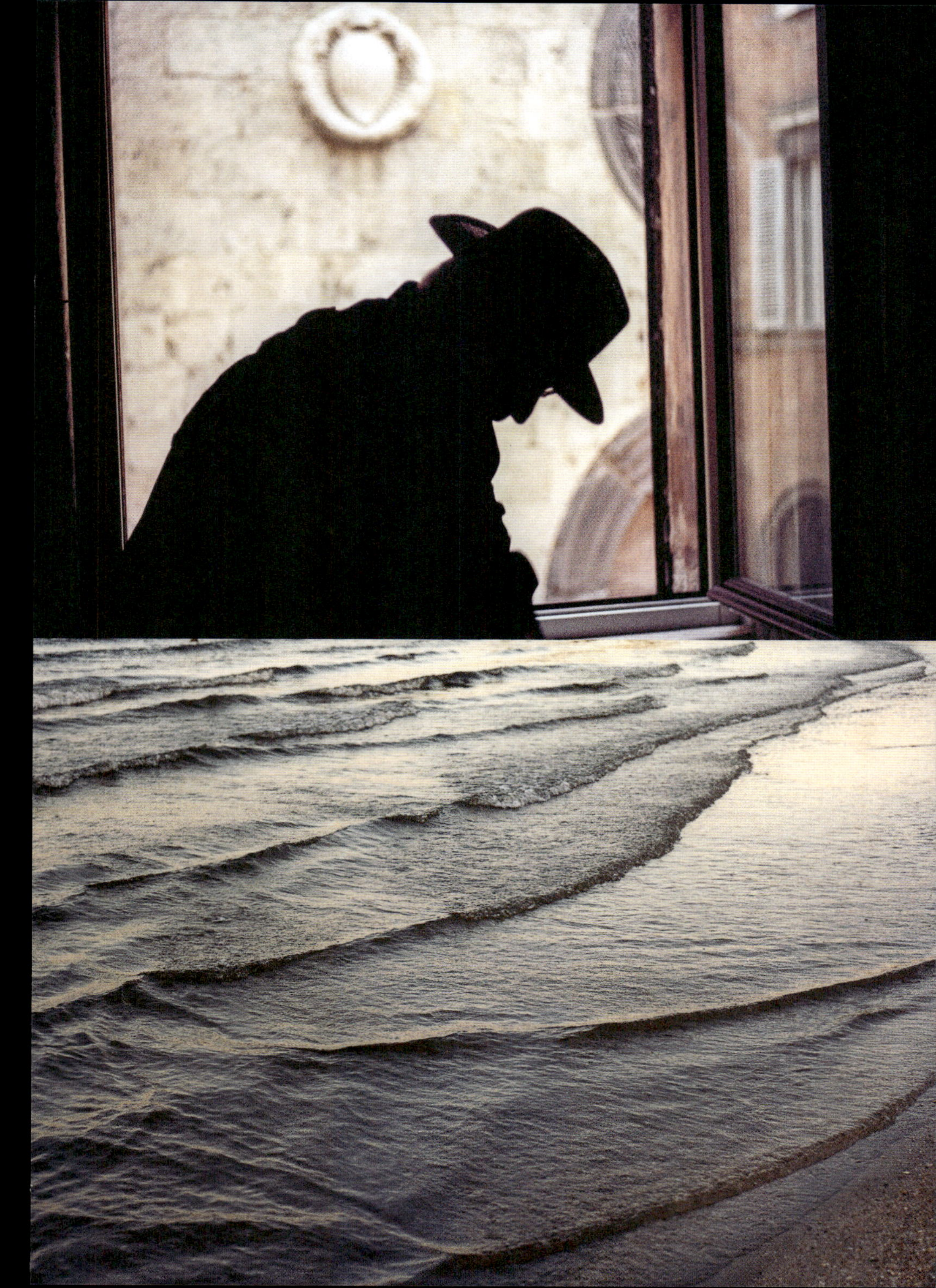

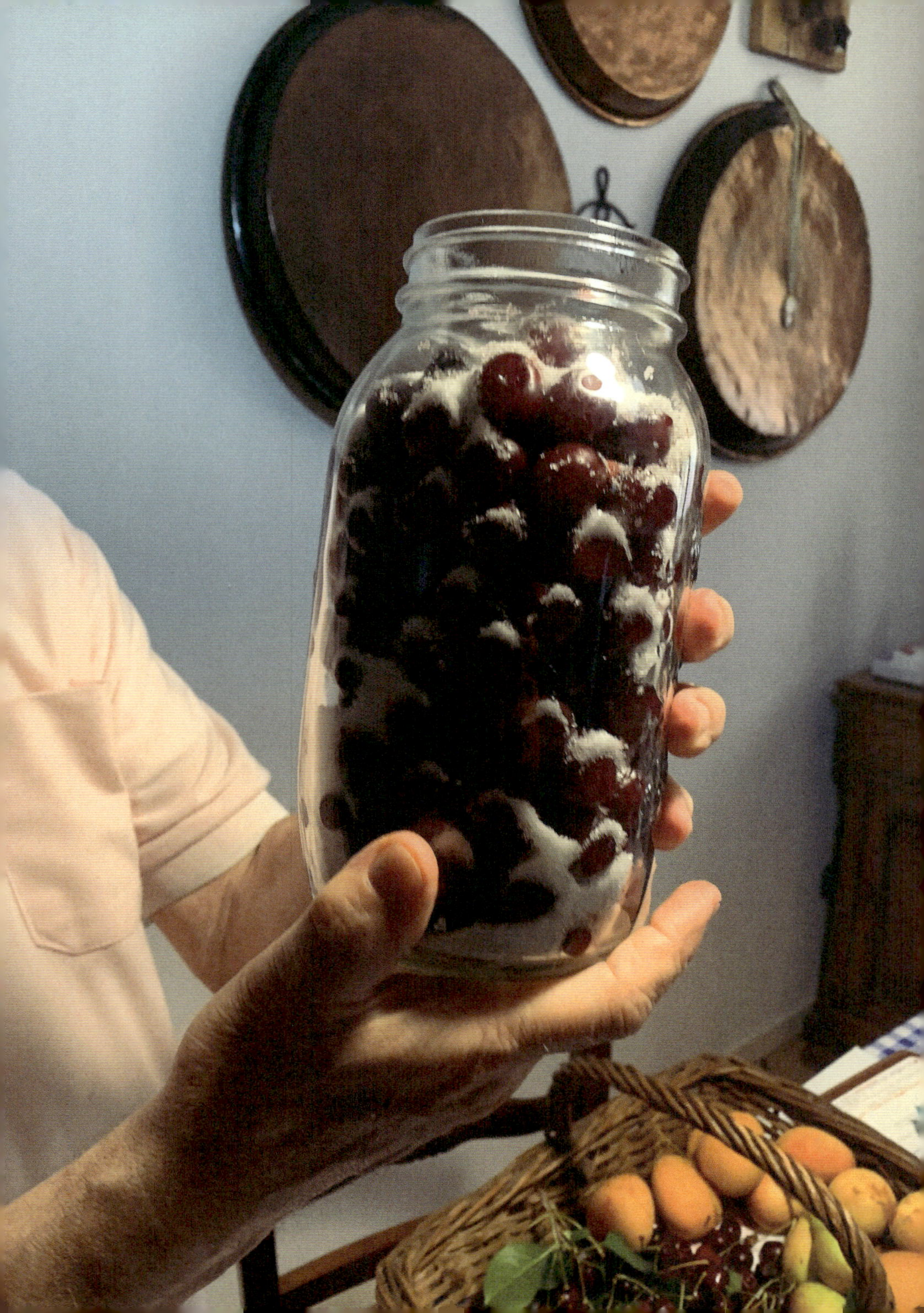

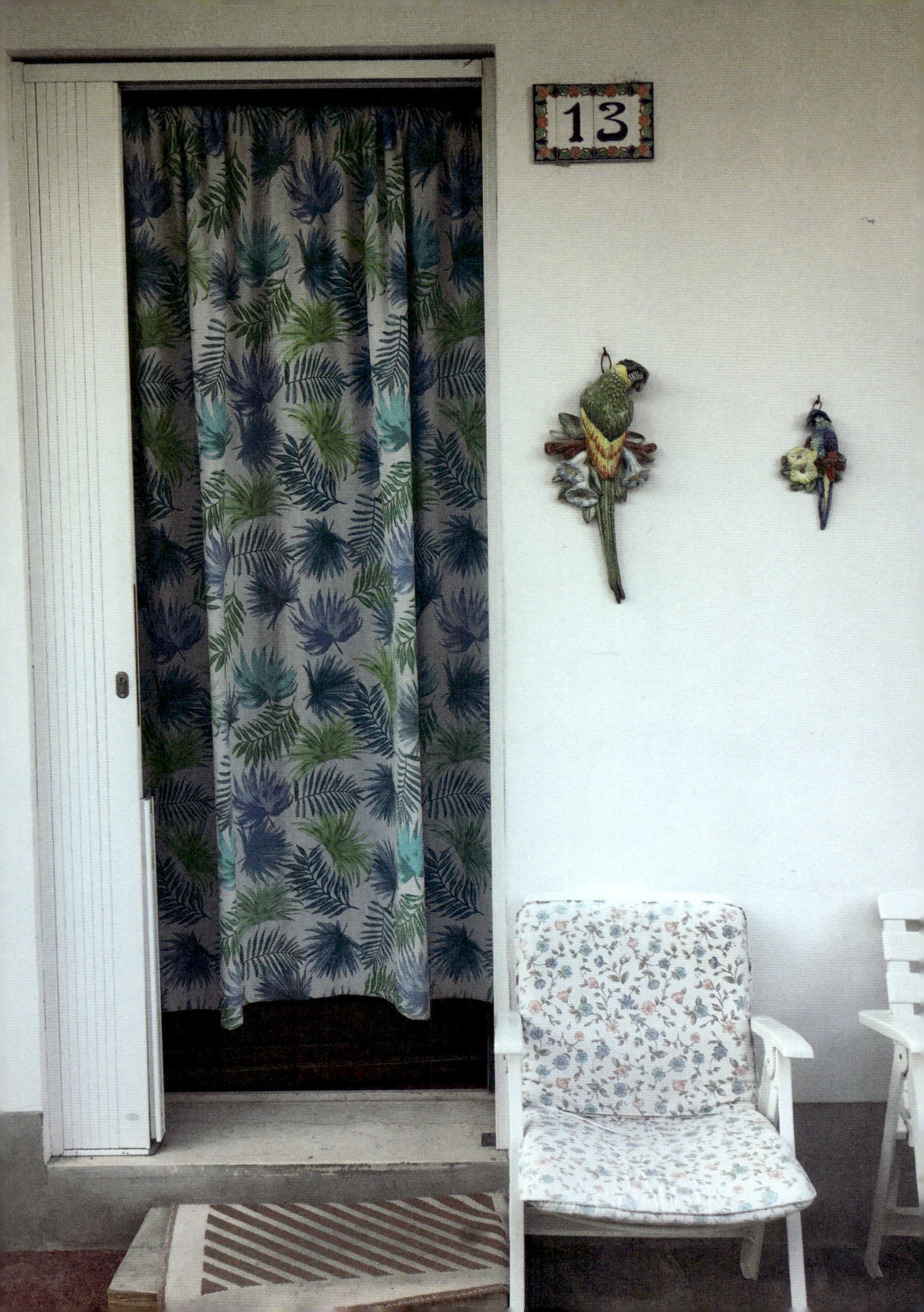

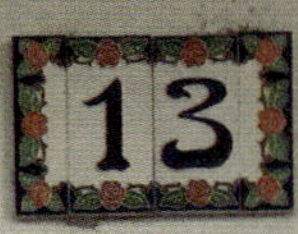
13
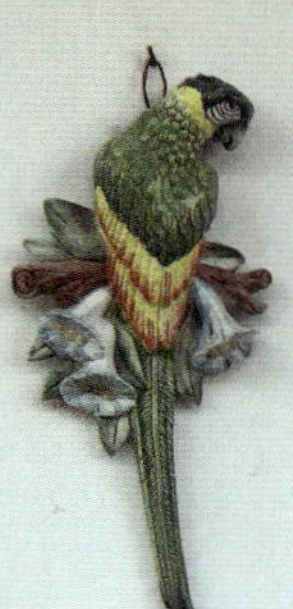
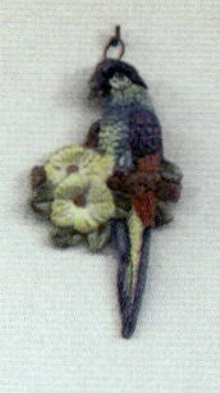
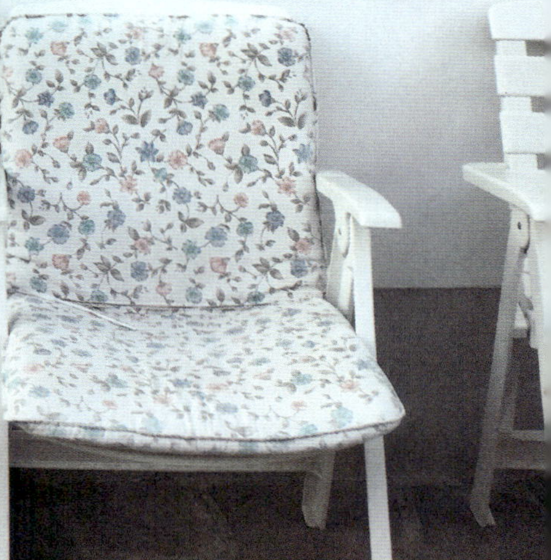

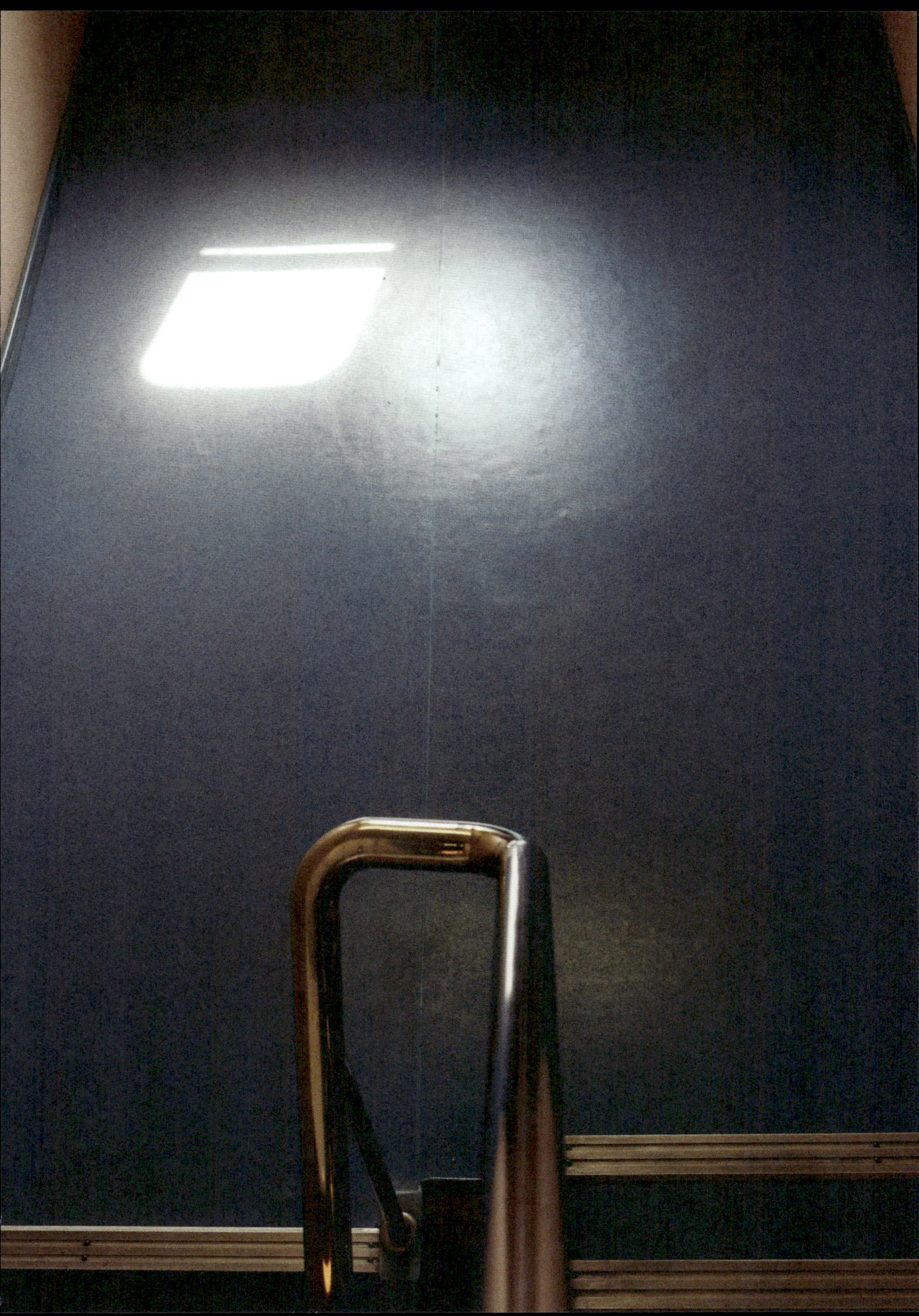

When I was 5 years old my parents gifted me a canary, I named it Mercoledina, little Wednesday. I wasn't sure about its gender but at the time I decided she was a girl. She was pale yellow with a funny fuzzy brownish topknot that stuck out from the rest of the body like a toupée. She used to scream all the time and attack anyone who came closer to her: she would open and shake her wings, scrunch her head down into her shoulders, and open her beak while running towards the wall of the cage. We used to say she was pretending to be a little eagle.

My cat, Briciola tried to get her many times, but Mercoledina resisted and after sometime, the cat, gave up and started sleeping placidly next to the canary's house on top of the kitchen cabinet. We thought the cat had changed her mind and now she was possibly guarding her.

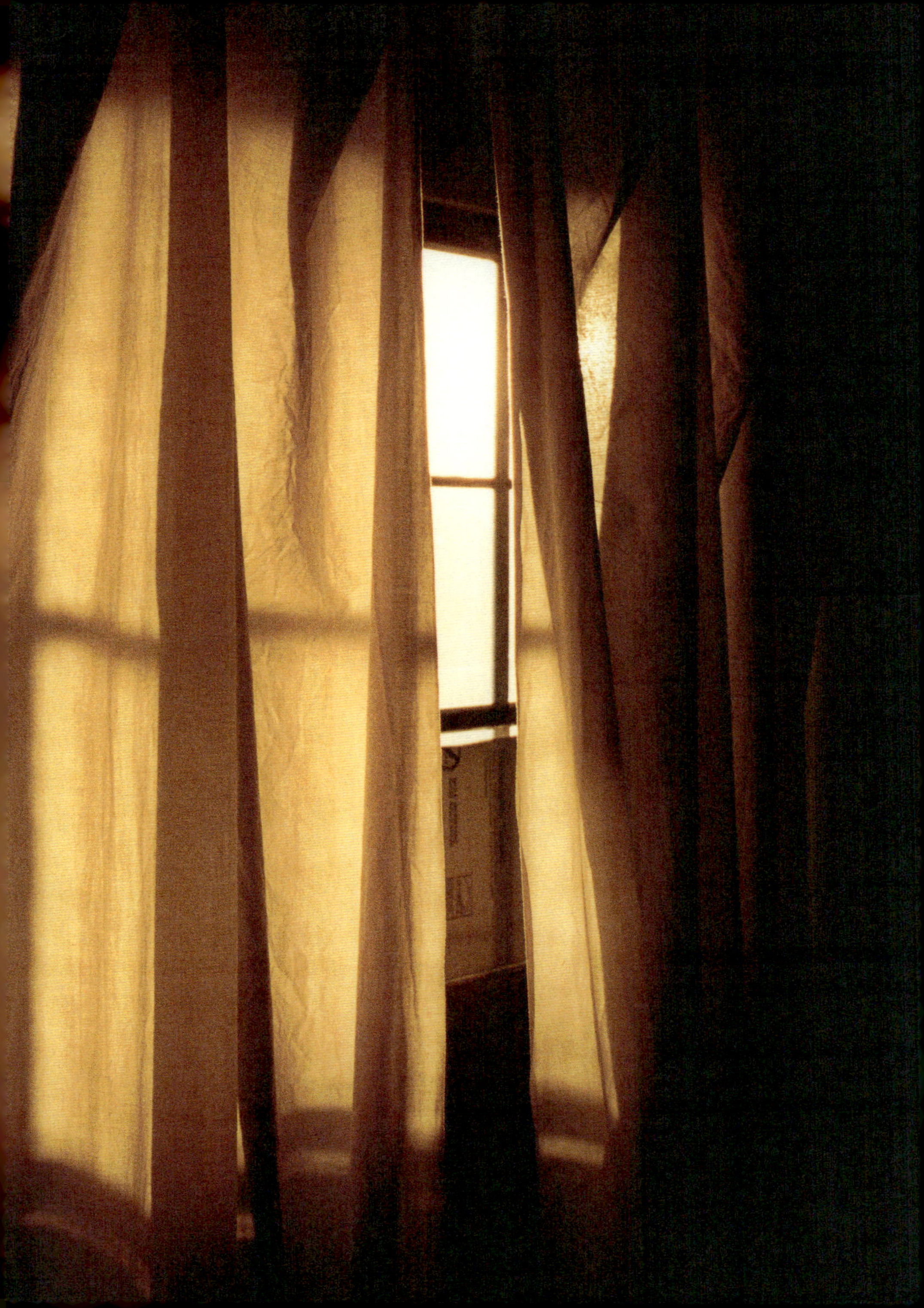

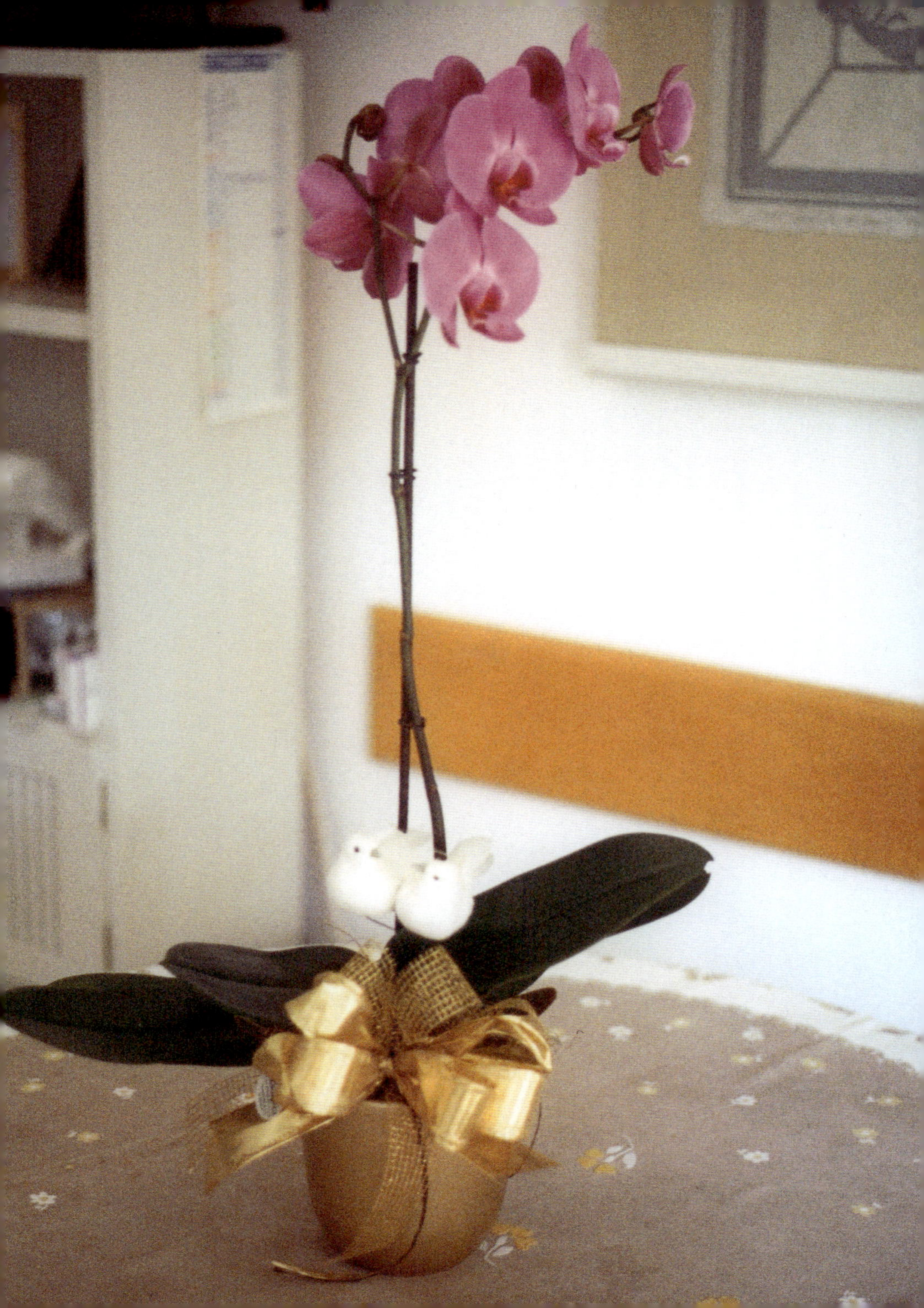

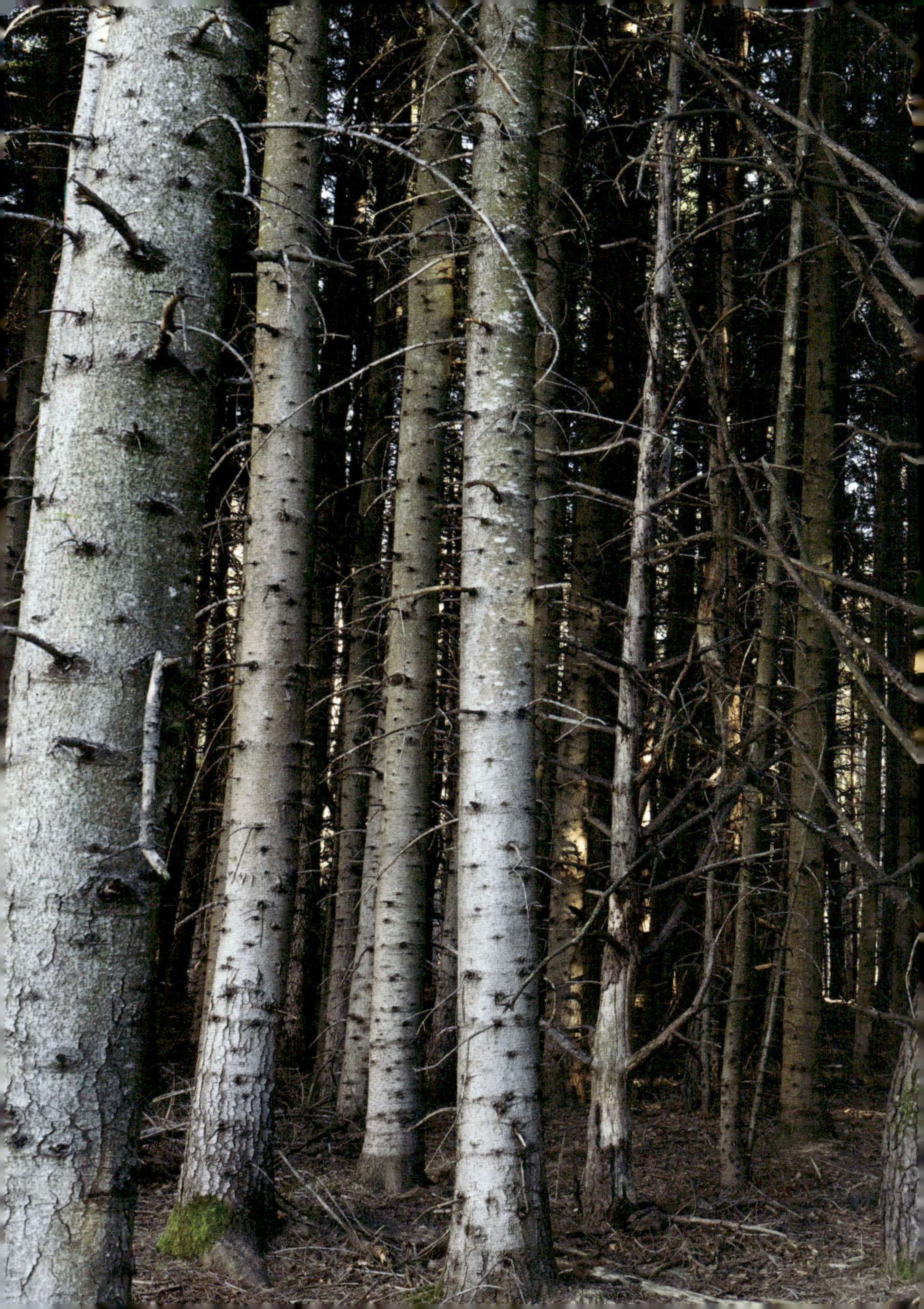

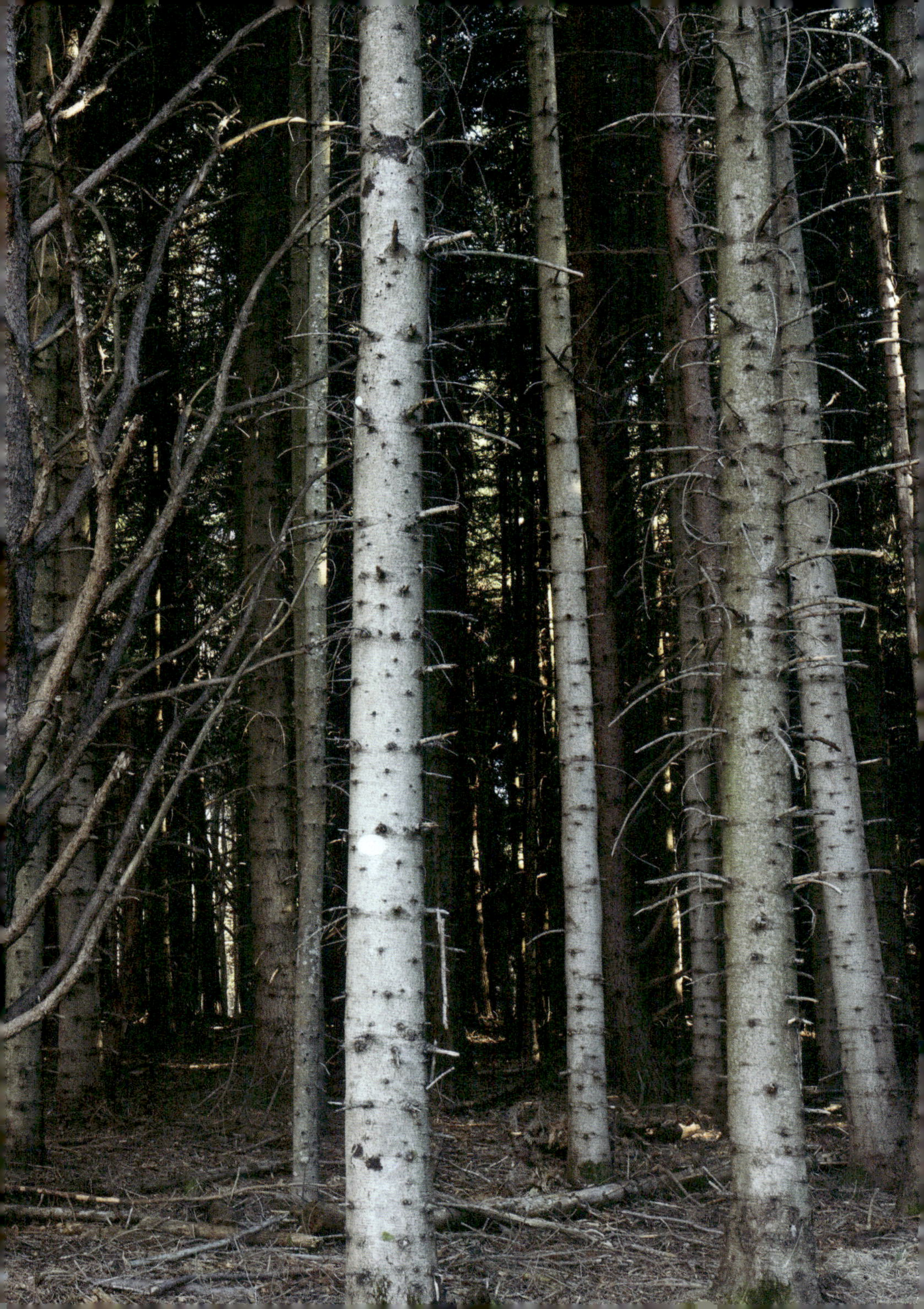

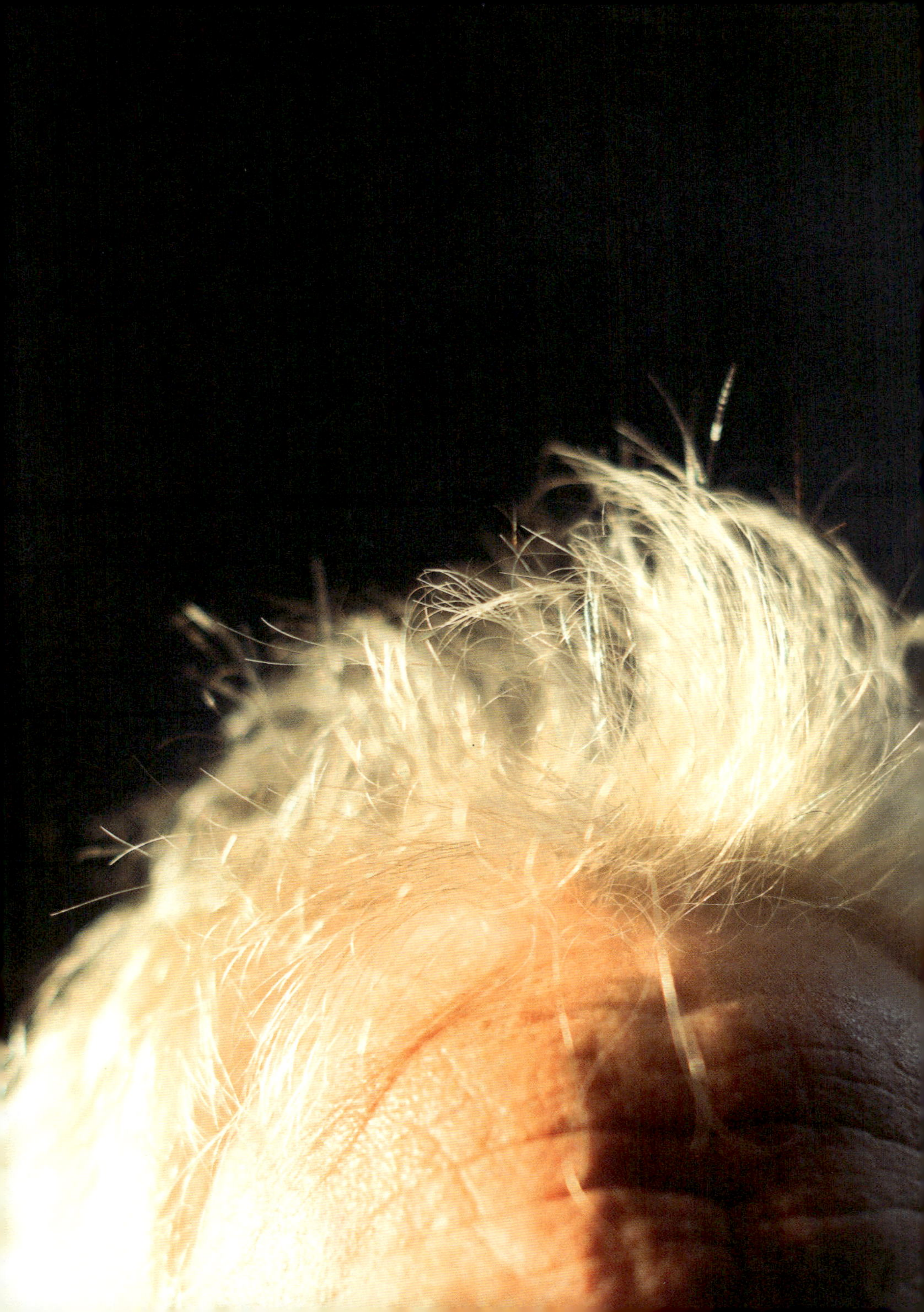

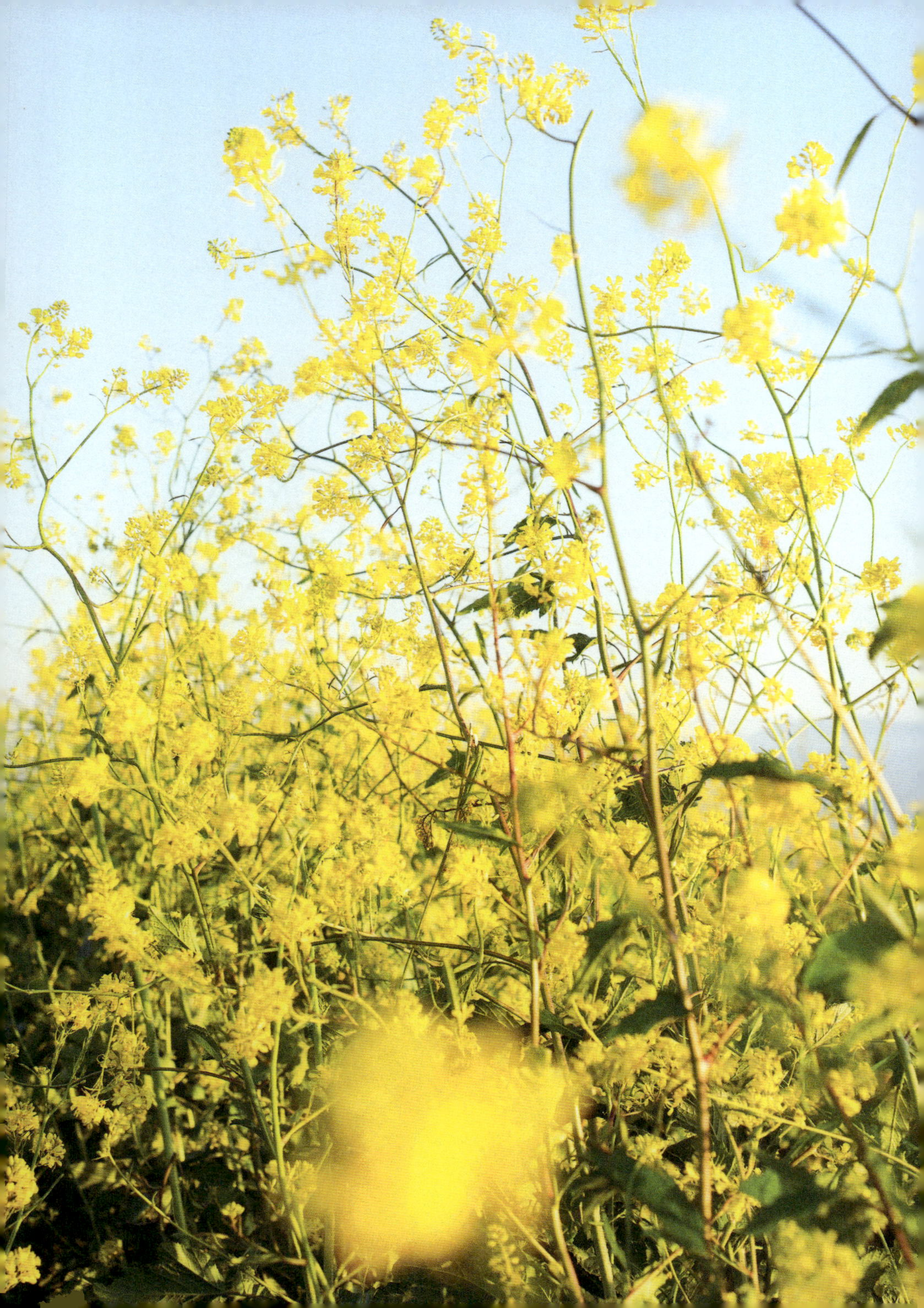

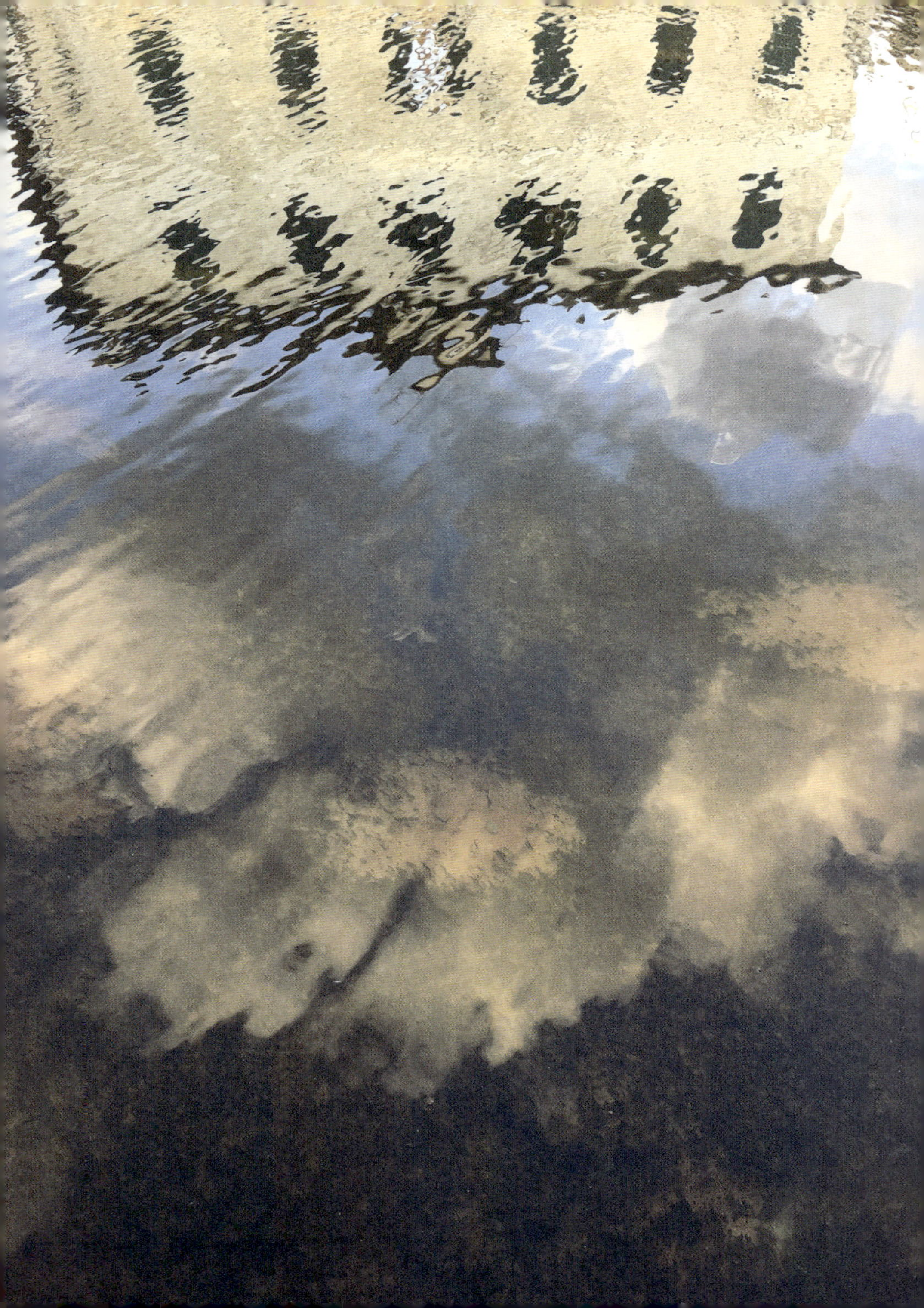

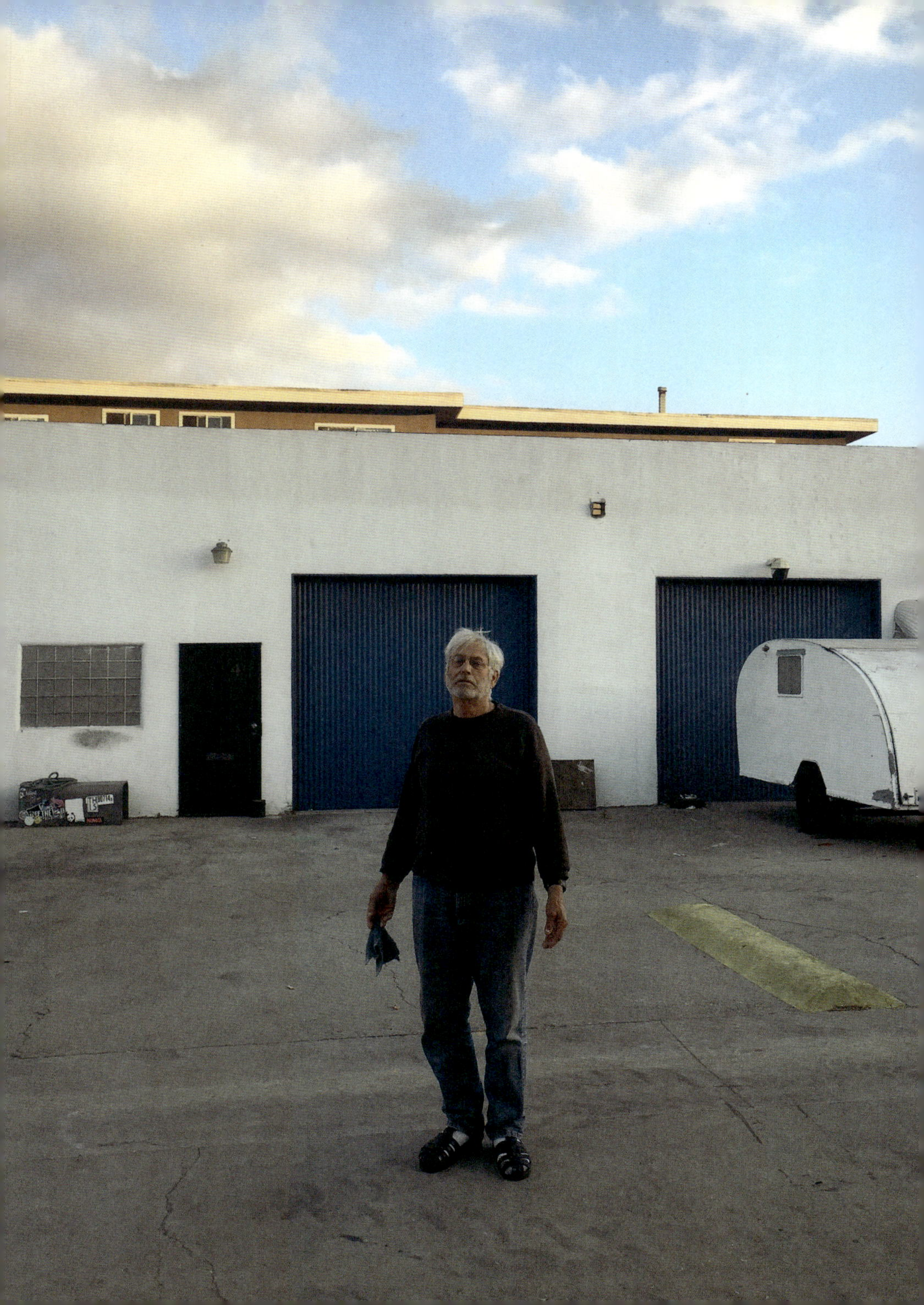

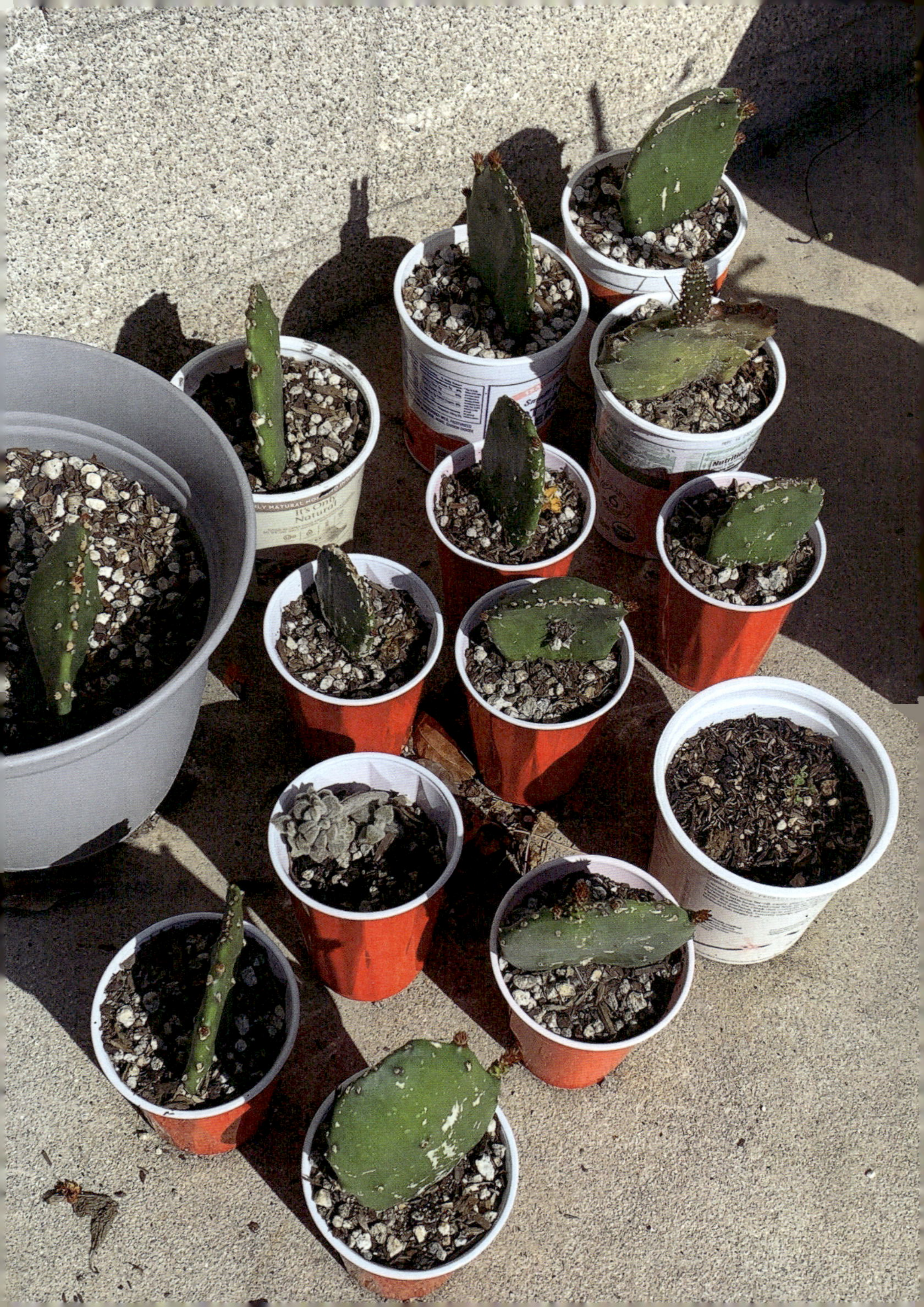

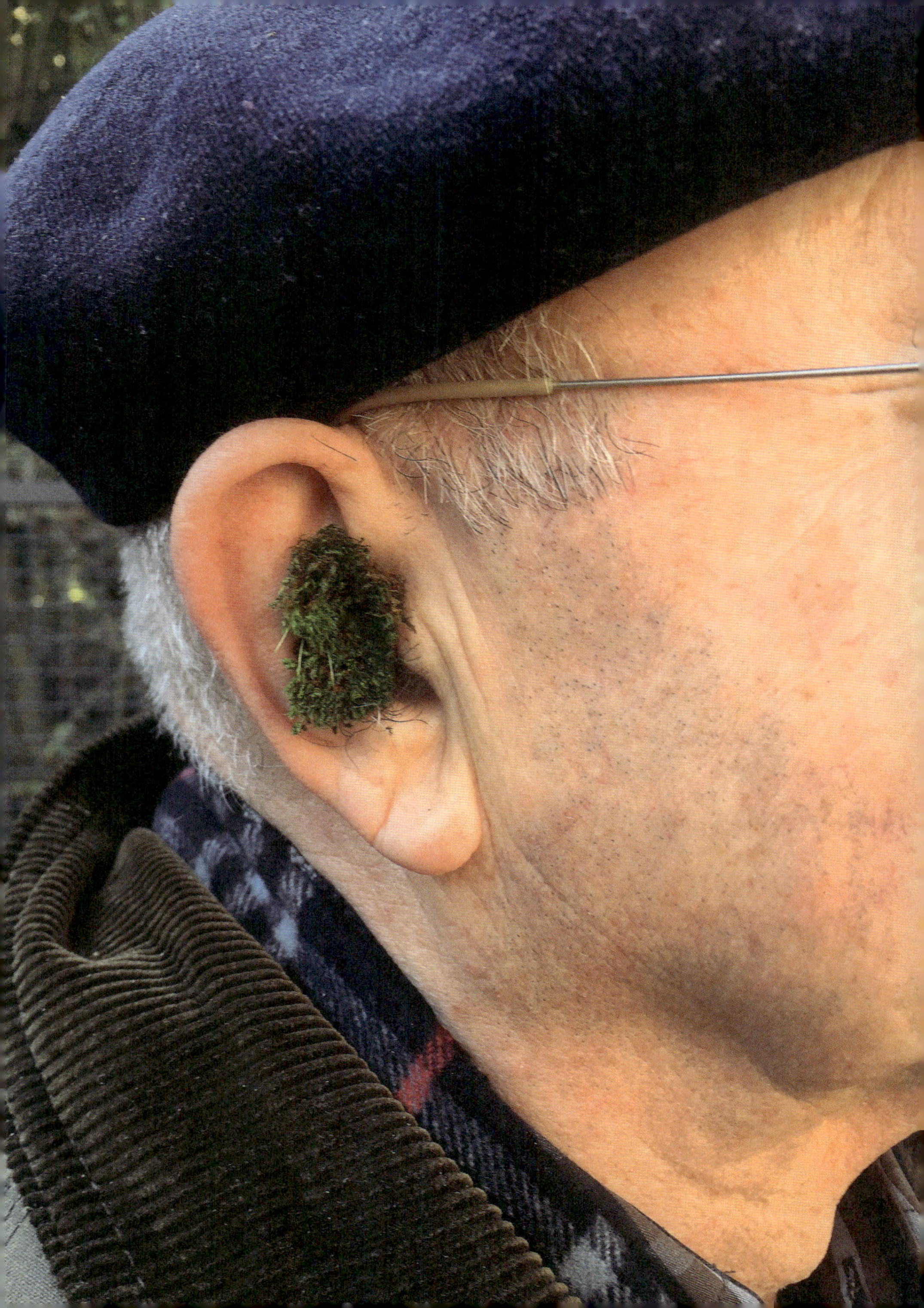

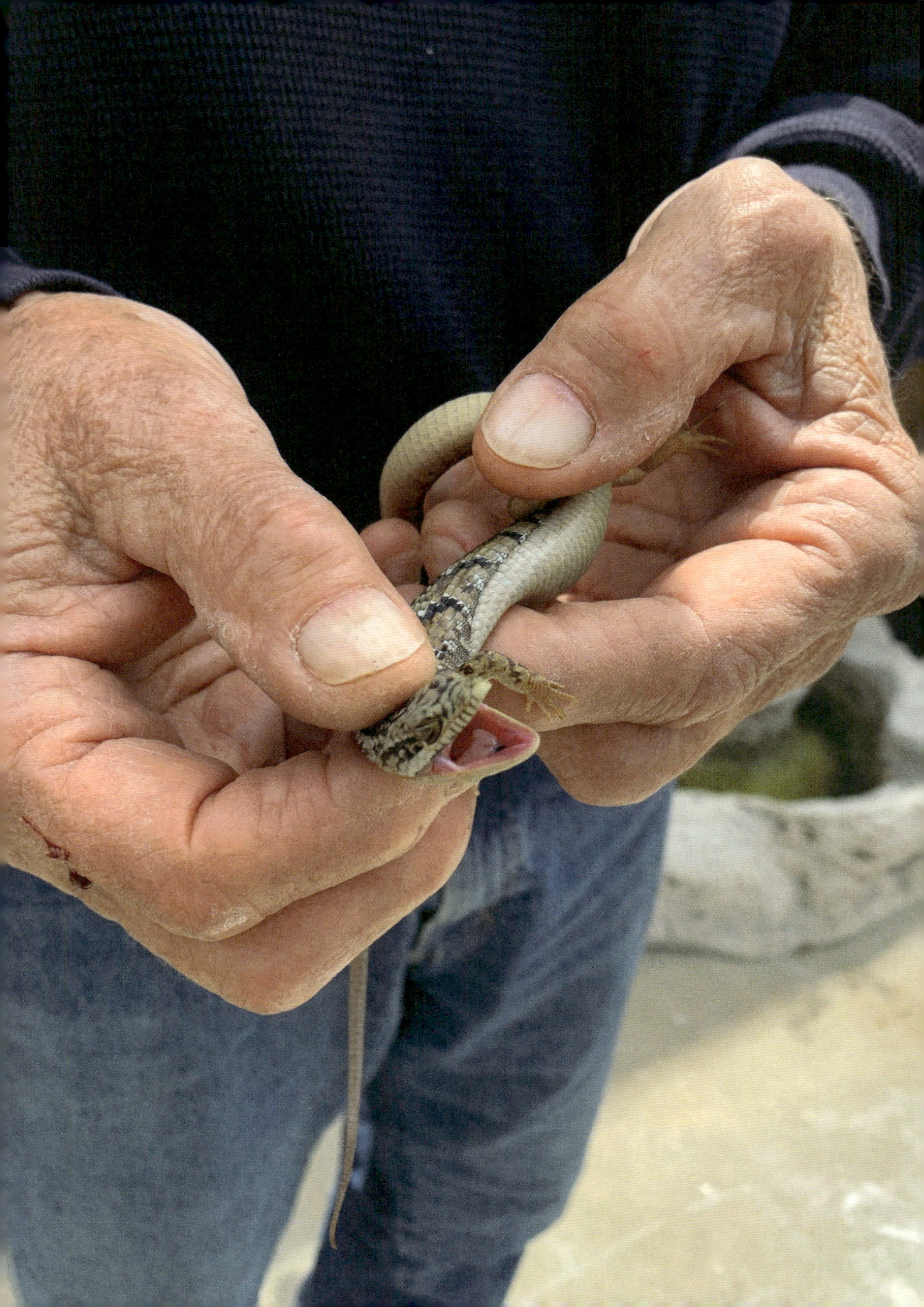

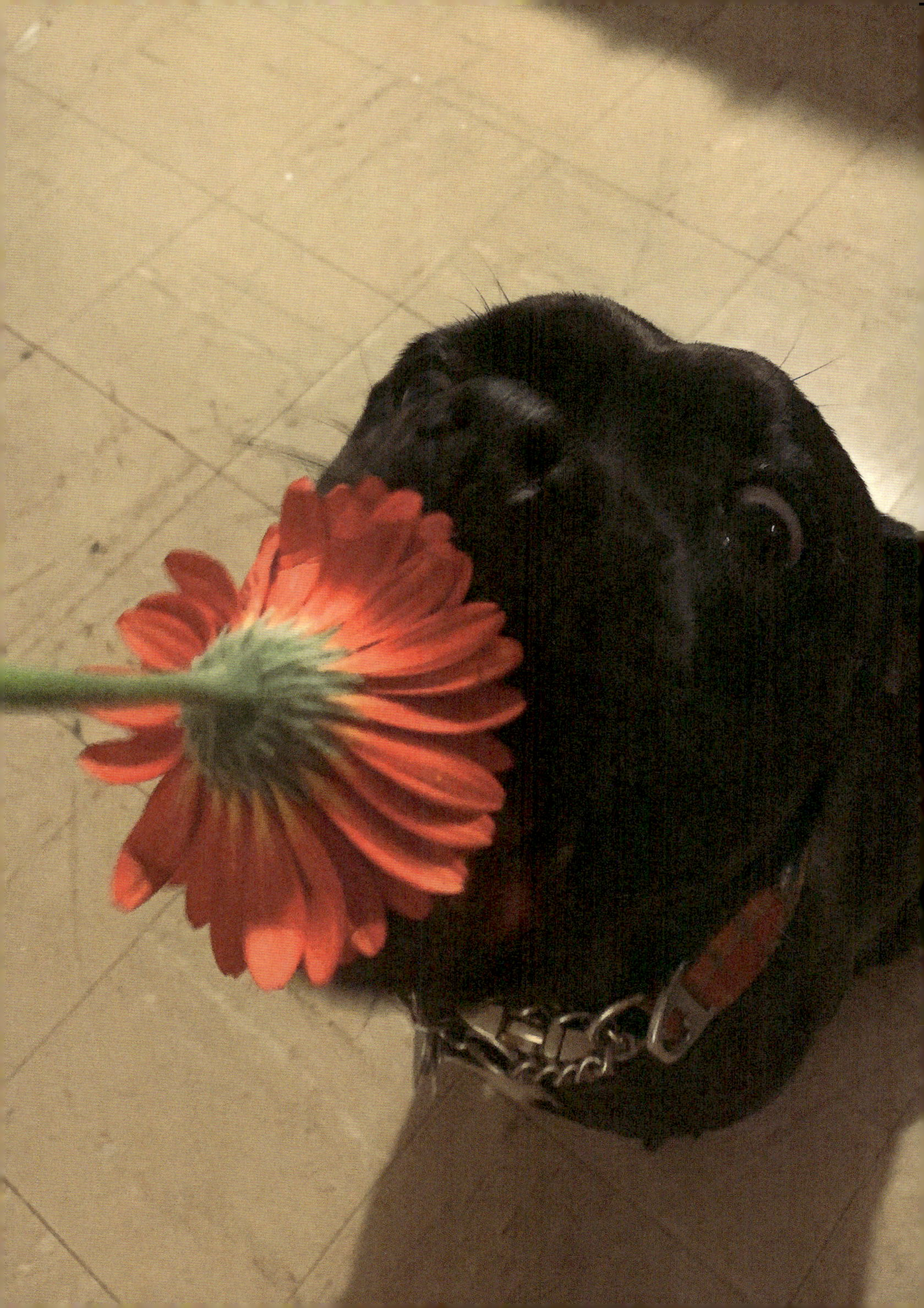

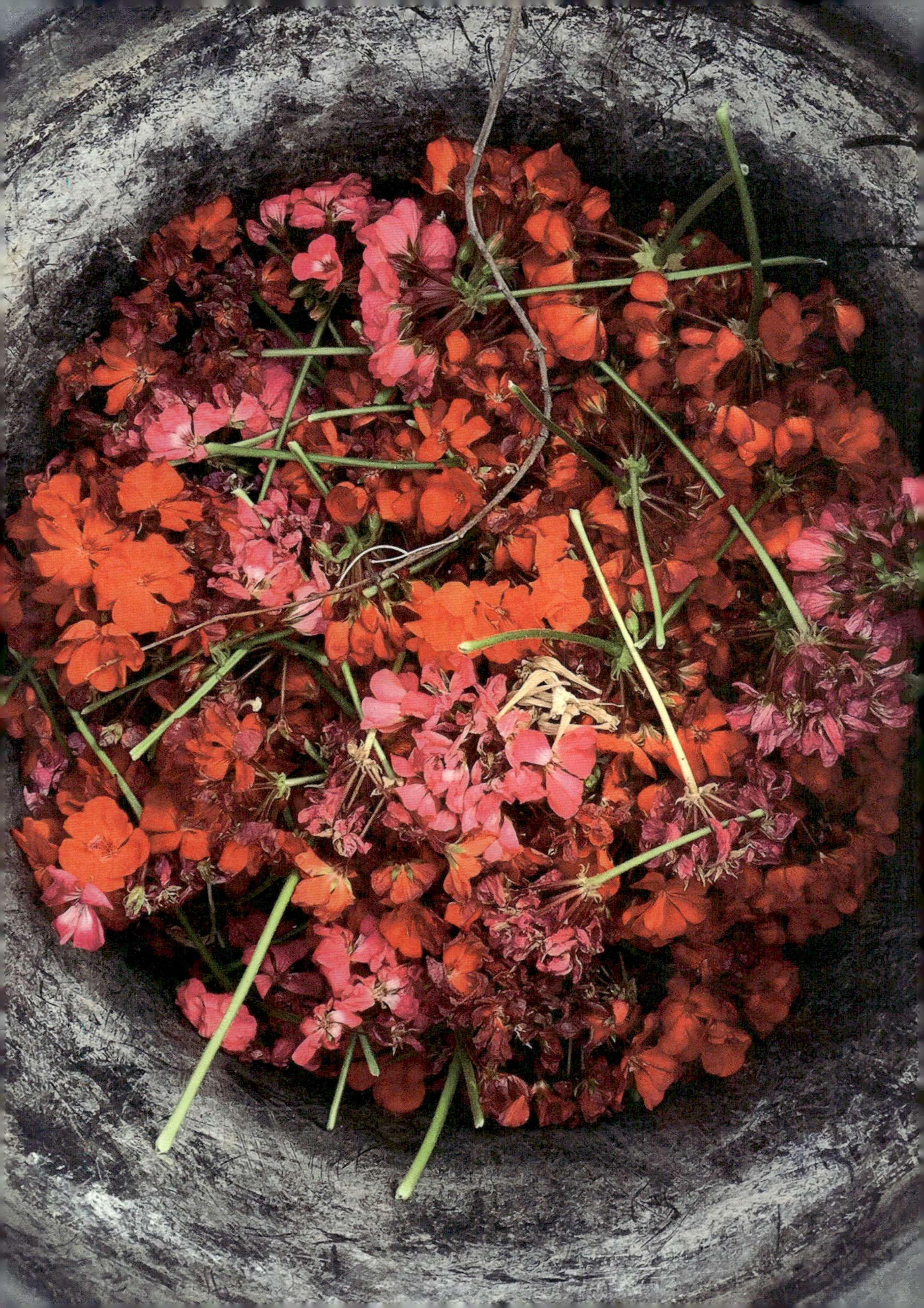

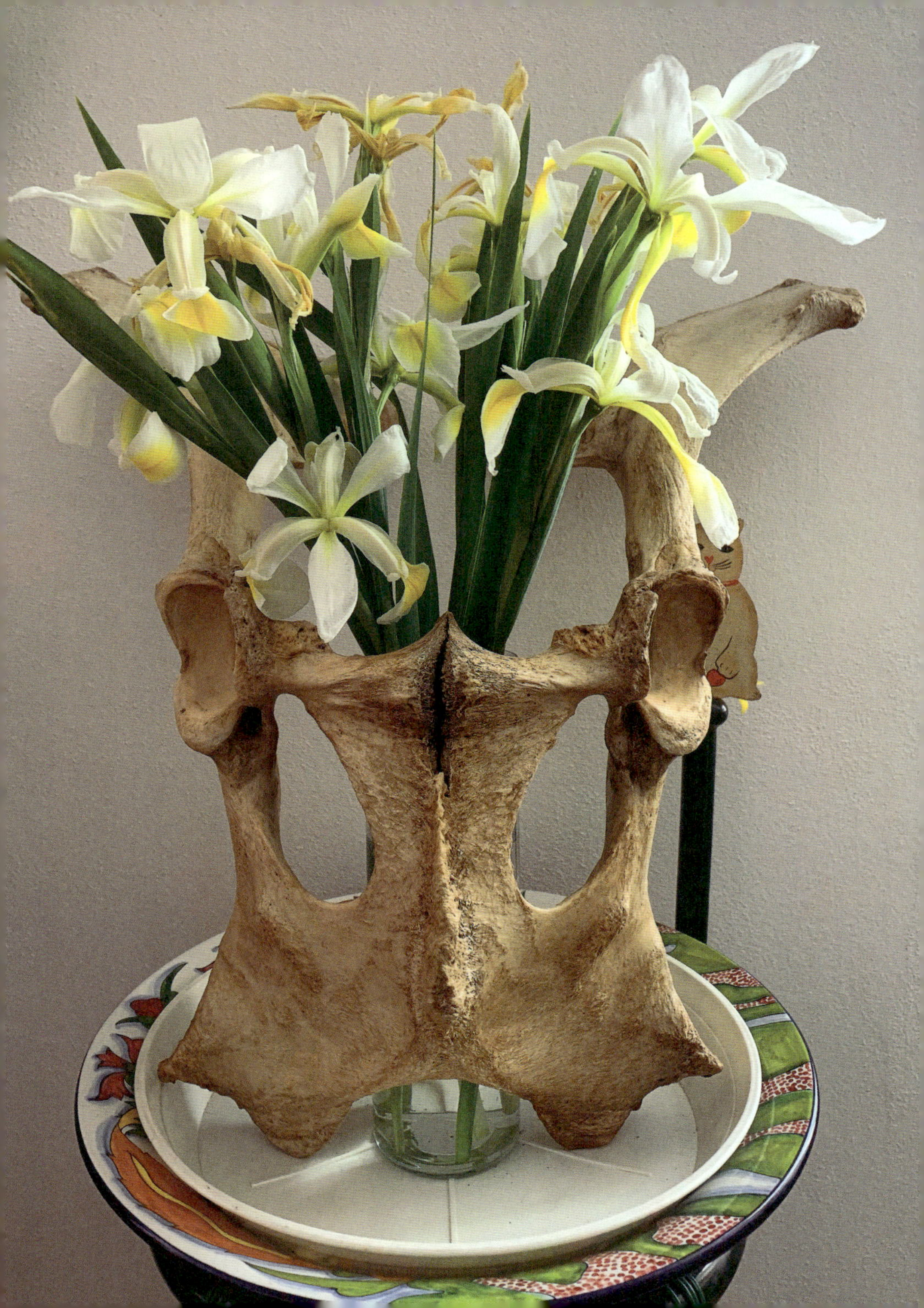

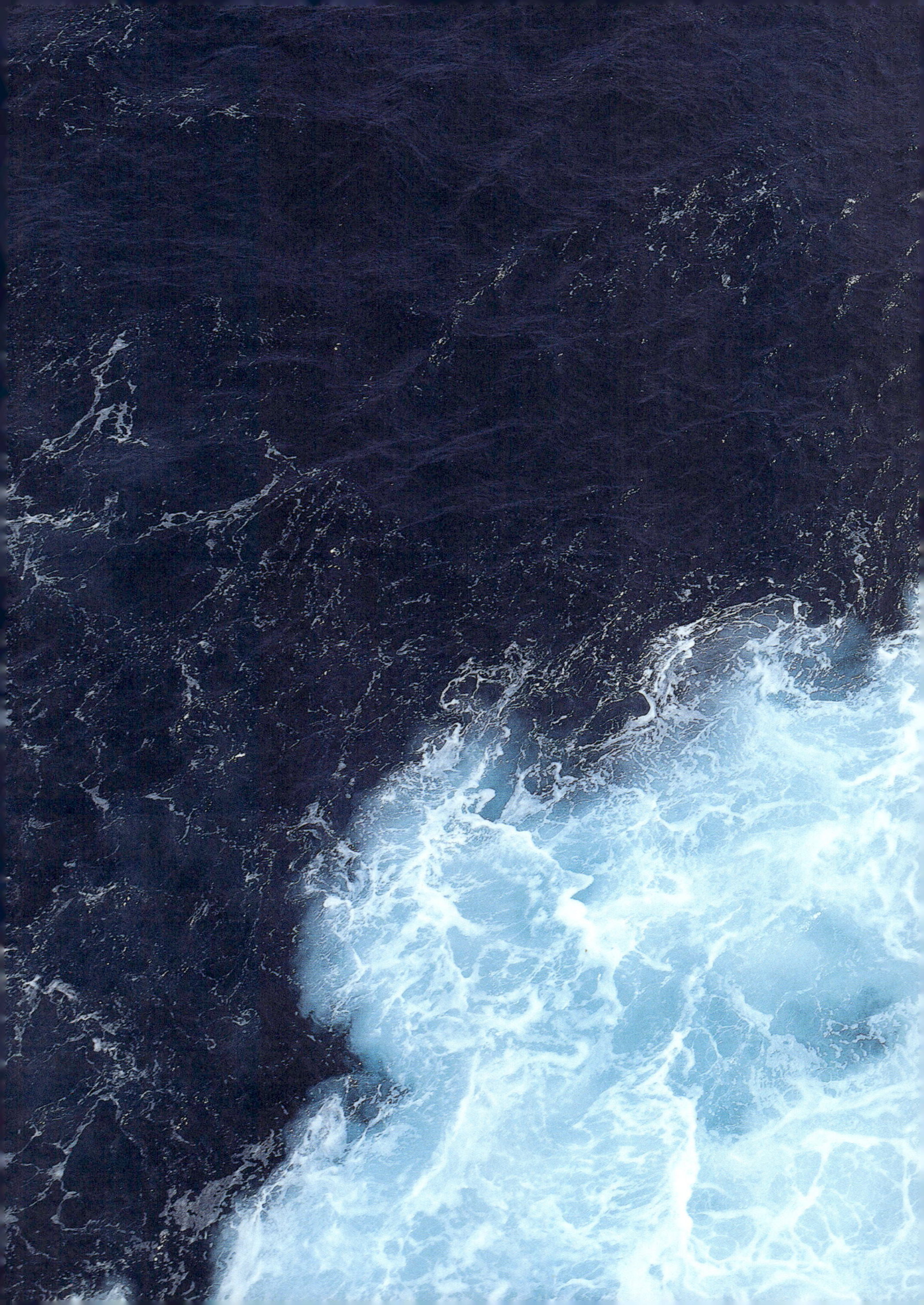

I have become aware that I have never felt completely comfortable being a woman. I could never cope with the expectations that were associated to my gender. I felt I had to be nice and pleasant, polite, quite, welcoming, accomodating, insecure, not too sensitive, in need of help or protection or guidance, in need of a man that could take care of me, that could fulfill my life, in need of being a mother, in need of being a daughter, in need. I could not accept the rules on how to be a woman, a daughter, a niece, a girlfriend, or a female friend. But, I had tried hard to fit into all of this. The suppression of my real self had a complicated and twisted effect on my life. The realization of it, however, was astonishing and powerful.

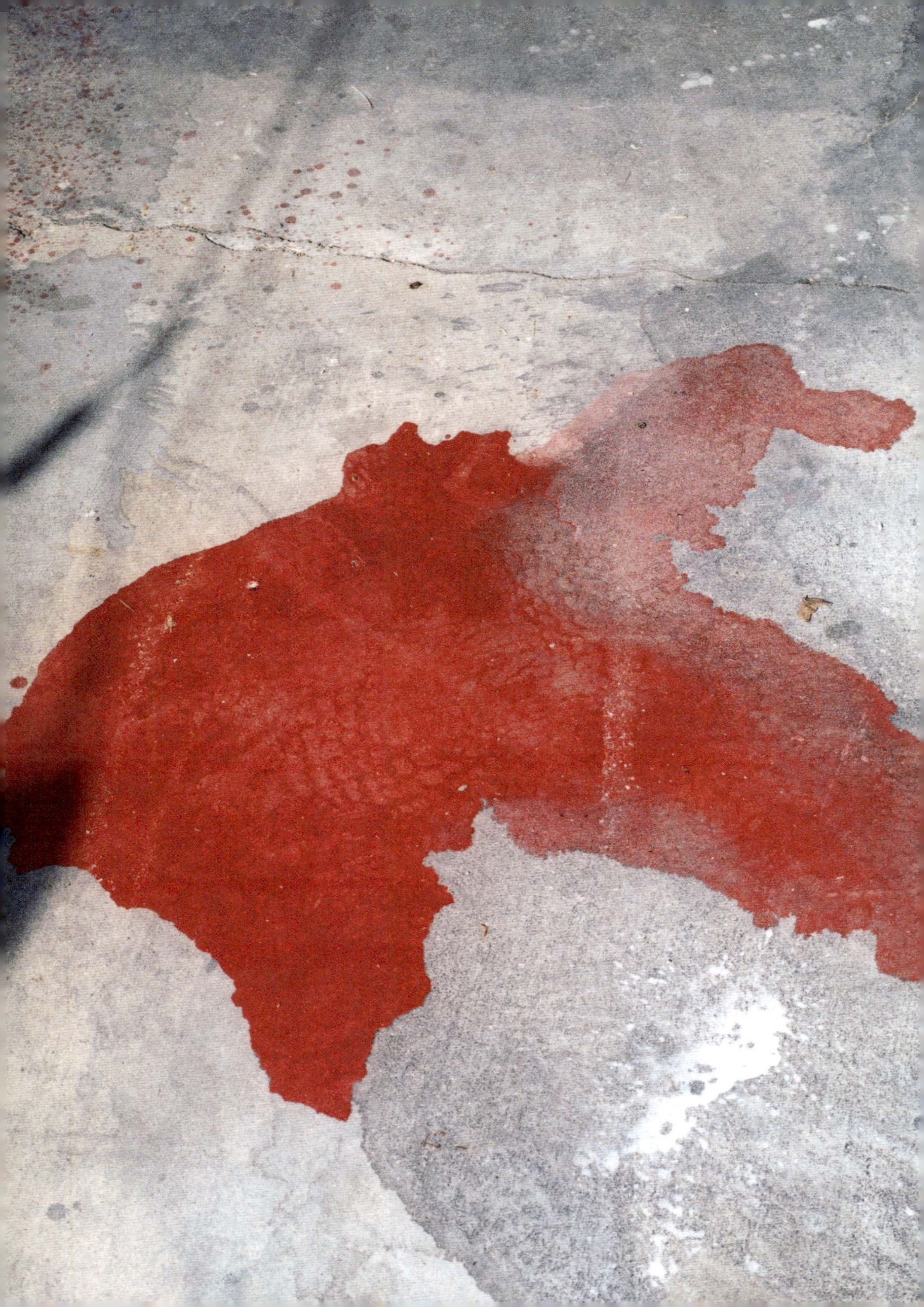

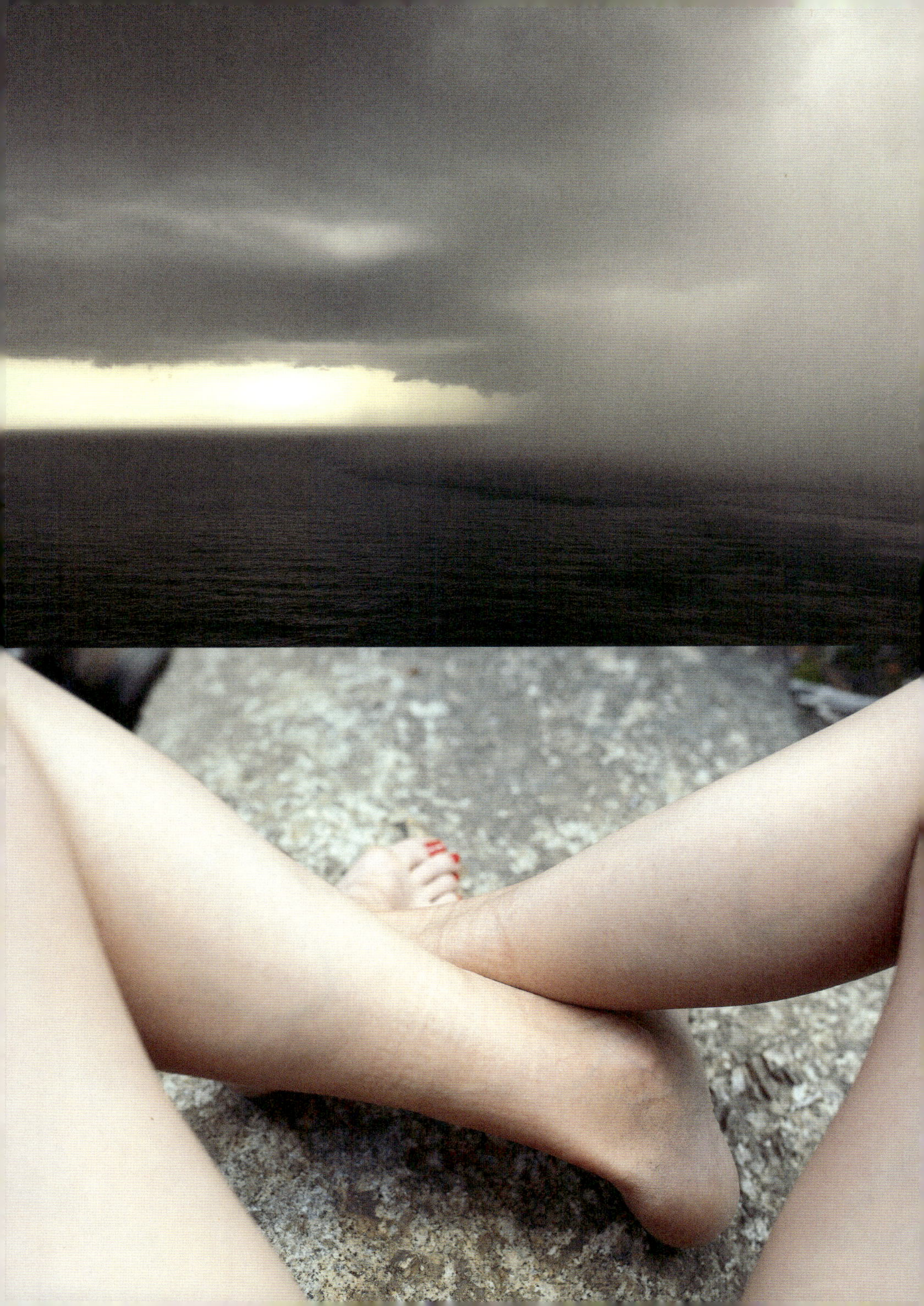

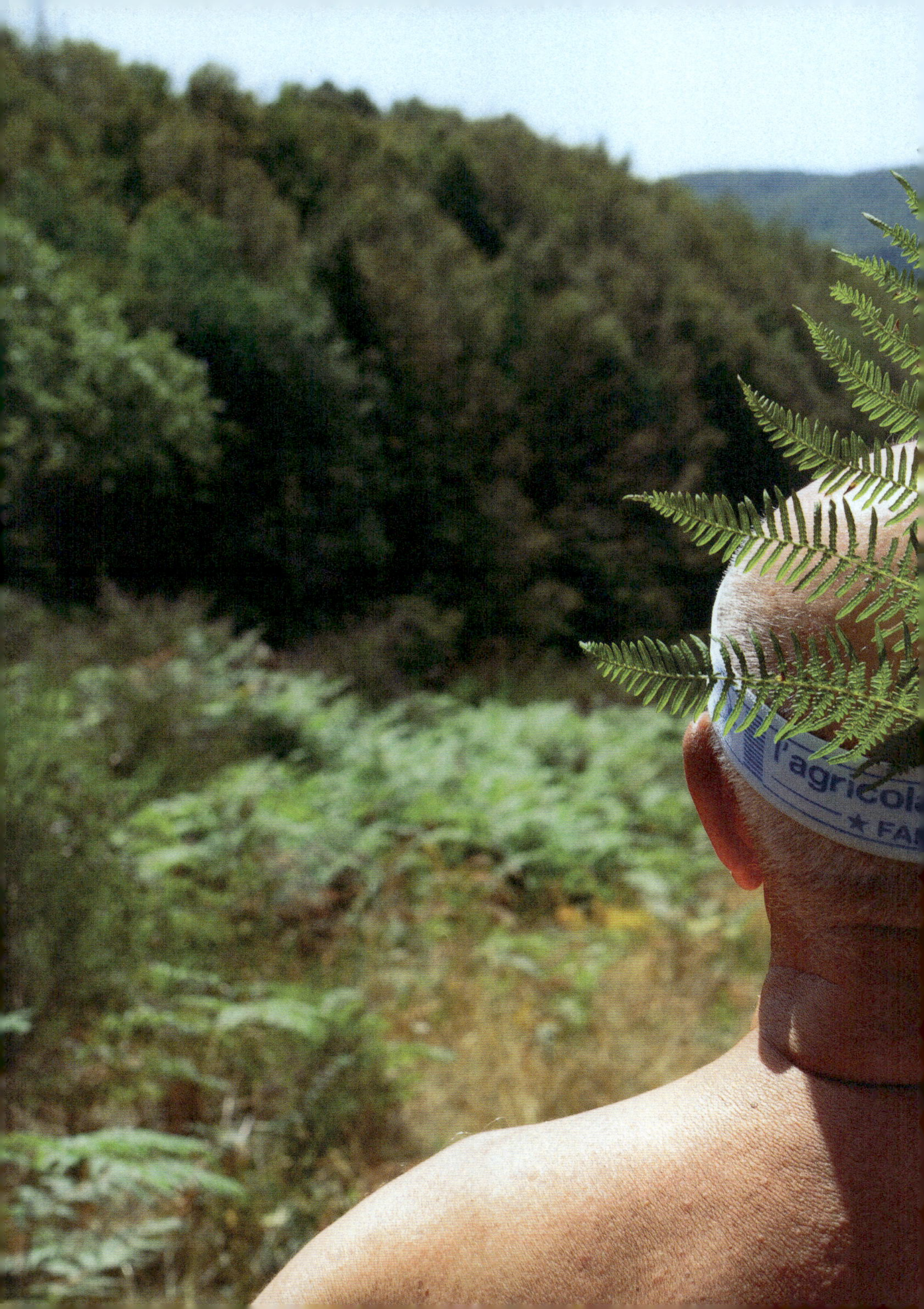

l'agricola
★ FA

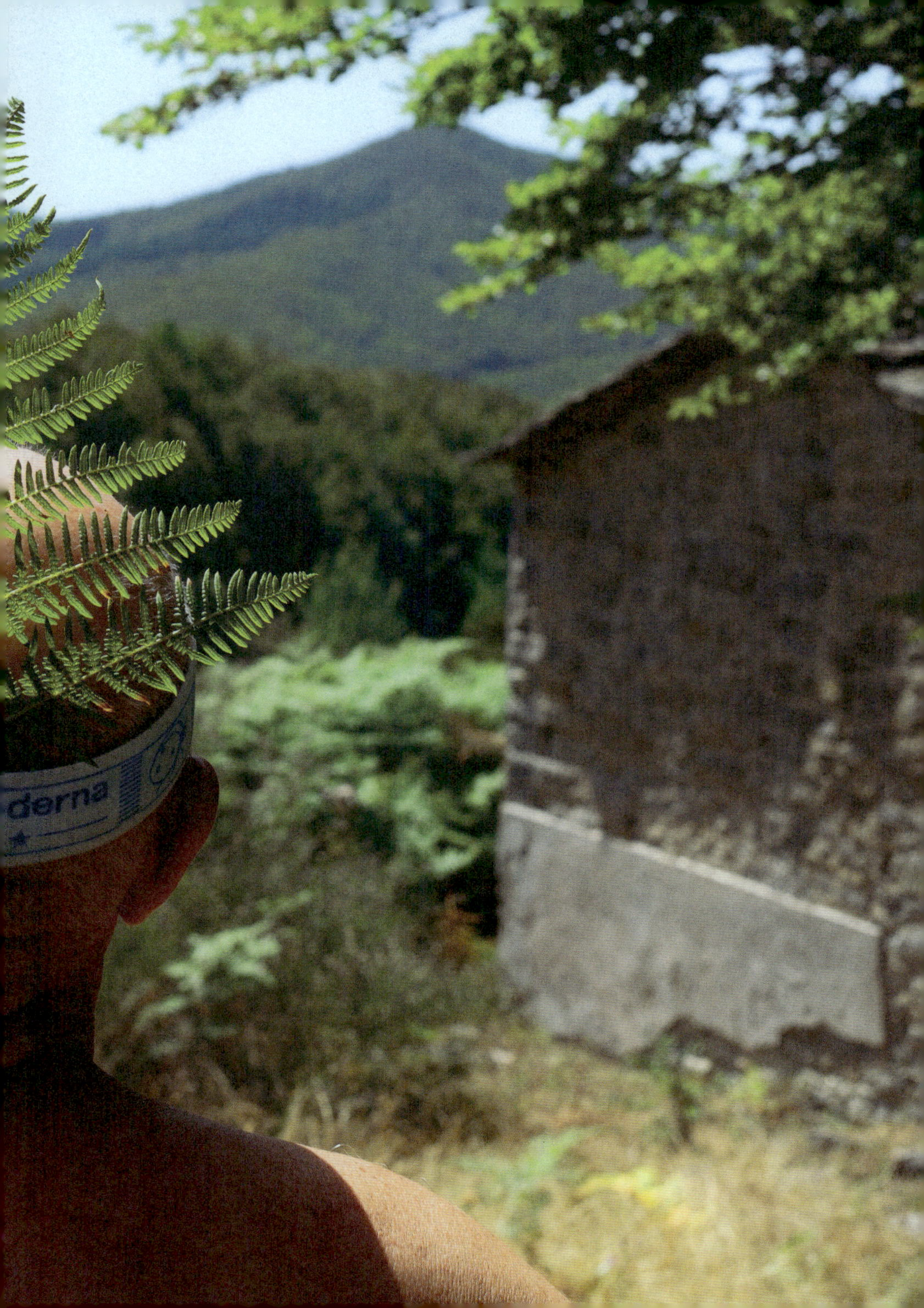
derna

When I was a kid, my dad taught me how to sprout little plants from seeds. We used to do it mostly with dry beans or my canary's food. It was our special thing together and a ritual for me. Every time the same simple steps seemed magical and made him look like a magician. It always happened after dinner on the kitchen table just before going to bed. We arranged cotton wool in an aluminium container, not too much, then we would carefully place the seeds in, one by one and, at the end, very precisely, like two chemists, the water. I remember the cotton changing its structure and becoming shiny and heavy. It looked like a nice and cozy nest for the seeds.

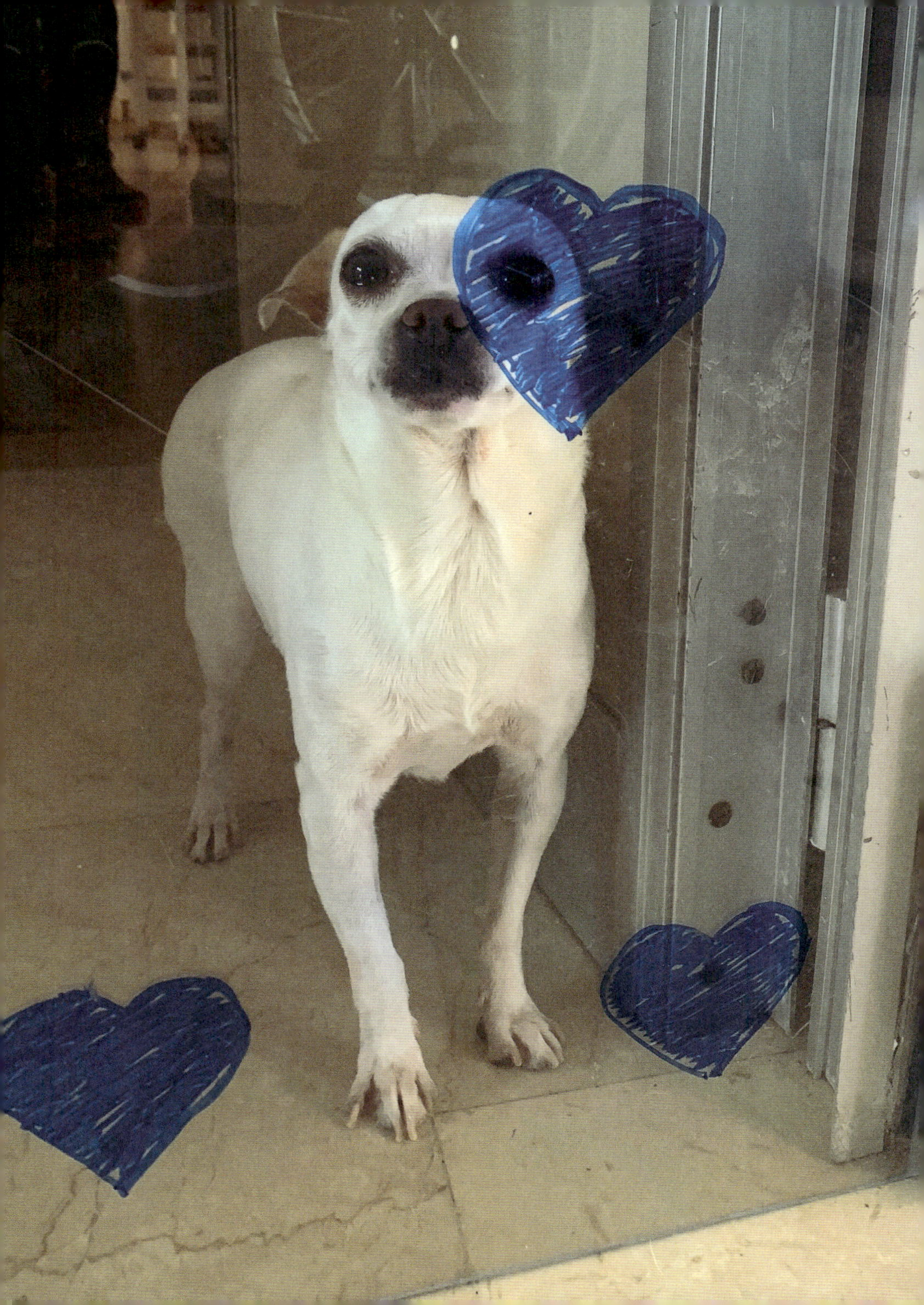

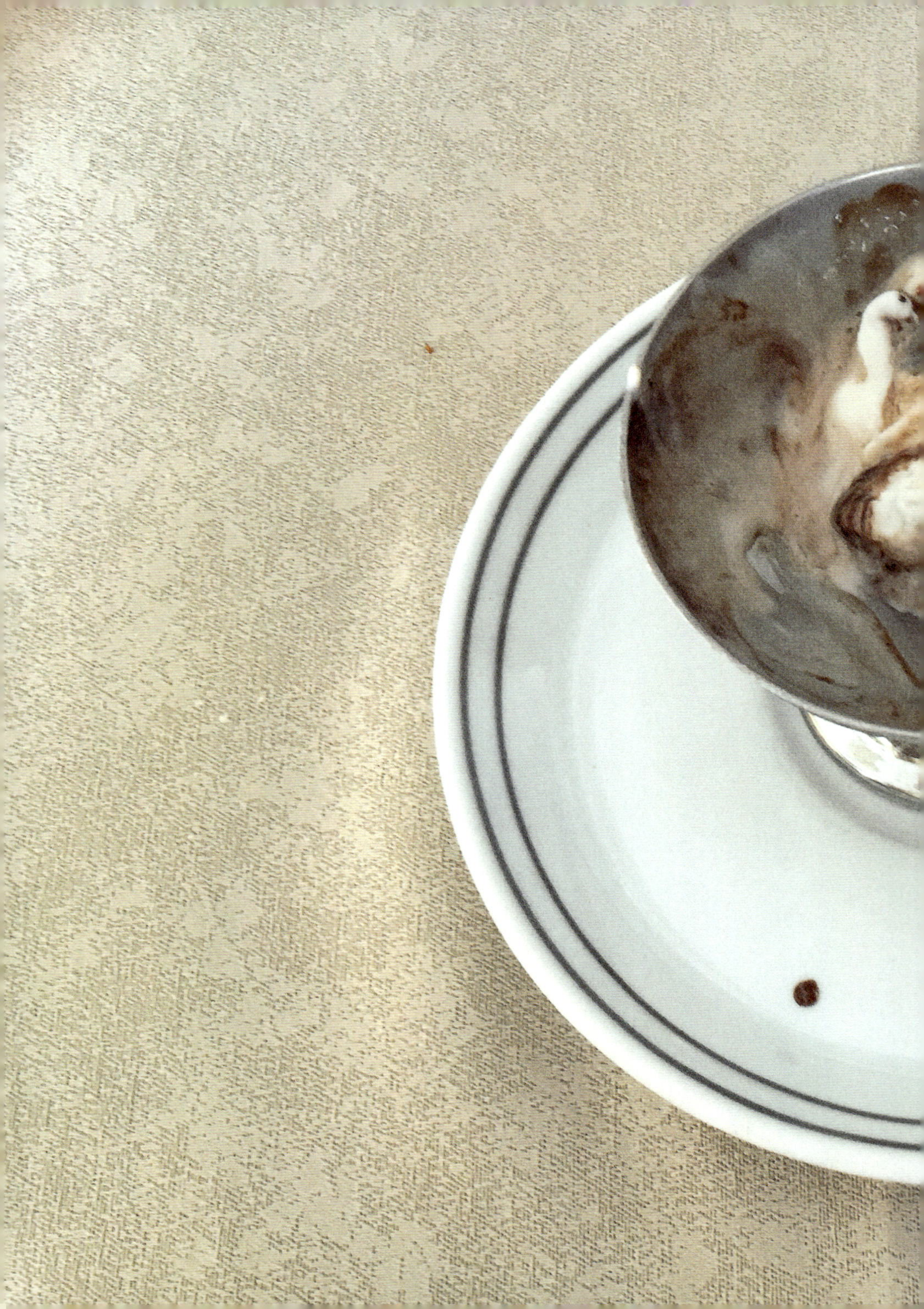

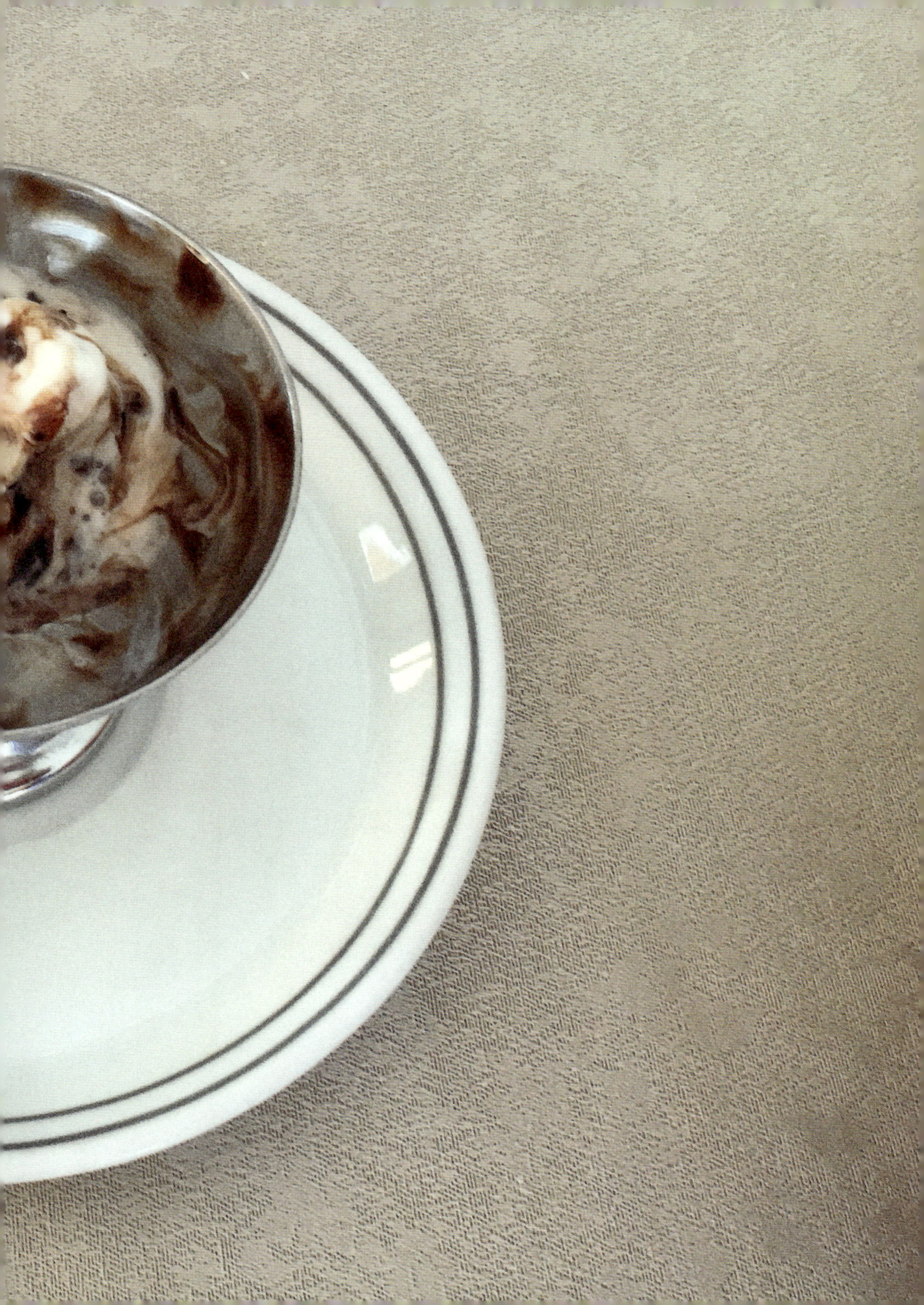

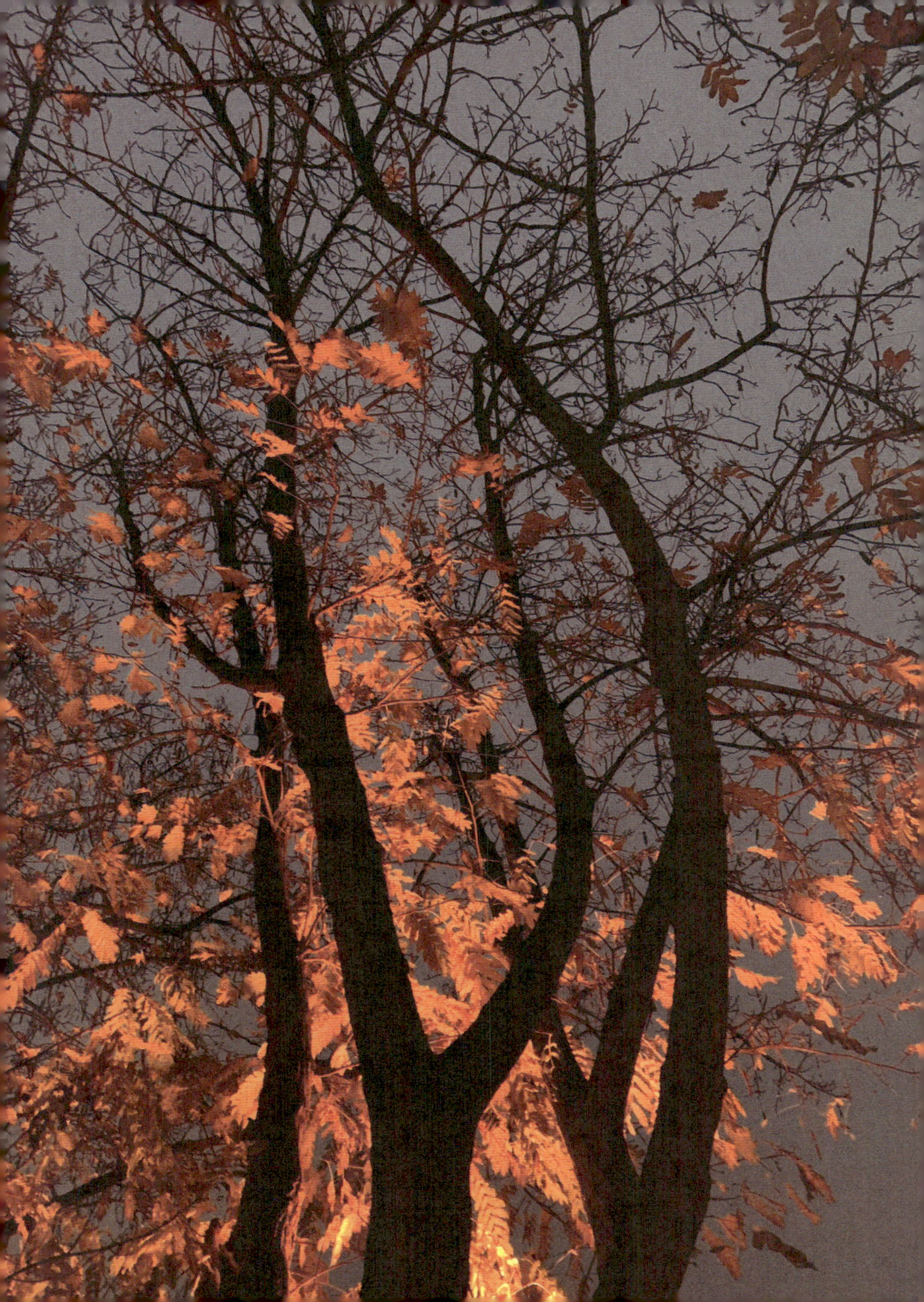

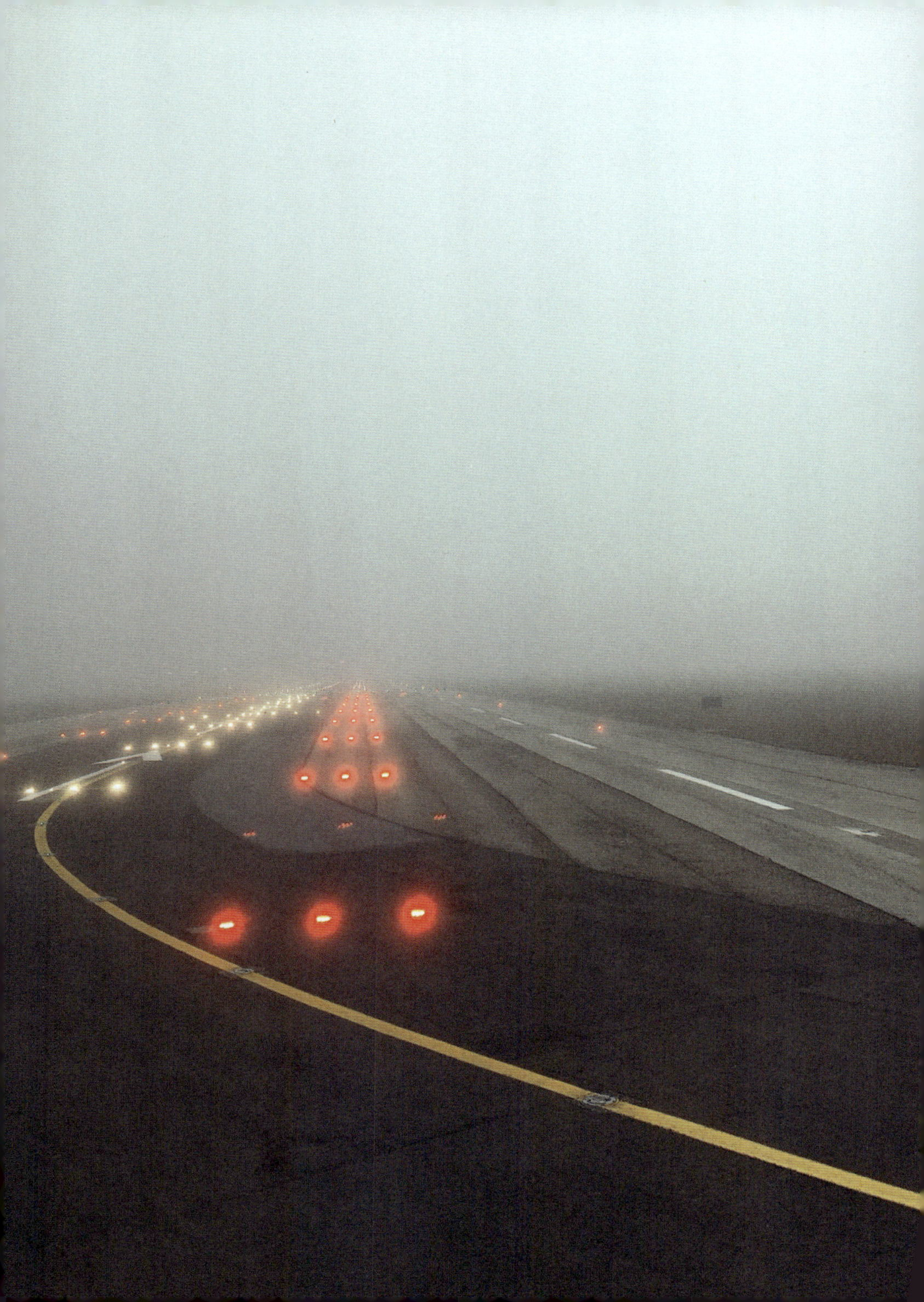

Have I ever told you about the book I want to write? The title will be, 'Quel posto dove non può succederti nulla', 'that place where nothing bad can happen to you'. It will be about the things that for a moment make everything else disappear and you feel so good and comfortable, like you could almost live forever.

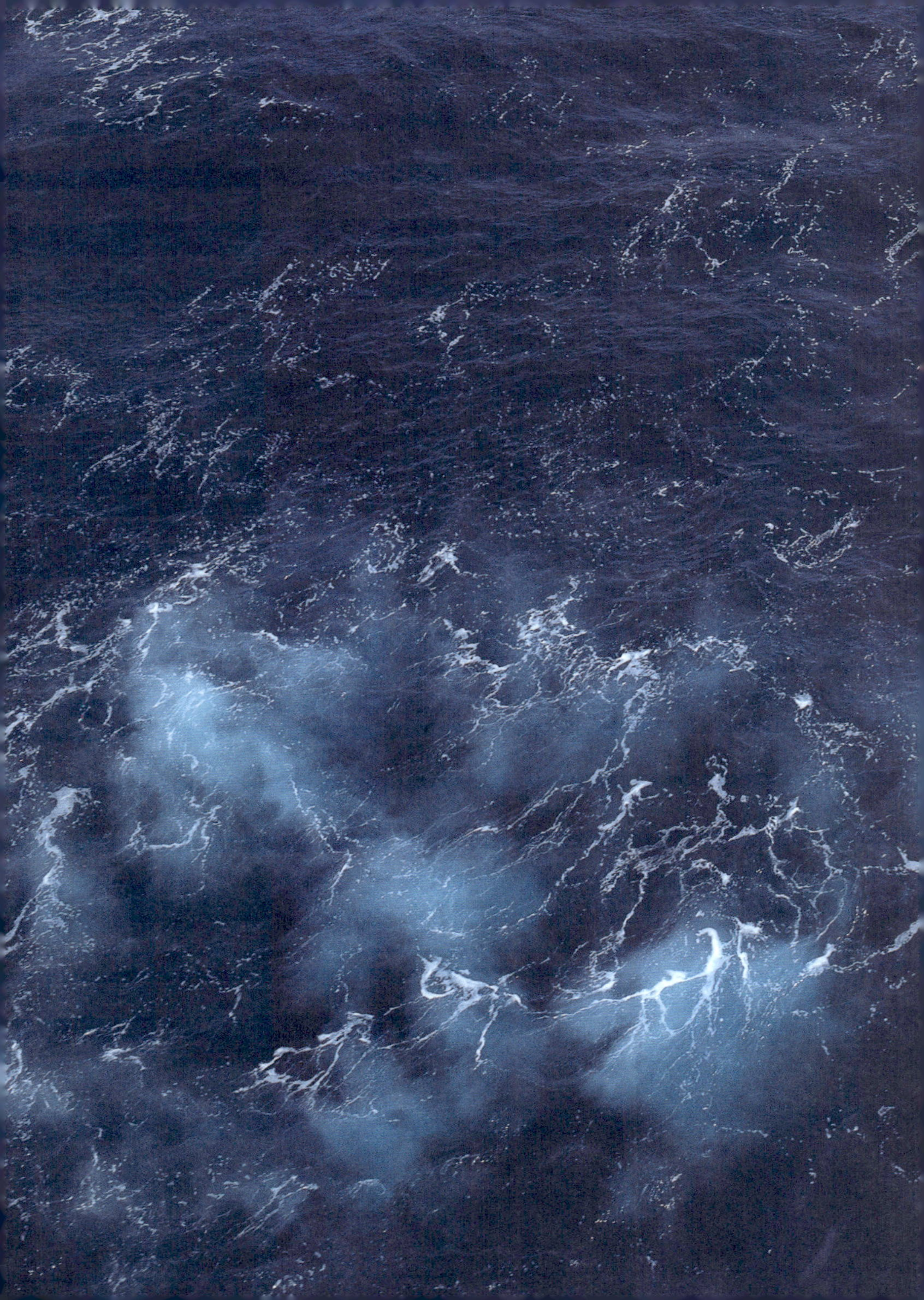

I thank :

Robert Wilhite for our life together and for constantly encouraging me to be myself.
My parents Bianca Lipparini and Domenico Guerra because no matter what, you are always there for and with me.
Angela Pelliccioni because you are you and you listened and supported me through this adventure.
Serena Carbone for our relentless vocal exchanges from Mantolino, Italy to Hawthorne, California, talking about projects, life, art, fears, love, death and naturally, "The Book".
Gaia Berezenska because you came into our lives and brought warmth, friendship and laughs.
Vanessa de Gruijter for you honesty and the push and for sometimes giving me hell. For helping me with the written section of the book and the selection of the texts.
Heine Pratt because without having met you, this project and everything that have led to its realization, would have never been possible.
Axel Wilhite for the talking and the listening.
Enrico Sassi because you and the Hotel Selene have been the source of fun stories, unique characters and creatures, encounters, good heart and heartfelt times.

Hannah Chewey for your effort on my texts. Sorry I didn't follow all your directions, I thought to keep it unvarnished.
Luca Muzzelleri because you went out of your way to help me as a friend and a professional.

Thank you to all the people who have kept asking me about my book during these years, who have shared their creativity, ideas, humor, care and spirit:
Helen Berlant, Denise Domergue, Paulin Paris, Scott Meskill, Alyssa Quigley, Karim Fazulzienov, Pedro Pablo Celedon, Sean P McGaughey, Alan Chin, Francesca Rebecchi, Eleonore Loricetti, Jennifer Drabke, Nicolette Tombe.

Alexa Becker for seeing something in this project when it was still a mess and for your kind, sensitive guidance throughout the entire process.
Hannah Feldmeier for your insightful work and your enthusiasm.
Verlag Kettler for standing behind this book.

Photographs: Carlotta Guerre
Texts: Carlotta Guerre
Editing: Hannah Feldmeier, Carlotta Guerre, Alexa Becker
Concept: Hannah Feldmeier, Carlotta Guerre
Design: Hannah Feldmeier
Image Processing: Humme, Leipzig
Publishing Consultant: Alexa Becker

Production: Druckerei Kettler, Bönen
Published by: Verlag Kettler, Bönen
www.verlag-kettler.de

Photographs © 2025 Carlotta Guerre
Texts © 2025 Carlotta Guerre
Publication © 2025 Verlag Kettler

ISBN: 978-3-98741-166-3

Printed in Germany